THE FRENCH
BIBLICAL EPIC

IN THE

SEVENTEENTH CENTURY

I. Saint-Amant, *Moyse sauvé*, 1653. Frontispiece

THE FRENCH
BIBLICAL EPIC

IN THE
SEVENTEENTH CENTURY

R. A. SAYCE

FELLOW OF WORCESTER COLLEGE
OXFORD

OXFORD
AT THE CLARENDON PRESS
1955

Oxford University Press, Amen House, London E.C.4

GLASGOW NEW YORK TORONTO MELBOURNE WELLINGTON

BOMBAY CALCUTTA MADRAS KARACHI CAPE TOWN IBADAN

Geoffrey Cumberlege, Publisher to the University

———

PRINTED IN GREAT BRITAIN

PREFATORY NOTE

A HISTORY of the Biblical epic in seventeenth-century France, at first sight an unrewarding task, proved in fact, as I hope to have shown, to touch upon important problems of religious and literary attitudes. The work first took shape as a dissertation for the degree of Doctor of Philosophy. It has since been shortened and largely recast (especially in Part III, most of which is new).

In the course of the work I have incurred many debts, which it is a pleasure to acknowledge. The greatest is to Professor Gustave Rudler, who guided my researches in the early stages and gave unsparing advice and criticism. Mr. W. G. Moore read the manuscript at a critical point in the development of the book, and I have discussed some of the problems with him. My wife has helped in the correction of proofs and in many other ways.

Of the friends and colleagues whom I have consulted on points of detail I should mention with special gratitude the late André Barbier, Professor A. M. Boase, Mrs. A. D. Crow, Professor A. Ewert, M. Lucien Febvre, Professor Francesco Flora, Professor Helmut Hatzfeld, M. Raymond Lebègue, the late Jean Plattard, M. Albert-Marie Schmidt, Mr. O. R. Taylor, and Mr. John Woodward. I am also greatly indebted to a number of librarians, in particular to Dr. A. F. L. Beeston of the Bodleian Library, M. Jacques Boussard of the Bibliothèque de l'Arsenal, M. Bruno Durand of the Bibliothèque Méjanes, Mr. D. M. Sutherland of the Taylorian Library, Oxford, and M. Jean Vallery-Radot of the Bibliothèque Nationale. I need hardly add that I am solely responsible for any errors which remain.

For permission to reproduce engravings and pictures I have to thank the Curators of the Bodleian Library, the Governors of Dulwich College, and the Bibliothèque Nationale.

R. A. S.

OXFORD
October 1954

CONTENTS

LIST OF PLATES

Plates II–VIII appear between pp. 224 and 225

PART I

THE BACKGROUND

CHAPTER I

Introduction

FROM Boileau's *Satires* to our day the French epic poems of the seventeenth century have been almost universally condemned as interminable and unreadable. *Jonas* and *David* and the rest have indeed continued to slumber in the dust to which Boileau consigned them. Even the recent revival of interest in the minor religious poets of the period has not extended its benefits to them. The only notable exceptions in the long catalogue of contempt have been Chateaubriand, who rather surprisingly found something to admire in Coras, and Remy de Gourmont, who at last revealed the authentic beauties of *Moyse sauvé*.[1]

It would be possible to demonstrate that even the other poems are not so utterly devoid of merit as literary historians have maintained. However, the object of this work is not to attempt rehabilitation or to rescue occasional passages from oblivion. Of the thirty poems studied here one, the *Moyse sauvé*, has high poetic qualities, though marred by serious blemishes; some, like the *Susane* of Montchrestien and the *Adam* of Charles Perrault, are estimable works of second-rate writers; some, like the *Esther* of Desmarets de Saint-Sorlin and the *Éliade* of Pierre de Saint-Louis, are interesting for their grotesque originality; others, like the poems of Morillon, attain a respectable mediocrity. The remainder, and it must be confessed the majority, present no redeeming features.

[1] Philarète Chasles also devotes a long and fairly sympathetic study to this poem (*La France, l'Espagne et l'Italie*, pp. 325–39).

B

Moreover, the subject has already been treated in two critical works, Duchesne's *Histoire des poëmes épiques français du XVIIe siècle* (1870) and Toinet's *Quelques Recherches autour des poèmes héroïques-épiques français du XVIIe siècle* (1899). The first contains penetrating observations but leaves aside all except the best-known works. The second is a bibliographical repertory, compiled with studious care and a most attractive modesty, but leads to no general conclusions. There is a more serious reason, however, for reviewing the material today. On the whole it may be said that (with important exceptions) the critics of the nineteenth century suffered from a certain lack of sympathy with the spirit of the classical period and with the very idea of a 'literary' epic. Thus Corneille and Racine were considered to have succeeded *in spite of* the limitations imposed on them by contemporary conceptions of literature and life. Virgil and Milton were thought *a priori* inferior to Homer or the *Chanson de Roland*. In the case of Duchesne and Toinet this attitude results not only in the depreciation of the literary value of our poets (which was largely justified) but in a decided hostility towards their aesthetic and cultural environment.

None the less the reader may inquire whether, in view of their limited poetic merit and the existence of previous studies, further investigation was justifiable. In fact, however, the subject raises questions which extend far beyond its apparent boundaries. First of all, why did the efforts of the epic poets end, for the most part, in such lamentable failure? Why did not French poetry produce its Tasso or its Milton? As we shall see, Du Bellay's conception of the epic as the greatest literary enterprise was hardly challenged throughout the century. The men who attempted it were often endowed with considerable, if not supreme, talent and with a sincere religious and literary faith. They were supported by a body of serious and intelligent critical work and, at any rate until Boileau's attacks, by the favour of the reading public (the numerous editions of *La Pucelle* and the *Moyse*, and the still more numerous imitations, are a sufficient indication). Several explanations have been offered, but none seems entirely satisfactory. Then again, why did the Biblical epic enjoy such a widespread vogue, and what were its origins? A solution to these problems clearly involves more than the fate of one literary genre.

When Phèdre invokes the sun,

> Noble et brillant auteur d'une triste famille,
> Toi, dont ma mère osait se vanter d'être fille,

the legend of Crete comes to life again, its absurdity vanishes. This is due not only to the genius of Racine but also to his education (and that of his audiences), which at Port-Royal, in the Jesuit colleges, or the schools of the Oratory was deeply marked by the gods of antiquity. In *Esther* and *Athalie* the same spirit and technique are applied to the completely different world of the Hebrew Bible, which was also familiar, though perhaps less so, to the dramatist and his audience. The Old Testament in turn is subjected to another different influence, that of Christianity. All three elements are certainly present in the plays, but by the mysterious process of poetic fusion the joints are concealed. This was possible for Racine alone, but the Biblical plays must derive from a background to which they themselves, precisely because of their poetic glory, hardly afford a key. The problem concerns not only Racine but nearly all the literature of the seventeenth century. What was the attitude of the people of the time to the Hebrew Bible? How could they reconcile it, not in abstract theology but in direct literary expression, with their Christian religion or with their poetic devotion to the gods of Greece and Rome (and poetic may well mean more real)? The answer to these questions may perhaps profitably be sought in works where the poetic tension is lower, where this fusion has not taken place and the constituent elements can be observed in a state of crude isolation.

These difficulties are almost equally evident if we turn from literature to the visual arts. While Saint-Amant was working on the *Moyse sauvé*, Poussin produced his great series of paintings on the life of Moses. Among them are the three 'Moïse sauvé des eaux', in which a pagan Nile god reclines unnoticed among the figures drawn from the Book of Exodus. Vouet too turned readily from classical to Biblical themes, as in his Moses tapestry, and Claude Lorrain was also inspired by 'Moïse sauvé', as well as by Old Testament themes such as Jacob and Laban, the Burning Bush, and the Golden Calf. At no point of seventeenth-century art is there such close contact between literature and painting, and the one may help to elucidate the other.

In particular, has the art-historian's conception of the baroque any significance for French literature? The question is, so to speak, *sub judice* and the word itself contains ambiguities which make it dangerous to handle. However, it may be said that to assume a baroque–classical antinomy would explain much that is obscure and that, though of course not identical, it presents many affinities with the Christianity–Antiquity antinomy which we have already remarked. The whole problem is bound up with religious expression and with the allegories and *merveilleux* which are the most important ingredients of epic.

Hence it may be claimed without undue presumption that the Biblical epic touches the heart of the seventeenth-century attitude to the relationships between religion, literature, and art. This work does not pretend to offer a final solution to any of the major problems indicated, but it is hoped that it will at least present some of the elements necessary to such a solution.

A word must be said concerning the title and the method followed. An attempt has been made to arrive at the definition of epic most generally accepted by contemporary critics, but in the choice of poems the net has been cast wide. Mere paraphrases have been excluded, but any work with some pretensions to epic form has been at least noted. What precedes will show clearly the reasons for the study of the Biblical rather than the historical epic and for the use of the word 'Biblical' in the common French sense—that is to say, that New Testament subjects have been omitted. The New Testament poems usually lack the essential characteristics of epic, and it is in the Old Testament poems that the problems discussed appear in most tangible shape.

The time-limits present on the whole little difficulty. It is impossible to make a clear division between sixteenth- and seventeenth-century works, and for that reason the earlier poems have been studied in outline. There is a hiatus in the middle of the century (about 1620–50), after which the epic appears with renewed vitality and with certain changes in form, though the gap is by no means unbridged. On the other hand, the disappearance of the genre coincides almost exactly with the end of the century. Perrault's *Adam* was published in 1697, and afterwards there is little in the same category with the exception of a few imitations of Milton and, later, Gessner.[1]

Except where precise textual problems are involved, references to the Bible are to the Authorized Version. In the case of the Apocryphal books the Vulgate has been preferred, with the same qualification. To avoid confusion the differences in nomenclature between Catholic and Protestant Bibles are appended:

Catholic	Protestant
I Kings	I Samuel
II Kings	II Samuel
III Kings	I Kings
IV Kings	II Kings

Where a particular translation is quoted (for example, the Geneva or Louvain versions), the system used there is followed.

Quotations from the poets usually refer to recent editions where possible, otherwise to the most satisfactory or accessible contemporary edition. The orthography has not been modernized,[2] but the ampersand (&) and the contractions for *us*, *n*, &c. have been consistently resolved.

Biographical details have been omitted where adequate information is available elsewhere, but in other cases a brief summary has been included so as to situate the writer in his professional and regional surroundings.

[1] I am indebted to Mr. O. R. Taylor for information about the epic in the eighteenth century.

[2] Except that when, in the titles of books, capitals have been transcribed as lower case, the modern distinction between *u* and *v* has been followed.

CHAPTER II

The Development of Epic Theory

BEFORE we can begin a study of the epic poems of the seventeenth century or even decide what was an epic or a *poème héroïque* in the seventeenth-century sense, it will be necessary to give a short account of the development of the theoretical attitude to the subject or at any rate of the main controversial points. The question has already been partially treated by Mr. Williams[1] and by Bray,[2] but the application of the theories to a set of practical examples demands a more detailed examination of some of the problems, especially as Bray only goes as far as 1670. It will also be necessary to refer occasionally to Italian theorists, since apart from his Italian commentators Aristotle was hardly known in France and their interpretations were the basis of French Aristotelian doctrine.

The Supremacy of Epic

One justification for a study of the seventeenth-century epic is the importance which the opinion of the century attached to it. According to Bray (p. 337), of all the critical writers up to 1670 only Hardy and La Mesnardière think tragedy superior to epic. After 1670 Boileau[3] and Rapin[4] (though not Le Bossu[5]) agree with the majority. It is surprising to the modern reader that an age whose supreme achievement lay in drama should prefer the epic, which attracted few of the writers who stood highest in general esteem. It is more surprising still since this opinion is directly opposed to that of Aristotle, who is often taken to have been the absolute ruler of seventeenth-century criticism. We may assume that it was, in part, the heritage of the Pléiade. Du Bellay in the *Deffence* declares that the production of a long heroic poem is to be the main object of the new poetry.[6] Peletier[7] also took this view,

---

[1] *Two Studies in Epic Theory*, I. *Verisimilitude in the Epic.*
[2] *La Formation de la doctrine classique.*   [3] *Art poétique*, iii. 160.
[4] *Reflexions sur la Poëtique* (en particulier), ch. ii.
[5] *Traité du poëme epique*, bk. i, ch. 2.   [6] Bk. ii, ch. 5.
[7] *Art poëtique*, ed. Boulanger, p. 194.

and his opinion is quoted by Pierre de Laudun in his *Art poetique françois* of 1597.[1] Vauquelin de la Fresnaye was clearly influenced by the doctrines of Du Bellay when he said that a great epic was still the aim of French literature.[2] Thus at the beginning of the seventeenth century we find—at any rate among critics—a tradition of the superiority of epic. Later Chapelain in the Preface to *La Pucelle* of 1656 affirms its supreme importance.[3] We can assume that Chapelain and the men of his generation were influenced by the attitude of the literary world in which they grew up. But this tradition was not in itself strong enough to outweigh the authority of Aristotle. A doctrine held by sixteenth-century poets and critics was indeed almost suspect for that reason alone. It is therefore in Italy that we must seek the principal source of the seventeenth-century reverence for the epic.

In Italy the critics who had most influence on French theory were convinced of its superiority. Vida, though he does not directly state his preference for epic, devotes most of his *Poetics* to it and makes his opinion clear in the lines:

> Sed nullum e numero carmen praestantius omni,
> quam quo post divos heroum facta recensent,
> versibus unde etiam nomen fecere minores.[4]

Scaliger also believed that epic was superior to tragedy, though he considered it inferior to the hymn and the ode.[5] Most important, however, was probably the opinion of Tasso, who in the *Discorsi del Poema Heroico* of 1587–94 refutes the arguments of Aristotle. If the Italians preferred epic it was probably because in sixteenth-century Italy epic was a living form in which the best work was being done. Finally it must be remembered that Aristotle's *Poetics* were made known in their entirety comparatively late[6]—the end of the fifteenth century—and by that time the reputation of Homer and Virgil was so firmly established that it would have been difficult to convince anyone that tragedy could be superior to the form they had chosen. On the whole, then, the high position of the epic in France was due to a literary tradition in France itself, to the success of Tasso's *Jerusalem*, reinforced by his own theoretical

---

[1] ed. Dedieu, p. 144. [2] *Art poetique*, ed. Genty, p. 26.
[3] *Opuscules critiques*, p. 258. [4] Bk. i, ll. 33–35. [5] *Poetices*, bk. i, ch. 3.
[6] There is a good account of Aristotle's appearance and treatment in Italy in Belloni, *Il Poema epico e mitologico* (p. 118). Cf. also Spingarn, *Literary Criticism in the Renaissance*, p. 17.

statements, and to the views of the Italian critics who enjoyed the greatest vogue in France. Ultimately all these sources may derive from one—the great reputation of Homer and especially Virgil. But of immediate sources the influence of Tasso, in theory and practice, stands out as the most important.

The Object of Epic

The object of the epic as of other poetry was generally considered to be utility, served by inclining the reader towards virtue and weaning him from vice. But the epic was to do this in a different way from tragedy, in the opinion of most critics. Here again seventeenth-century opinion diverged from Aristotle, who assumes in the *Poetics* that the object of poetry is the pleasure of the reader, though because of its purgation of the passions tragedy can be defended on utilitarian grounds. He does not, however, suggest any use for epic. Horace gives equal weight to usefulness and pleasure. Italian and French critics made the principles of Aristotle and Horace the foundation of their views but by changes of emphasis arrived at very different conclusions. On the whole, French opinion tends more and more to the magnification of the idea of utility at the expense of pleasure. Thus Chapelain says in the *Lettre sur l'Adone* that utility is the object of poetry, though this utility is effected by means of pleasure.[1] Later Le Bossu sheds the idea of pleasure almost entirely.[2]

There was, however, some disagreement on the special usefulness of epic. By 1656, in the Preface to the first six books of *La Pucelle*, Chapelain had come to the conclusion that the epic poet has a special moral task, different from that of the writer of tragedy:

J'ajouterai que la poésie, et principalement celle qui chante les héros . . . cherche à élever les cœurs aux actions extraordinaires . . .[3]

The epic here conceived is not concerned like tragedy with the purging of evil passions but with the inspiration of good. Marolles takes a similar view:

. . . dans le Poëme Epique, il n'est pas tant question de fléchir la dureté

---

[1] *Opuscules critiques*, p. 85.
[2] *Traité du poëme epique*, bk. i, ch. 3. A detailed account of the utilitarian view and its development is given by Bray, pt. ii, ch. 1.
[3] *Opuscules critiques*, p. 270.

du cœur par vne commiseration pathetique, que de faire triompher la vertu par vne representation poëtique.[1]

Chapelain, when he approaches the question of the effect of epic poetry, considers that it should act on the morals of the individual. Marolles thinks that its effect is primarily political:

... qui serve ... sur tout à faire conceuoir vne haute idée de l'amour de son païs et des respects qui sont dubs aux Loix diuines et humaines.[2]

This bias becomes very marked in epic theory after 1660.[3] For Rapin even more than for Marolles the instruction is not moral but political.[4] Le Bossu also stresses this element: the purpose of the *Iliad* was to show the evils of disunity among princes, of the *Odyssey* to show what will happen if a king leaves his country, of the *Aeneid* to prove the advantages of a monarchy over a republic. From this political effect he perceives an essential difference in aim between epic and tragedy, which at the same time explains the differences in form between them. It is that epic, to influence moral attitudes and conduct, must work slowly, tragedy, to influence passions, must work fast:

L'Epopée est plus pour les mœurs et pour les habitudes que pour les passions. Celles-ci naissent tout à coup, et leur violence est de peu de durée; mais les habitudes sont plus tranquilles, et cessent ou s'impriment plus lentement.[5]

But to understand the elaborate system of Le Bossu it is necessary to return to the *Lettre sur l'Adone*.

Allegory

From the principle that the poet must reward the virtuous and punish the wicked, Chapelain deduces a more important conclusion:

... je ne considère pas plus Enée pieux et Achille colère ... que la piété avec sa suite et la colère avec ses effets, pour m'en faire pleinement connaître la nature.[6]

Therefore, what the poet intends and what the reader sees is not

---

[1] *Traité du poëme epique*, p. 74. [2] Ib., p. 12.
[3] Cf. also Bernard Lamy, *Nouvelles Réflexions sur l'Art Poëtique*, p. 213.
[4] 'Elle ne parle que de Rois et de Princes; elle ne donne des leçons qu'aux grands pour gouverner les peuples' (*Reflexions sur la Poëtique* (en particulier), ch. iv).
[5] Bk. i, ch. 2. [6] *Opuscules critiques*, p. 86.

merely the actions and relations of human beings but the clash of abstract virtues and vices. He goes on to say (p. 89):

L'*allégorie* donc, de la commune opinion des bons esprits, fait partie de l'idée du poème . . . .

Here then is a further development in the moral object of epic. Not only are lessons to be drawn from the behaviour of the characters, but this behaviour itself is simply the lesson made concrete.

But Chapelain only says that allegory is an essential part of the structure. Le Bossu takes up the idea and makes it the keystone to which all is subordinate. Without it a poem, though it may be in externals exactly similar to Homer or Virgil, cannot be an epic.[1] The poet must build his plot in terms of abstract moral ideas, then give each idea a name.[2]

Truth and Fiction

The moral conception of epic naturally influenced views on the material which could be used to construct a poem. It was disputed whether the poet should draw on truth (i.e. on history) or fiction. The argument was conducted on moral and aesthetic grounds. From the latter point of view it was the problem of verisimilitude raised by Aristotle in the *Poetics*. There he says that poetry deals with what ought to happen, history with what has happened. But he assumes that the poet will in general use historical facts as a basis, because this will make the story seem more probable to the hearer or reader. There seems to be a contradiction here. If the public will believe a thing more easily because it is historical, why should not everything historical be probable? But Aristotle, unlike the Renaissance and seventeenth-century critics, did not make the beliefs of the public the only criterion of probability. He is concerned also with general philosophical truth, whether apparent to the public or not. This distinction was, I think, missed by most Italian and French critics.

However, the Italian critics showed on this question great independence from Aristotle. Scaliger[3] rejected his distinction between poet and historian and argued that the distinction was purely one of form. The poet might follow historical truth as closely as he liked. Piccolomini and Tasso took a more positive

---

[1] Bk. i, ch. 15.   [2] Bk. i, ch. 6.   [3] *Poetices*, bk. i, ch. 2.

view, maintaining that truth *must* be the material of poetry. Tasso draws a further argument from Aristotle's theory of imitation: a thing which does not exist cannot be imitated, and this leads him to the principle: 'la perfettissima poesia imita le cose che sono, che furono, o che possono essere'.[1] This admits things which might be but are not: but the criterion is again the experience of the reader, since it is declared that centaurs and flying horses are not things which might be.

In France critical opinion was much more inclined towards the use of fiction. Chapelain took up in the *Lettre sur l'Adone* an extreme position. Not only are truth and verisimilitude not the same, they are directly contrary, and the verisimilitude of a poem is in inverse proportion to the amount of truth it contains. Therefore the more invention there is the better.[2] On the other hand, he defends himself for having burned Jeanne in *La Pucelle*: the poet must follow the truth if it is so widely known as to make alteration incredible.[3] The opinion of Boileau is well known: epic, he says, 'Se soutient par la fable et vit de fiction'.[4]

Marolles approaches the question from a different angle. So far from declaring fiction to be the essential of epic poetry, he finds it necessary to defend its right to a place, which he only grants under certain conditions.[5] For Chapelain and most seventeenth-century critics it is to historical truth, in particular, that the test of *vraisemblance* must be applied: for Marolles above all to fiction. His position is close to that of Tasso: like him he believes that truth must provide the basis of epic and that the criterion of probability is the attitude of the public. Marolles looks at the subject from a Christian (and therefore largely moral) point of view. Boileau, Le Bossu, and Chapelain are more concerned with the principles of classical aesthetics.

Le Bossu shifted the question more completely on to a moral plane. He gives equal importance to truth and fiction, but by truth he means general moral significance. So long, therefore, as the poem has this significance it does not matter whether its incidents (external symbols to Le Bossu) are true or false.[6] That is to say, like Aristotle, he is considering the question in a sphere where truth and falsehood, in the sense of Chapelain and Tasso, are irrelevant.

---

[1] *Discorsi*, bk. ii (*Prose diverse*, i. 100). [2] *Opuscules critiques*, pp. 88–89.
[3] Ib., p. 308. [4] *Art poétique*, iii. 162. [5] *Traité*, p. 25. [6] Bk. i, ch. 14.

The 'Merveilleux'

The question of truth and fiction leads to that of the *merveilleux*. Two books have already been devoted to this subject:[1] here it will only be necessary to indicate the positions of the principal critics and their importance. There was no real divergence on the meaning of *merveilleux*. Rapin gave this definition: 'Le Merveilleux est tout ce qui est contre le cours ordinaire de la nature'.[2] It was generally restricted to the intervention of supernatural beings in the action of the poem. There was also agreement on the necessity for this intervention in the epic. Aristotle had said that the incredible could go farther in epic than in tragedy because there was no visual test of realism. The Italian critics were mostly content to repeat Aristotle, but Tasso develops his theory to the conclusion that the *merveilleux* is the essential of epic, the main source of the pleasure it gives, and even the basis of its utility.[3] French critics did not go quite so far as this, but they all believed the *merveilleux* to be an integral part of the epic which helped to give it its special form.

The real problem, however, was the source of divine intervention. Was the epic poet to continue to use classical deities, should he turn to the supernatural elements in Christianity, or could he combine both? From the point of view of the Biblical epic, only the last two are of interest. It is not surprising that of all the critical problems discussed in the seventeenth century, this provoked the longest and bitterest controversy. In fact, it concerns the foundations of the aesthetic and religious conceptions of the period. It is connected with the question of utility (is an essential part of epic to be an addition intended only to give pleasure?) and with that of verisimilitude (can something which nobody believes be probable?), but it is even more fundamental, because the relation between art and religion was much more vital than that between art and morals or art and philosophy.

The controversy had begun in Italy, where Giraldi Cinthio, Tasso, and others had argued for the use of the Christian supernatural. In France, after Du Bartas, Vauquelin called for a Christian epic.[1] The idea of pillaging the classics, as the Israelites

---

[1] Delaporte, *Du Merveilleux dans la littérature française sous le règne de Louis XIV*; Williams, *The Merveilleux in the Epic*. Mr. Williams's book is devoted entirely to the theoretical discussions.   [2] *Reflexions sur la Poëtique* (en général), ch. xxiii.
[3] *Discorsi*, bk. i (*Prose diverse*, i. 83–85).

had pillaged the Egyptians, has a long history, going back to the Greek Fathers, and after Vauquelin it was considerably modified.[2] But apart from this, he states the position of the seventeenth-century believers in Christian inspiration. On the one hand, poetry must gain from closer contact with the spiritual realities of the present; on the other, religion must gain from the support of art. This explains at least partly why the problem was so immediate and aroused so much passion in France. Strong religious feeling, demanding expression in art, came into conflict with Renaissance classicism, which had consolidated its position, hardened its dogma, and made its power felt far beyond the ranks of the scholars who had been its principal champions in the sixteenth century.

Chapelain's *Lettre sur l'Adone* is not directly concerned with the question of the *merveilleux*. Thirty years passed before he made a definite statement (at least, in his critical works). In the meantime the Christian position found many more defenders. One of the most important was Godeau, who discusses the question in the *Discours* prefixed to his *Œuvres chrestiennes* in 1633. His argument is that of Vauquelin, but with all the stress on the religious necessity that poetry should be Christian.[3] He joined to his appeal for Christian poetry a practical injunction to look to the Old Testament for material.[4] This probably had some part in encouraging the efforts of the Biblical poets, though it may be doubted whether they needed encouragement. After Godeau the arguments for the *merveilleux chrétien* are to be found in the prefaces of published epics. The most important are those of Le Moyne, Chapelain, and Scudéry. All of them are based on the central point of the Christian position, the lack of verisimilitude in paganism, and all are summarized in chapter iii of Mr. Williams's book. Marolles in 1662 takes up the same position, with severe

---

[1] Portez donc en trophé les despouilles payennes
  Au sommet des clochers de vos citez Chrestiennes.
    Si les Grecs, comme vous, Chrestiens, eussent escrit,
  Ils eussent les hauts faits chanté de Iesus Christ.
  Doncques à les chanter ores ie vous inuite,
  Et tant que vous pourrez à despouiller l'Egipte,
  Et de Dieu les autels orner à qui mieux mieux
  De ses beaus parements et meubles precieux . . . (ed. Genty, p. 135.)

[2] Cf. p. 34 below; also Curtius, *Europäische Literatur*, p. 462.

[3] *Poësies chrestiennes*, 1646, p. 13. Cf. Bray, *Formation*, p. 300.

[4] 'L'histoire du Peuple Iuif leur peut fournir des sujets admirables de Poësmes' (*Poësies chrestiennes*, 1646, p. 50).

condemnation of the mixture of pagan and Christian wonders.[1] Until this time the Christian point of view had encountered no serious opposition. But after Boileau's attacks on the Christian epic in the *Satires* and the *Art poétique* the controversy became violent. In the *Satires* Boileau attacks individual poets: it is only in the *Art poétique* that he presents a reasoned summary of his objections to the *merveilleux chrétien*. There are in fact only two arguments: one religious, that Christianity is degraded by contact with the fiction which is essential to the epic; the other literary, that Christian wonders are either dull or ridiculous, as in the case of Satan *hurlant contre les Cieux*. This was Boileau's only serious answer to the polemics conducted for a period of five years by Desmarets de Saint-Sorlin.[2]

Desmarets begins by using the stock argument founded on the authority of the ancients. The Greeks and Romans celebrated their own gods, not those of foreign countries. Christians must look to their own religion for the marvellous element in their work.[3] From a purely literary point of view it was probably the strongest argument on the side of the Christian poets since it is founded on the premises of their adversaries. But from a religious point of view it admits a kind of relativity: paganism and Christianity are equally probable at different times. Such an argument could not be congenial to Desmarets and here it is considerably modified: if the classical poets obeyed the laws of a false religion, how much more should we obey those of the true religion!

In fact, however, this attitude was not the result only of piety. Stung by the comparisons of Christian poems (especially his own) with the classical epic, he is driven to a counter-attack on the latter. In 1670 he describes the classical poems as *si beaux, si reverez*, and argues that the modern poet should imitate them in their attitude to religion (a different religion, of course). Later he condemns them as improbable and at the same time proclaims the

---

[1] *Traité*, ch. vi.

[2] Desmarets first expressed his views on the possibilities of Christian poetry in the *Advis* prefixed to the 1st ed. of *Clovis* (1657). Here his tone is reasonable, though confident. It is in 1670 that he begins to write violently and to publish a large number of treatises and pamphlets: *Traité pour juger des poetes grecs, latins, et françois* (1670); *L'Excellence et les Plaintes de la Poësie Heroïque* (1670), prefixed to *Esther*; *La Comparaison de la Langue et de la Poësie françoise avec la Grecque et la Latine* (1670); *Discours pour prouver que les sujets Chrestiens sont les seuls propres à la poesie Heroïque*; *Epistre au Roy* (both in the 3rd ed. of *Clovis*, 1673); *La Deffense du Poëme Heroïque* (1674).

[3] *Excellence et Plaintes*, p. 9.

necessary superiority of Christian poetry.[1] In contradiction to the arguments of the *Excellence et plaintes*, he maintains that the classical poets themselves did not believe in their gods, which destroys still more completely their claim to probability.[2] From this view of the classical epic a moral principle is deduced which also serves to discredit it. As they invented their divinities the classical poets could have made them models of virtue: instead they painted them with every vice. Desmarets expresses this view in a violent tirade which has considerable rhetorical force.[3] It was legitimate to apply to the gods the rigid standards of decorum maintained by Boileau and those who thought like him. It was the more effective since Boileau himself argued that the classical deities were invented by the poets. But in his search for any valid argument Desmarets commits another inconsistency which complicates the question and restores it to a purely religious plane. He draws on the tradition, well known through Fontenelle, that the classical gods were demons and had therefore an existence outside the imagination. The consequence is that the poems of Homer and Virgil are not merely aesthetically bad but directly inspired by the Devil.[4]

Desmarets does not, however, exclude the *merveilleux païen* from all poetry. In epic it is permissible to introduce classical gods in the mouth of a pagan.[5] This is a detail which does not affect the main theory. Yet it suggests that the poet is anxious to exploit the poetic possibilities of classical mythology if he can find a plausible excuse. Since he has denied the poetic merit of this mythology and condemned it from a religious point of view, his position is necessarily weakened. More than this, in spite of his attacks on the classical poets, he argues that it is legitimate for the Christian poet to take from them anything that is useful to him.[6] We have already seen the history of this argument. Desmarets adds nothing to it except a more vigorous rhetoric.

Up to the present we have examined arguments for the *merveilleux chrétien* which are mainly negative. Desmarets's positive reasons must depend on a religious basis, to which aesthetic considerations are secondary. He summarizes his position in

---

[1] 'Ainsi les Chrestiens, qui seuls ont la verité, ont seuls le vrai-semblable, et seuls peuvent faire vn bon Poëme Heroïque' (*Discours*, e2 v⁰).

[2] *Traité pour juger des poetes*, pp. 93-94.

[3] *Traité pour juger*, p. 85.

[4] Ib., p. 95.

[5] *Discours*, i6.

[6] *Traité pour juger*, p. 96.

five points which attempt to show the necessary relationship between this religious principle and the principles of criticism.[1] But Desmarets goes farther, and here he is certainly original. Not only are Christian subjects in general necessarily superior to pagan subjects but any particular Christian poet is necessarily superior to any particular pagan poet. He would not maintain the superiority of the Christian poet in every respect, but the general conclusion is clear. Desmarets compares himself to Homer and Virgil:

Par sa grace, et par les lumieres de la Foi, il m'a bien élevé au dessus d'eux, sans que je puisse en tirer de vanité, puisque ce qui est de sa grace n'est pas de moi.[2]

This is so naïve as to be almost modest. But in it the theory of Desmarets has reached an absurd point. At the same time it is connected with a principle which contains a great deal of truth and which is expressed in the apology for *Clovis*.[3] We have here, expressed in a noble form, an idea which lies beneath all the attempts at Christian epic, which takes into account both the religious devotion and the monarchical nationalism of the time. *Clovis* is not the true poem of France, but its guiding principle might have made it so. Twenty years before the quarrel came to a head Desmarets puts forward all the arguments used by the *Modernes*.[4]

From this welter of contradictory arguments two essential facts emerge. One is the firm religious foundation of Desmarets's theory. The other, less obvious, is the influence of the classical ideal and the spell of classical epic. The bitter attacks on Homer and Virgil are attempts to break this spell. Desmarets does not propose to substitute for the classics a new kind of epic. His object is to conquer their position for Christian poetry by using their methods. Seen in this light, many, if not all, of the inconsistencies can be reconciled. It is the idea of pillage which is most significant. The attacks are mainly tactical and conceal an admiration no less real because it takes the form of envy.

Perrault's *Paralelle des Anciens et des Modernes* is best considered

[1] *Traité pour juger*, p. 94.   [2] Ib., p. 92.

[3] 'C'est le veritable Poëme de la France, où l'on void les admirables exploits de ce grand Roi qui en fit la conqueste, et qui lui donna le nom de France, et où la sainte Religion triomphe du triomphant' (ib., p. 97).

[4] Cf. Gillot, *Querelle*, pp. 488 ff.

here as it expresses a doctrine which is fundamentally that of Desmarets. The central point of his theory is the greater probability of the Christian *merveilleux*: his merit is a sharper historical sense than earlier critics had revealed.

Le Bossu is not concerned with the modern epic: when he says that the poet 'se fait instruire par les Dieux, qui savent tout'[1] he is speaking as the historian of the classical epic. But he does justify the invocation of the Muses by the Christian poet, though in very general terms.[2]

Biblical Subjects

The question of the propriety of Biblical subjects is closely connected with that of the *merveilleux*. Needless to say, the opponents of Christian poetry included Biblical subjects in their condemnation. But even among its supporters there was disagreement. The logical conclusion of the religious arguments for Christian material is that the source of this material should be the Bible, since it is there that the heroic and miraculous elements of the Christian religion are to be found. In fact the majority of critics took this view and used only Biblical examples to support their arguments. We have already seen how Godeau encouraged poets to take their subjects from the Bible. Desmarets was more impassioned and perhaps reaches his highest flights of eloquence in his apology for Biblical subjects.[3]

Those who believed in a lay Christian epic argued that it was impossible in a Biblical subject to introduce the necessary invention. This is put clearly by Scudéry.[4] Their opponents had an answer: the Biblical epic was to contain invented elements, but only additions and alterations of doctrinally unimportant details. This is explained by Saint-Amant in his Preface.[5] Desmarets gives

---

[1] Bk. ii, ch. 12.

[2] Because the Muses are not divinities but the forces of poetic genius allegorized (bk. iii, ch. 4).

[3] 'Et parce que les saints livres presentent des histoires incomparables, des richesses et des magnificences au dessus de la puissance humaine, et des merveilles veritables, surprenantes, et infiniment plus dignes d'admiration et d'étonnement, que tout ce que la fiction la plus libre et la plus hardie a pû jamais inventer' (*Traité pour juger*, p. 95).

[4] 'Il faut donc que l'Argument du Poëme Epique soit pris de l'Histoire Chrétienne, mais non pas de l'Histoire Sainte: d'autant qu'on ne peut pas sans prophanation en alterer la verité; et que sans l'inuention, qui est la principale partie du Poëte, il est presque impossible que l'Epopée puisse auoir toute sa beauté' (Preface to *Alaric*, 1654, a4).   [5] *Œuvres*, ed. Livet, ii. 141.

this argument more force by a comparison between Biblical epic and Biblical painting.[1] It was, however, condemned on religious grounds by Le Moyne in his *Dissertation du Poëme Heroïque*. According to him it is wrong to combine invention (which he calls *Mensonge*) with sacred truth.[2]

It is difficult to pronounce on the merits of these arguments since the dispute is purely religious, both sides being agreed on the critical principles involved. Superficially the party of Scudéry and Le Moyne is more strictly orthodox. But in fact Desmarets and those who thought like him are closer to the union of Christianity with classical art which was the prime object of the movement for Christian epic.

The Characters and the Hero

After these general questions had been settled the critics discussed in detail the requirements of epic material. They all agreed on the first essential—the epic must deal with illustrious characters and events. By an illustrious character Aristotle seems to have meant a morally admirable one, but the modern critics generally gave it a social sense: the epic deals only with kings and princes. Rapin and Le Bossu insist that only royal personages are suitable characters.[3] In fact, this condition was taken for granted, and I do not think anyone opposed it.

For most critics, however, the moral character of the hero had at least some importance. Rapin argues that the characters must offer examples of virtue and vice.[4] Le Bossu, like Rapin, thinks that a character in epic may be entirely good or entirely bad, but, unlike Rapin, he thinks the hero may be bad. He justifies this mainly by a very unfavourable analysis of the character of Achilles,[5] to which he adds the reason given by Rapin: the object of epic is to discourage vice as well as to encourage virtue.[6] On the other hand, the hero may be virtuous, as in the case of Aeneas. The question is of practical importance for the epic poems themselves,

---

[1] 'Jamais il n'a esté dit qu'vn excellent tableau, representant vn miracle de l'ancien ou du nouveau Testament, fust vne chose contraire à la verité; bien que le Peintre y eust feint diverses choses, que le saint Texte ne particularise pas mais qui sont convenables au sujet' (*Discours*, 17).   [2] e3.

[3] Rapin, *Reflexions sur la Poëtique* (en particulier), ch. iv; Le Bossu, *Traité*, bk. i, ch. 2.   [4] *Reflexions* (en general), ch. x.

[5] Marolles also criticizes the character of Achilles (*Traité*, p. 78). But he does not draw the logical consequences of his criticism.

[6] Bk. iv, ch. 5.

but it is doubtful whether the theory had much influence. More important were the example of Virgil and the heroic tradition of Corneille, the Fronde, and the novel.

Peace and War

There was not quite such unanimity on the question of illustrious action. It was agreed that this meant above all war, but there was uncertainty as to whether epic could describe a peaceful action also. Bray says (p. 338): 'Tous les critiques sont de cet avis: l'épopée raconte des guerres.' But he cites only Saint-Amant, Coras, and Bernard Lamy, the first two of whom are not precisely critics. On the other hand, Chapelain in the *Lettre sur l'Adone*[1] maintains that an epic may have a peaceful action. According to Bray, however, none of this is to be taken seriously. Chapelain was defending what seemed to him indefensible and what he said was intended to damn with faint praise. *La Pucelle* proves what he really thought. This view is plausible enough. Chapelain in his letters speaks cynically of the *Adone* and the Preface he wrote for it at the request of his friends. Still, his view was a perfectly tenable critical position, as is proved by the fact that Le Bossu followed it, using a different argument. He bases his opinion on the *Odyssey*, which, he says, contains no war.[2]

Another approach to such an epic is seen in Vauquelin, who considers it a different genre with its own laws. He confirms this idea with classical examples, the *Georgics* and Ovid's *Fasti*.[3] It is in fact surprising that seventeenth-century criticism does not seem to have given any attention to the classification and regulation of such didactic poems as the *Georgics*. Both these opinions are of importance in considering Saint-Amant.

Structure and Plot

Before we approach the general aspects of structure there are two practical recommendations, both of some importance for the consideration of the epic poets, especially Saint-Amant. The first concerns the selection of material. According to Tasso, the main plot must not be too full of incident,[4] because if it is the poem will be of such a length that there will be no room for episodes and

---

[1] *Opuscules critiques*, p. 77.   [2] Bk. ii, ch. 19.
[3] *Art poétique*, ed. Genty, p. 42.   [4] *Discorsi*, bk. ii (*Prose diverse*, i. 127).

other necessary adornments. This must be remembered when judging both those poets who ignored it and those who, like Saint-Amant, followed it all too closely. The second concerns the plot itself. It is the need for what Aristotle calls peripeteia, a sudden revolution in fortune. Aristotle thought that it was principally a method of tragedy, but he declares it to be necessary in epic also.[1] Chapelain goes farther: he thinks it an indispensable part of the structure.[2]

The main story must be supported and varied by episodes which, though not essential to the plot, are connected with it. The necessity for intimate connexion is emphasized by Aristotle in his praise of the *Odyssey*. In Italy this doctrine was followed, but nothing of great importance was added to it. Castelvetro sums it up with considerable force, comparing the poem to an animal, the episodes to its food.[3]

In France, however, Le Bossu treated the question systematically and attempted to decide what an episode was, under what circumstances it could be used, and what intimate connexion with the narrative really meant. He defines an episode as part of the action which is not strictly essential to the narrative but which occupies a place that must be filled.[4] The example he puts forward is that of the *Odyssey*: it is essential to the allegorical theme that Ulysses should be away from home, but the poet may fill this time with episodes as he wishes. Each of these episodes could in fact be removed but would have to be replaced by another.[5] Le Bossu then lays down three conditions for the preservation of unity of action:[6] all episodes must be part of the action; they must all be closely bound together; and they must not be complete in themselves. The first two conditions are evident from Le Bossu's definition. The third is equally important. The poet may make an episode incomplete in two ways. He may leave the action itself unfinished, as in the duel between Paris and Menelaus in the *Iliad*. Or he may make it complete for the central character of the episode but incomplete for the central character of the whole poem, who provides the link between the two. The episode of Dido is complete for Dido but not for Aeneas.

---

[1] 'The parts of epic are the same, for it requires revolution, discoveries and disasters . . .' (Twining's translation).
[2] *Opuscules critiques*, p. 100.   [3] 1576 ed., p. 536.
[4] Bk. ii, ch. 4.   [5] Bk. ii, ch. 5.   [6] Bk. ii, ch. 7.

In the development of the action itself, Horace urged the poet to approach the centre of the story as soon as possible and condemned those who returned laboriously to the remote sources of the action. This maxim, under the influence of the *Odyssey* and the *Aeneid*, was considerably modified by later critics, who said that it was wrong to relate events in their natural order, and necessary to return to those omitted by introducing a recital. Vida seems to have been the first: the recital has the object of keeping the reader in suspense. He is not dogmatic, however, and confines himself to the remark that this is the practice of the majority of poets.[1] Tasso sees the relation between this question and that of historic truth and treats them together. He considers it wrong to follow the order in which things happened and attacks Lucan on this ground, as well as for a too close adherence to history. For the natural order of Lucan he would substitute an artificial order in which the events are arranged to suit the necessities of the poem.[2] In France, Chapelain lays down as a rule that the narrative must not follow the actual order of events.[3]

The Unity of Time

Aristotle had said that, in contrast to tragedy, the duration of epic action is indefinite. Italian critics seem mostly to have repeated this, perhaps introducing certain qualifications. In France we see an interesting example of the restriction of critical opinion. Ronsard had said that the action of epic was limited to a single year and criticized Virgil for not following this rule exactly.[4] His source appears to have been Minturno.[5] It will be noticed that the time is taken from the beginning of the poem to the end: that is to say, a recital counts as the time taken to recite it, not as the duration of its contents. Thus Ulysses' story of his wanderings and Aeneas' tale of the sack of Troy, though important parts of the main story, do not disturb the unity of time. Chapelain also makes a year the limit.[6] Marolles, who takes the trouble to distinguish carefully between the total time and the duration of the actual narrative, also adhered closely to the position of Ronsard.[7]

Le Bossu discusses the question in detail and arrives at a stricter conclusion still (bk. iii, ch. 12). According to him a single summer

---

[1] Bk. ii, ll. 60–61. [2] *Discorsi*, bk. iii. [3] *Opuscules critiques*, p. 99.
[4] 1587 Pref. to *Franciade* (ed. Laumonier, vii. 79). [5] Cf. Bray, *Formation*, p. 285.
[6] *Opuscules critiques*, p. 101. [7] *Traité*, p. 39.

is the limit of epic action. It is not necessary to enumerate all his ingenious, sometimes fantastic, arguments for fitting Virgil into his scheme. What is interesting is the motive for the construction of this elaborate theory. Le Bossu wished to press farther the parallel between epic and tragedy, which Chapelain and Marolles had already suggested. The more severe critics had limited the action of tragedy to daylight (*le jour naturel*). For the same reason Le Bossu wished to limit the epic to that part of the year in which heroic action is possible (presumably because of the difficulty of conducting military operations in the winter). The theory is typical of the tendency to regulate and rationalize literature, which became more apparent as the century went on.

Questions of Setting and Adornment

Tasso makes one or two interesting remarks on the best setting for epic, which seem to have had some influence on French poetry, even though they find little echo in French criticism. He thinks that a distant country makes a good setting, because the poet is at liberty to introduce fabulous stories without arousing incredulity.[1] For the same reason he objects to subjects set in the present time. On the other hand, he objects just as strongly to a subject taken from the distant past, because it is too remote from the reader's world.[2] He therefore recommends that the poet should choose a subject which lies between these two extremes (as he himself had done in the *Jerusalem*). In France Marolles repeated the condemnation of subjects taken from the present or the near past, and for the same reason.[3]

Tasso believes that it is necessary for an epic to be enriched with descriptions of such things as sunrise and sunset, storm and calm, or battles, arms, buildings.[4] He adds a warning, however, on the need for proportion and the danger of excessive length. Chapelain repeats this principle with regard to the epic of which the *Adone* is the type (though without Tasso's warning).[5] The reflection of

---

[1] *Discorsi*, bk. ii (*Prose diverse*, i. 122).
[2] Ib. (*Prose diverse*, i. 111–13).
[3] *Traité*, p. 25.
[4] *Discorsi*, bk. ii (*Prose diverse*, i. 124).
[5] '. . . tout l'effort se mette aux descriptions et à la particularité, et ce plus des choses pratiquées en paix . . . comme de palais, jardins, architecture, jeux et autres semblables' (*Opuscules critiques*, p. 81).

such maxims in poetry, together with the neglect of this warning, led to Boileau's attack on exaggerated descriptions:

> S'il rencontre un palais, il m'en dépeint la face;
> Il me promène après de terrasse en terrasse.[1]

Boileau says in a note that this was directed against Scudéry, but it could have been applied to other poets.

Homer and Virgil had begun with a short statement of the theme of the poem or the acts of the hero. Horace declared that this should be as modest as possible and mocked poets who began by vaunting the glorious deeds of their hero. In Renaissance criticism it was called the proposition and was considered an indispensable part of epic. Already Vida presents this as a universal rule.[2] In France Boileau repeated Horace's satire, but, as often, it was left to Le Bossu to discuss the question in detail.[3] He amplifies what Horace said and describes the faults which are possible in the proposition.

Closely connected with the proposition was the invocation, the appeal to a god or a noble patron. Vida confines it to the invocation of the gods and says that it should be repeated throughout the poem, not made once and for all at the beginning.[4] Piccolomini divides invocations into three classes: invocations to the Muses, to other deities (*altro Nume divino*), and to a person, a patron or a mistress for example.[5] All these kinds of invocation are to be found in French epic. Where earlier critics had argued whether the invocation was a sign of modesty or presumption, Tasso sees in it simply a sign of piety. This leads him to attack the invocation of pagan deities, though he makes an exception for the Muses, who are simply personified abstractions.[6] Marolles goes farther than Tasso and would exclude even the Muses from the invocation.[7] Le Bossu also emphasizes the influence of piety on the invocation. In fact, however, he thinks, consistently with his general theory, that the significance of these deities is mainly allegorical, a symbol of poetic inspiration. Finally he too believes that the invocation should be repeated at intervals.[8]

[1] *Art poétique*, i. 51–52. [2] Bk. ii, ll. 17–20.
[3] Bk. iii, ch. 3. [4] Bk. ii, ll. 20–29. [5] 1575 ed., p. 382.
[6] *Discorsi*, bk. iv (*Prose diverse*, i. 189–90). [7] *Traité*, p. 70.
[8] Bk. iii, ch. 4.

It is not necessary here to discuss figures of speech. They were considered the province of the rhetorician and grammarian, not of the critic proper. Le Bossu, for instance, typically relegates his opinions *Des Sentimens et de l'Expression* to the brief final book. However, there are one or two problems connected with similes and metaphors which require brief mention. It is well known that the Pléiade thought poetry should draw on the stock of technical words of various trades. The importance of this for the sustained epic simile is emphasized by both Ronsard[1] and Pierre de Laudun.[2] Seventeenth-century poets followed this advice faithfully, but it does not seem to figure in seventeenth-century criticism.

The second question concerned the relation in poetic dignity between the object of comparison and the thing compared to it. The root of the problem was Homer's liking for such comparisons as that of Ajax to a donkey or the Greek army to ants, and the difficulty the critics had in reconciling them with their notions of poetic decorum. In Italy Vida deals with the problem: he turns Virgil's practice into a rule—the great may be compared to the small. But he objects strongly to what is low and for that reason condemns the comparisons of Homer.[3] Unfortunately he gives no definition of what is low or why flies round a jug of cream are ignoble while ants are not. Tasso is of the same opinion but defines the noble and the ignoble. The former, he says, is that which is pleasing to the senses: the latter is the opposite and in general anything plebeian or vulgar.[4]

Le Bossu begins by laying down general rules for comparison, made from a psychological point of view. The two main conditions are that the comparison should be accurate and that the thing introduced in the comparison should be better known than the original object, thus making the latter more intelligible.[5]

Desmarets and Perrault succeeded in arriving at consistent conclusions. It was difficult for the orthodox critics to reconcile their exclusion of the ignoble and their admiration for Homer. Desmarets and Perrault laid stress on the former principle and used it as a weapon in their condemnation of Homer. Desmarets repeats with satisfaction what he considers to be the ridiculous compari-

---

[1] 1587 Pref. to *Franciade* (ed. Laumonier, vii. 87–88).
[2] *Art poétique*, ed. Dedieu, p. 149.   [3] Bk. ii, ll. 282–9.
[4] *Discorsi*, bk. iv (*Prose diverse*, i. 197).
[5] Bk. vi, ch. 3.

sons of Homer, Ajax compared to a donkey and Ulysses ship-
wrecked to a judge in his court.[1] Perrault chooses the same
faults for censure: he analyses the narrative of the *Odyssey* so as
to make it appear ridiculous.[2]

Metre

Both Aristotle and Horace lay down that there is one suitable
metre for epic and Aristotle makes the use of this metre part of his
definition. The Italian critics also attached some importance to it,
though they found difficulty in deciding what the Italian heroic
metre was. Tasso discusses at length the merits of each metre,
finally deciding on that which he had used himself, the *ottava
rima*.[3] In France there was no such hesitation after the beginning
of the seventeenth century. Ronsard maintains that the ten-
syllable line is superior to the Alexandrine for epic purposes.[4]
Vauquelin is more hesitant: clearly the Alexandrine had gained
still more ground since Ronsard wrote.[5] Afterwards the Alexandrine was not challenged and by the middle of the century its
use was taken for granted. Only Marolles seems to have taken the
trouble to condemn the decasyllable.[6]

The Definition of Epic

The Italian critics had to distinguish not only epic and tragedy,
but also epic proper and romance, which was the name usually
applied to the *Orlando Furioso*. Many critics condemned the romance
because of its irregularity. Those who liked it escaped this difficulty by saying that it was a new poetic form, which required
a new set of rules. Pigna and Giraldi Cinthio were apparently
the first to lay down this principle.[7] It was repeated by Tasso[8] and
became in France a favourite way of avoiding Aristotle's rules
without denying their authority. Thus it is the keystone to Chapelain's defence of Marino and it is used by Saint-Amant and Coras.
We are now in a position to decide what the seventeenth

---

[1] *Traité pour juger*, ch. xxviii.

[2] *Paralelle des Anciens et des Modernes*, vol. iii, *passim*.

[3] *Discorsi*, bk. vi (*Prose diverse*, i. 265–9).

[4] His main reason is 'la honteuse conscience que i'ay qu'ils sentent trop leur prose'
(1572 Pref. to *Franciade*, ed. Laumonier, vii. 70).

[5] En vers de dix ou douze apres il le faut metre:
  Ces vers la nous prenons pour le graue Hexametre. (ed. Genty, p. 26.)

[6] *Traité*, p. 96.   [7] Belloni, *Il Poema epico e mitologico*, p. 127.   [8] *Discorsi*, bk. iii.

century thought an epic was. The highest common factor of critical opinion was, it may be said, that epic was the narration (as opposed to representation) in verse of an illustrious action within very wide limits of length.[1] 'Illustrious' meant that the main characters should be of high rank (and according to some critics of exemplary virtue). It should be noted, however, that just as the gods could be illustrious characters in the pagan epic, saints and prophets satisfied this condition in the Christian epic. The other accepted elements of illustriousness were the *merveilleux* and allegory. The relative importance of these elements was different in the view of different critics, but all admitted their necessity.

The last essential of epic is contained in the word 'action', which is in a way equivalent to *fable*. It was necessary that the plot itself, even without the marvellous elements, should have its own pleasurable appeal. Thus Chapelain, as we have seen, makes peripeteia an essential of epic. By its variety and the vicissitudes of its narrative as well as by its subject the epic must follow the model set by Homer and Virgil. This provides a criterion for dealing with the poems of doubtful character, mostly on Biblical themes, which were common in the seventeenth century. The deciding point is whether their religious significance is expressed in meditation or in action.

[1] Formulated by Tasso: 'Il Poema Heroico sia imitatore d'attione illustre, grande e perfetta fatta, narrando con altissimo verso' (*Discorsi*, bk. i; *Prose diverse*, i. 82).

CHAPTER III

The Origins: I. The Sixteenth Century

CRITICAL theory, we have seen, was influenced by Italian models, beside which the native tradition of the Pléiade is of limited importance. The origins of epic production are complicated by the fact that this native tradition must itself be divided into two streams, the sources of which are Ronsard and Du Bartas (a division which had no effect on theoretical developments). Apart from the primary sources—the Bible, Homer, and Virgil—there are thus three immediate sources which must be taken into consideration. Critics have generally chosen one as predominant, to the exclusion of the other two. Thus Sainte-Beuve[1] decides that the seventeenth-century epic proceeds from Du Bartas—it is true that he does not discuss the influence of Tasso. His contemporary Saint-Marc Girardin[2] less dogmatically suggests an affiliation to the neo-Latin epic of Vida and Sannazaro. Since then critical opinion has emphasized the role of Tasso and neglected the other sources. This tendency has been accentuated by the works of M. Cioranescu[3] and Professor Beall,[4] which enable us to appreciate the full extent of Italian influence in the seventeenth century. Finally M. Cottaz[5] attributes entirely to Tasso the doctrine, the methods, and the failure of the seventeenth-century epic.

These conclusions are based on study of the epic as a whole and evidence from the Biblical poems alone must be of limited value. However, it is possible at once to qualify Vianey's statement:[6] the titles of the poems show, he says, that the religious epic is no longer principally Biblical, as it was in the sixteenth century. This again he attributes to the influence of Tasso. It is true that the profane, or medieval, epic is considerably developed in the

---

[1] 'C'est bien à sa manière plutôt qu'à celle de son rival [Ronsard] qu'il faut rapporter tous les ampoulés poèmes épiques du temps de Louis XIII' (*Tableau de la poésie française au XVIe siècle*, 1876, i. 175). 'Il est bien le père ou le grand-père de cette mauvaise lignée de poètes plus ou moins gascons et pesants' (ib. ii. 244).

[2] *Tableau de la littérature française au XVIe siècle*, 1862, pp. 237–87.

[3] *L'Arioste en France*, 1938.   [4] *La Fortune du Tasse en France*, 1942.

[5] *L'Influence des théories du Tasse*, 1942.

[6] *Revue des Cours et Conférences*, 1922, p. 482.

seventeenth century, but Biblical subjects keep an important place, as Toinet's catalogue proves.[1]

Before examining each of these sources in detail it will be advisable to consider briefly the three great movements which lay behind them—Humanism, Protestantism (or more strictly Calvinism), and the Counter-Reformation. The debt of the epic to Humanism is vast—models, technique, form, ornament, the gods and the spirit of antiquity, all belong to it. Here we may mention one important aspect, the rapid development of Biblical and Oriental scholarship under the influence of Humanism. In general this led to a growing public interest in the historical, geographical, and critical background of the Bible, culminating in the *Geographia Sacra* of Samuel Bochart, Saint-Amant's friend (1646). To this may be added the popularity of books of travel and collections of Oriental costumes.[2]

Of more particular interest for us is the vulgarization of the works of Josephus and Philo Judaeus. Josephus was translated into French by Gilbert Génébrard, Archbishop of Aix, in 1578. Seven editions had appeared by 1646. Other translations were made by François Bourgoing (1558), Le Frère and Kiber (1569), and La Faye (1597). None of these attained the popularity of Génébrard's work, which held the field until the appearance of Arnauld d'Andilly's version in 1667, thenceforward the standard translation. The importance of Josephus in seventeenth-century literature is considerable. Thus Arnauld in his plan of studies for Port-Royal devotes as much time to the reading of Josephus as to the Bible,[3] Thomassin considers his work a part of sacred history,[4] Desmarets places him on the same level.[5] In painting he is used to provide supplementary material for Biblical subjects: Poussin draws on him for at least two pictures.[6] In the Biblical

---

[1] Of 94 poems mentioned by Toinet, 32 are on Old or New Testament subjects.

[2] For example, d'Avity's cosmographies, the works of Jacques Gaffarel, and La Chappelle, *Recuel de divers portraits des principales Dames de la Porte du Grand Turc*, Paris, 1648.

[3] *Œuvres complètes*, vol. xli, quoted by Lantoine, p. 286.

[4] *Methode d'étudier . . . les lettres humaines*, e8.

[5] 'Chacun sçait l'histoire de la belle et sage Esther, tant par l'histoire Sainte, que par celle de Iosephe' (Preface to *Esther*, 1673 ed., a3 vº).

[6] 'Moses trampling on Pharaoh's Crown' (Louvre), which depicts an incident contained only in Josephus, and the detail of the floating weapons in the 'Crossing of the Red Sea' (National Gallery of Victoria, Melbourne). See Friedlaender, *The Drawings of Poussin*, London, 1939, i. 7, 11.

epic Josephus is employed almost universally, and for the same reason, to permit an expansion of the Bible narrative which can be justified by reference to an authority carrying only slightly less weight than Scripture itself. This use of Josephus begins early. In Thierry Petremand's *Judith* (1578) there are already many marginal references to the *Antiquitates*. In view of the date it is not certain whether he used Génébrard's translation, which is important mainly as a symptom of general interest. However, Saint-Amant, who made numerous borrowings from Josephus, certainly read the translation.[1]

The influence of Philo Judaeus is less extensive (he is used particularly by Saint-Amant and Coras). A translation by Pierre Bellier appeared in 1575, with reprints in 1588 and 1598. It was republished in 1612 by Fédéric Morel the younger as a revised translation. In fact there are a few grammatical corrections and some slight alterations in the marginal rubrics. This version was reprinted in 1619.

The growth of feminism in the sixteenth century may also perhaps be attributed to the influence of humanism. In the epic the movement is reflected in the appearance of two women writers (Gabrielle de Coignard, Marie de Pech de Calages) and in the popularity of the Biblical heroines Judith, Susanna, and Esther.

The supreme contribution of Protestantism to our subject was the Bible itself. The earliest translations were those made by the men of the Reform, Lefèvre d'Étaples (1530) and Olivetan (1535). The Catholic Bible of Louvain which appeared in 1550 was closely modelled on Olivetan's version. Such differences as there are are either very small or have a clear doctrinal significance. This remained the standard Catholic translation for most of our period,[2] until the publication of Le Maistre de Saci's version, beginning in 1667. Of course the official Catholic Bible was the Vulgate, which most men of letters would read in preference to a French translation (Saint-Amant was a notable exception).[3]

But these translations are only one aspect of a wider phenomenon, the diffusion of Biblical ways of thought and speech brought about

---

[1] See below, Ch. VII.

[2] Ostensibly new translations, like those of René Benoist (1566) and Pierre Frizon (1621), were in fact merely reprints from it.

[3] For a fuller account see Pétavel, *La Bible en France*; Berger, *La Bible au XVI*[e] *siècle*; Sayce, *Modern Language Review*, 1942, pp. 147 ff.

by Protestantism. Of far-reaching importance for the literature
of the Protestant countries, this Biblical spirit is also typical of
the French Huguenots (*Les Tragiques* provide the most striking
example). That it was equally typical of the mass of French Protestants, and well into the seventeenth century, is shown by an
anecdote of Tallemant des Réaux: 'Une huguenotte ayant à passer
une grande cour au grand soleil, dit: Il faut passer ce torrent
de Cedron.'[1] With this must be coupled a pride in plain speaking
and a contempt for courtly and precious phraseology.[2]

It is not therefore surprising that in France the first Biblical literature on humanist models was the work of Protestants—
Buchanan's Latin tragedies *Baptistes* and *Jephthes* (*c*. 1540), followed
by the Biblical plays of Bèze and Des Masures.[3] The first Biblical
narrative poem I have been able to trace was also written by a
Protestant—*Le livre de Iob traduit en poesie françoise selon la verité
Hebraique* by A. Du Plessis (1552).[4] The author is described as
Parisien and the poem is dedicated to Edward VI of England. It
was written at Geneva.[5] The poem is merely a verse paraphrase
with a theological and didactic object, though a reference to heroic
style in the Preface and the division into three parts suggests
a rudimentary attempt at literary form.

After Du Plessis the Biblical poets of the sixteenth century were
frequently Protestant. In the seventeenth century they were nearly
all Catholics (Saint-Amant and Coras were converts to Catholicism). It is noteworthy, however, that the majority originated
from provinces, the whole of the Midi and Normandy, which were
deeply influenced by Protestantism.

Calvinist conceptions of morality are also of importance in the
development of the Biblical epic. A story like that of Jacob and
Esau presents a serious problem for the modern reader, and such

---

[1] ed. Mongrédien, viii. 81.

[2] A significant text is a statement of Du Moulin (1609): 'Nous ne parlons point
de "barriquades de convoitises" ni d' "escalades de vertus". Nous n'appelons point
Jésus-Christ "le Dauphin du Ciel". . . . Il nous suffit de parler françois. Nostre but
seulement est d'estre entendu' (quoted by Pannier, *L'Église Réformée de Paris, 1621–9*,
i. 340).

[3] See Thibaut de Maisières, *Les Poèmes inspirés du début de la Genèse*, p. 12; Lebègue,
Tragédie de la Renaissance, p. 24.

[4] No place is given, but it was printed at Geneva (*de l'imprimerie de Iean Gerard* on
title-page).

[5]   Parmy ces rocz, en terre Geneuoise
            Loue Angleterre en ma langue Françoyse (p. 8).

problems occur frequently throughout the Old Testament. There
seem to be three possible solutions. Many Christians today would
say that such actions, wrong in themselves, must be considered
in the light of local and contemporary circumstances; but, whatever its merits, this attitude was hardly possible in the sixteenth
and seventeenth centuries. Secondly, an attempt may be made to
reconcile the conduct of the patriarchs with Christian standards,
using the methods of casuistry. This was the choice of most
Catholic poets of the seventeenth century. From a literary point
of view, as we shall see, it leads almost inevitably to a distortion
of the atmosphere of the Bible, to grotesque anachronisms or
contradictions. Finally it may be argued that human standards of
morality are an illusion, that the just man with divine guidance is
superior to human law, and that the fulfilment of the divine
purpose justifies such apparent crimes. This was approximately
the position of Zwingli and Calvin.[1] Thus in his *Sermons sur le
Deuteronome* Calvin considers similar questions in detail. God
commands the Jews to kill their enemies without mercy. Does
not this show that they act with no feeling for pity or humanity?
Calvin replies that, while men must in general follow the commandments of love, special orders of God, even though apparently
inconsistent with those commandments, must be obeyed without
hesitation.[2] That this attitude was generally assumed by Protestant
poets of the late sixteenth century explains their superior understanding of the spirit of the Bible, for it approaches most closely
the conceptions of the Old Testament. Its absence in later poets
goes far to account for their insipid flatness in the treatment of
such episodes.

The broad effects of the Counter-Reformation were the renewal
of spiritual life, described by Bremond,[3] and the attempt to
rechristianize art and letters.[4] Both are of consequence for the
Biblical epic, but they have been treated elsewhere, and here it will
be necessary only to refer briefly to those aspects which touch
the subject closely.

---

[1] Well summarized by Zanta: 'Pour le juste par excellence, il n'est point de loi;
si bien que l'adultère, l'homicide, crimes en tant qu'ils sont l'œuvre de l'homme,
ne le sont plus, en tant qu'ils sont l'œuvre de Dieu' (*La Renaissance du Stoïcisme*, p. 53).
[2] *Sermons sur le Deuteronome*, pp. 289 ff.
[3] *Histoire littéraire du sentiment religieux*.
[4] See Dejob, *L'Influence du Concile de Trente*; Mâle, *L'Art religieux après le Concile
de Trente*.

The perpetual aspiration of the time, says Mâle,[1] was the union
of heaven and earth. Two manifestations of this tendency were
the cult of angels (half-way between the human and the divine)
and the rapid development of conventional allegory, in which
ethical and spiritual conceptions take on human form. In particular, belief in a Guardian Angel who accompanies everyone from
the cradle to the grave began to exert a considerable influence
on religious life. The origin of the belief was no doubt the Bible
story of Tobit, and there is some New Testament authority for it.
It is possible to trace a classical influence also at work: Thomassin[2]
compares the relationship to that between Ulysses and Minerva.
But as a doctrine it seems to have taken shape only in the sixteenth
century and in France. The first mass of the Guardian Angel was
celebrated at Rodez in 1526.[3]

Allegory was not of course an innovation of the Counter-
Reformation, but during the period it was developed into a
conventional system. We must distinguish between the allegorical
significance attached to a whole work (see Chapter II) and the
occasional appearance of abstractions in human form. In the
first we pass from the human to the superhuman, in the second
the order is reversed—both are facets of the desire to join heaven
and earth. This second kind of allegory is of special importance
for the plastic arts—it was reduced to a code by such works as the
Iconologia of Ripa[4]—but it was of almost equal importance for
literature.

Another result of the Counter-Reformation was the treatment
of incidents in the Old Testament simply as prefigurations of the
New. Thus the rescue of Moses represents the Infant Christ saved
from Herod. This belongs to the oldest traditions of Christianity
—the novelty consists in its systematic application to the arts.
In the epic it leads to the multiplication of Messianic prophecies,
which add another allegorical sense to the poems.

A somewhat similar conception influenced the treatment of
Biblical figures in art, in opposition to the historical exactitude
encouraged by Biblical scholarship and Protestantism. During
the sixteenth century a striking change occurred in painting:
instead of being represented in modern dress (still to be found in
Tintoretto and Veronese) Biblical personages were attired in a

[1] Op. cit., p. 301.   [2] *Methode d'étudier*, i. 366.
[3] Mâle, p. 302.   [4] Ib., pp. 383 ff.

manner which was neither historical nor modern. A significant text for our purpose is a collection of engravings by Antonio Tempesta depicting battle-scenes from the Bible.[1] The scenes resemble each other to the point of monotony. Each warrior—Joshua or Samson or David—wears a large plumed helmet, a loose tunic, and sandals; his expression is one of noble ferocity. The disparate elements of these figures are no doubt principally classical, perhaps especially Roman. In fact, however, they correspond to a timeless ideal of heroic dignity.

Engraving is of special importance for the study of seventeenth-century literature. Painting was on the whole difficult of access; engraving brought it within reach of the general public and added a large original production. Intimately connected with the technique of printing and publishing, it may well have affected the imagination of the poets: and if, as is more probable, the influence was mostly in the contrary direction, it still enables us to seize that imagination in visible shape. Figures like those of Tempesta reappear frequently in the frontispieces and plates of the epic poems.

Of even greater importance were the illustrated Bibles and sets of Biblical engravings which appeared in France, though here an equal part must be ascribed to the Protestant spirit. The prototype, as far as France is concerned, may be found in the woodcuts of Bernard Salomon (*le petit Bernard*), published at Lyons in 1553.[2] Bernard himself was a Catholic, but his employer, Jean de Tournes, was a convert to Calvinism: the work issues from a typically mixed environment. It was reprinted, at Geneva, as late as 1681.[3] In the meantime there appeared the engravings, sometimes attributed to Jean Cousin[4] and published by Jean Le Clerc in 1596,[5] very different in style but similar in iconography (thus in both works the Golden Calf is represented in two plates, once on a low altar, once on a high column). Le Clerc's work was reprinted at frequent intervals throughout the seventeenth century (and later—the Bibliothèque Nationale has an edition of 1724). Later came the illustrations to Pierre Frizon's Bible (1621), published separately by the Jesuit Antoine Girard in 1653,[6] which

---

[1] Rome, 1612; reprinted as *Sacra Bella* at Antwerp (no date).
[2] See Rondot, *Bernard Salomon*; Schubart, *Die Bibelillustrationen des Bernard Salomon*.
[3] *Icones historicae Veteris et Novi Testamenti*, Geneva, 1681.
[4] Cf. Duportal, *Étude sur les livres à figures*, p. 76, n. 4.
[5] *Figures de la Saincte Bible . . .* , Paris, 1596. Cf. Didot, *Jean Cousin*, p. 143.
[6] *Les Peintures sacrées sur la Bible*, Paris, 1653.

continue the same tradition, and the *Bible de Royaumont* of 1670, which for the most part reprints Merian's *Icones Biblicae*.[1] It seems probable that the way in which people of the seventeenth century imagined the scenes of the Bible was that of Bernard Salomon and his imitators. They make a much more serious attempt at local accuracy than Tempesta. The landscape backgrounds are remarkable in this respect. The buildings and costumes, on the other hand, are exotic but in no way historically true. They are half Roman, half fanciful. The most characteristic Oriental element is the camel, a strange beast with slender swan-like neck and a horse's head. Biblical, classical, and modern features are assembled but finally make up a realm of pure fantasy.

If the Counter-Reformation encouraged this sort of semi-classical inspiration, it made a determined attack on paganism both in thought and in the mythological apparatus of poets and painters. Montaigne's difficulties with the Roman censors over the word 'Fortune' will be remembered. One Biblical epic—Ansaldo Cebà's *Esther*—was even placed on the Index because, says Baillet, 'Ceba avoit deshonoré et souillé la vérité de l'Histoire Sainte par un tas de petits contes.'[2] The attitude of the Church must therefore be taken into account, as well as the conclusions of the theoretical critics.

At the same time ecclesiastical opinion supported and propagated the doctrine of pillage of the ancients (see Chapter II). Bremond shows that among the French theologians of the early seventeenth century, such as Richeome and Binet, the idea was so widespread as to be commonplace.[3] Later Thomassin, whose work is in part an amplification of the same theme, ascribes its origin to the early Fathers:

Saint Gregoire Evesque de Nysse veut qu'à l'imitation de Moyse, nous volions l'Egypte avant que d'en sortir, et que nous luy enlevions les richesses dont elle ornoit les temples de ses fausses Divinitez, pour les transporter dans l'Eglise, qui est le temple du veritable Dieu.[4]

These then were the external factors which influenced particularly the development of the Biblical epic (those religious and

---

[1] Strasbourg, 1625. Cf. Duportal, *Étude*, p. 128.

[2] *Jugemens des Sçavans*, v, no. 1399.

[3] 'Fils de l'humanisme, nos dévots prétendent . . . que les richesses de l'Égypte, je veux dire, ce qu'il y a de vraiment exquis chez les classiques, appartient au peuple de Dieu' (*Sentiment religieux*, i. 194).   [4] *Methode d'étudier*, a8v°.

social phenomena which affected all literary forms have been passed over). It will be seen that the three great movements we have discussed—Humanism, Protestantism, and Counter-Reformation—correspond, very approximately, to the three immediate sources proposed—Ronsard, Du Bartas, and Tasso. This correspondence is by no means rigid, however. Thus it is impossible to separate either Du Bartas or Tasso from the influence of Humanism, to which they owed a large part of their inspiration. Ariosto must be considered a poet of the Renaissance, with none of the characteristics of the Counter-Reformation, but he influenced French poetry through Tasso, as well as directly. Du Bartas owed much to the Pléiade, especially in his technical characteristics. Tasso's *Mondo Creato* was perhaps inspired, certainly influenced, by Du Bartas.[1] We are confronted at the very beginning with a *chassé-croisé* of influences, which already tends to cast doubt on too decided affirmations.

The first Biblical poem produced by the Pléiade was Du Bellay's *Monomachie de David et de Goliath*, published in 1560. It consists of about five hundred decasyllabic lines in *huitains*, strictly limited to the single episode of David's battle. It is not an epic, but it might well be an epic fragment. In any case it is interesting as the first attempt in French to treat a Biblical subject on the model of Homer and Virgil. Already we find many of the external features, which later become standardized: the proposition, still in a very loose form; the double invocation, divine and human (almost universal in later poems and probably derived from Ariosto); sustained similes and long tirades. However, there is no *merveilleux* and no attempt to vary by episodes the simple movement of the Bible narrative. Du Bellay's treatment of the Bible is interesting—he proceeds by suppression, not by expansion. Thus there is no mention of the details of David's preparations, the sling and the pebbles, which stand out so vividly in the original.[2] In this way the two adversaries and the course of the battle are isolated, and the narrative acquires a certain dramatic tension. These characteristics, however, are important for later poems only by contrast. More interesting is Du Bellay's own consciousness of his departure from pagan themes, which anticipates some

---

[1] See Thibaut de Maisières, *Poèmes inspirés*, pp. 47 ff.
[2] I Sam. xvii. 40.

of the arguments used by the seventeenth-century defenders of
Christian poetry:[1]

> Chantez mes uers, cest immortel honneur,
> Dont uous auez la matiere choisie:
> Ce uous sera plus de gloire et bonheur,
> Que les uieux sons d'une fable moisie . . .
> Si auez uous plus saincte fantaisie,
> Que le sonneur des Pergames de Troye.[2]

Remy Belleau's *Les Amours de David et de Bersabee* followed in
1572 in the second edition of *La Bergerie*. It is brief, it has no
proposition or invocation, the opportunity for presenting illustrious action (Uriah's death) is neglected, the description of the
setting, which was to become an integral part of the epic recipe, is
omitted. On the other hand, there are some of the devices which
characterize epic, especially the daring employment of the *merveilleux*. And it is written in Alexandrines.

Cupid, who sets the plot in motion by his intrigues, occupies a
position of prominence and authority. A serious ambiguity results.
We find *Dauid choisi de Dieu* (where *Dieu* is Jehovah) and three
lines further on, referring to Cupid,

> Mais qui peut resister à la force indomptable
> De la main de ce Dieu . . . ?[3]

Such a juxtaposition, aggravated by the attribution of omnipo-
tence to Cupid, is characteristic of the Pléiade's attitude to pagan
and Christian *merveilleux*. It could certainly not be found in any
Biblical poet after 1620. In the Bible[4] God inspires Nathan to
charge David with his crime. In Belleau an angel is dispatched to
instruct the prophet. We are here in the presence of one of the
most constant of epic devices. Its original source must be sought in
the divine messengers of classical epic, Mercury and Iris. At what
point the divine messenger became an angel is not quite clear,
though the origin is probably Italian. A striking example occurs in
Sannazaro's *De partu Virginis*.[5] Belleau also introduces the allegorical figures of the Justice and Clemency of God, who debate on the
punishment of David.[6] This idea is used in an exactly similar way

---

[1] See Ch. II, above; also Chamard, *Histoire de la Pléiade*, i. 302.
[2] *Monomachie*, p. 6.   [3] p. 104 v°.
[4] II Sam. xii. 1.   [5] See below, p. 49.
[6] *Les Amours de David*, p. 107.

by Coras in *Jonas*.[1] It was no doubt intended as a substitute for the council of the gods in classical epic.

About the same time (before 1570) Vauquelin de la Fresnaye began his *Israëlide*, which also deals with the history of David.[2] In 1576 Pierre de Brach published *La Monomachie de David et de Goliat*, dedicated to Montaigne. The title must have been copied from Du Bellay, but there are few signs of imitation. It is again a miniature epic or self-contained episode. It begins with a proposition, like Du Bellay's, showing the poet's evolution from war to the works of God, though the conventional *je chante* is avoided. There follows a regular invocation to God, but there is no description of the setting—the reader is plunged at once into the war between Hebrews and Philistines. Epic conventions had not yet hardened. Like Belleau, de Brach uses the pagan gods rather dangerously. Jupiter and Mars appear as the effective lords of thunder and war.

Vauquelin and de Brach were not members of the Pléiade but they wrote under its influence. That de Brach was also the friend of Du Bartas, who admired him greatly, is one more link between the two schools, another proof that the division between them must not be made too rigid. This said, it is remarkable that all the four Biblical poems of the Pléiade group should deal with the story of David. The subject was in the air, no doubt, but more precise reasons may be sought. The Hebrews and the Philistines may well represent the two parties whose dissensions were ravaging the country.[3] At any rate the realism in the scenes of battle and carnage was probably due to the contemporary reign of violence. The theme of single combat links the Bible with classical epic and Italian romance. Another explanation, perhaps fanciful, is the blossoming of springtime and youth in David, which caught the imagination of Donatello and Michelangelo and was in harmony with the spirit of the Pléiade.

In the meantime Ronsard's *Franciade* had appeared in 1572. It is of no interest from a narrowly Biblical point of view, but its position as the first French Renaissance epic on a grand scale and its

---

[1] Pp. 34 and 170 (1665 ed.).

[2] See Ch. V below. Cardinal Du Perron also planned in his youth to write an epic, the *Mosaïde*, of which he quotes the opening line (*Perroniana et Thuana*, Cologne, 1694, pp. 310–11).

[3] Explicitly stated by de Brach (*Œuvres*, ed. Dezeimeris, ii. 6).

formal characteristics give it considerable importance. Its composition in decasyllables represents, historically at least, a step back, since the Alexandrine was already established as the heroic metre in the works of Belleau and de Brach. On the whole, in comparing it with the seventeenth-century poems one is struck by the differences rather than the resemblances. Above all Ronsard is much closer to Homer, not only in form but in spirit (the familiar contact with everyday things). It is difficult to judge the structure as the poem is not complete, but it appears to follow the classical model more strictly than later poets. However, to this Homeric basis much is added—magic, Christian *merveilleux*, clumsy attempts at psychological analysis.

The divine messenger plays an important part, and the contrast with the angels of Christian epic is so marked that the passage may be quoted in full:

> A peine eut dit que Mercure s'appreste,
> Sa capeline affubla sur sa teste,
> De talonniers ses talons assortit,
> D'vn mandillon son espaule vestit,
> Prist sa houssine à deux serpens ailée :
> Puis à chef bas enfonçant sa volée,
> Ores à poincte, ores d'vn grand contour
> Hachoit menu tout le ciel d'alentour.[1]

The first part—Mercury's preparation—is vividly recorded and Olympus is illuminated with a wholly terrestrial beauty. The second part, the flight, fails to convey rapidity of movement or a sense of divinity.

It is not necessary here to repeat in full the fortunes of Ronsard in the seventeenth century.[2] Among the Biblical poets Coras quotes the *Franciade* in the Preface to *Jonas*.[3] Carel de Sainte-Garde in the *Defense des Beaux Esprits*[4] gives high praise to Ronsard, *ecrivain incomparable*, but this must be attributed partly to the choice of a weapon against Boileau. Direct borrowings from Ronsard are, however, rare. Negative conclusions in such cases are of limited value, but only one obvious imitation is to be found—in the *David* of Coras. Here David is loved by two sisters, Merab and Mical, the daughters of Saul. There is thus an exact parallel

---

[1] *Franciade*, bk. i (ed. Laumonier, iii. 16–17).
[2] See Fuchs, *Revue de la Renaissance*, viii–ix, 1907–8.
[3] 1665 ed., p. 23.   [4] p. 30.

between the characters of the two poems—David and Francus; Goliath and the giant Phovère; Saul and Dicée; Merab and Hyante; Mical and Climene. It is true that the two sisters are from the Bible,[1] though there only Michal is in love with David, and that the whole situation bears a general resemblance to the story of Aeneas and Dido grafted on the Nausicaa episode of the *Odyssey*. But there are more particular coincidences between the two poems and it is clear that Coras was influenced by the analogy in the development of the situation. Merab, like Hyante, has magical powers and uses them to ensnare the hero. The magic powers of the Witch of Endor are almost certainly modelled on those of Hyante (though a common Italian source cannot be completely excluded):

> Et la Lune a paru dans son cours diligent,
> Toute preste à tomber de son trône d'argent,
> On a veu le haut front des superbes montagnes,
> S'abaisser jusqu'au sein des plus humbles campagnes,
> Vers leur source on a veu les fleuues remonter.[2]

> Par sa magie elle peut attirer
> La Lune en bas, le Ciel faire virer
> A reculons, et des fleuues les courses
> Encontre-mont rebrousser à leurs sources.[3]

Another striking resemblance is to be found in Ronsard's description of Hyante in her chariot[4] and Coras's triumphal entry of the two sisters into Gaba.[5] Here, however, the question is complicated by the fact that for this passage Coras also drew on Saint-Amant's princess of Egypt in the *Moyse sauvé* and that Saint-Amant may himself have been influenced by Ronsard.[6]

A poem which does not fit into any group, but which also indicates certain future tendencies, is the *Judith* of Thierry Petremand (Lyons, 1578). It appeared four years after the *Judith* of Du Bartas, but there is no evidence of any connexion between the two. The author was a Catholic, as is shown by the *nihil obstat*. The poem follows the Bible closely. There is no *merveilleux*, except for superficial mythological allusions, no recitals, no unity

---

[1] I Sam. xviii. 17 ff.   [2] *David*, p. 77.
[3] *Franciade*, bk. iii (ed. Laumonier, iii. 91).
[4] Bk. iv (Laumonier, iii. 128).
[5] *David*, p. 108.   [6] Cf. p. 94 below.

of time (Petremand goes back to the very beginning and carries on the story until the death of Judith at the age of 105), no episodes, except for the history of the Jews, which is contained in the Bible and is not fully exploited. But there is plainly an attempt to mould the poem in an epic form and it shows certain qualities of narration.

The clearest evidence of Petremand's epic intentions is to be found in the marginal rubrics, which reveal an acquaintance with critical theory—*Proposition, Inuocation, Narration, Mutation de Fortune* (to stress the Aristotelian peripeteia of Arphaxad's fall), *Comparaison.* Such a proceeding shows that the main ingredients of the epic recipe were already fixed, even for an obscure poet.

Petremand's attitude to the moral problems raised by Judith's deed is simple. He has no doubts and no humanitarian scruples. Judith's maid tells her:

> Si en ce tu l'amuses
> Pour lui donner la mort, ce sont tressainctes ruses.[1]

Before she kills Holofernes she debates with herself in a long monologue. But there is never any suggestion of a moral problem in the actual killing. The object of this hesitation is merely to screw up the heroine's courage by means of previous examples and the shame of failure. The death of Holofernes is described with sardonic brutality:

> Et auecque la vie,
> Va perdant le desir de sa nouuelle amie.[2]

There are no excuses for Judith and no useless irades against Holofernes. This attitude, diametrically opposed to that of later poets, is, we have suggested, essentially Protestant in origin. There is no reason to modify this opinion, though it appears that Catholics too were influenced by it.

Petremand is typical of a large category of Biblical poets: a provincial, far removed from the prevailing literary schools, impelled by religious motives but equally eager to employ (or display) a store of classical culture. He differs from his successors principally by a fresher enthusiasm, a more vigorous talent. Historically he may be regarded as occupying a place half-way between the Pléiade and the school of Du Bartas.

[1] p. 68. [2] p. 72.

The *Judith* of Du Bartas was first published in 1574.[1] The *Semaine* followed in 1578 (it was continued by the *Seconde Semaine*, published from 1584 to 1603). Both are written in Alexandrines, but apart from their metre the two works are very different. The *Semaine* ranges over the whole course of Biblical history, and outside it, to cover wide fields of scientific knowledge—astronomy, zoology, botany, mineralogy. There is no hero who could unify these diverse elements by his continual presence. The work is truly epic in its proportions and vast scope, but the form of classical epic with its unity of time and action, or even the looser structure of Italian romance, is submerged in this many-sided development. In fact the sources of the *Semaine* are to be found elsewhere—in the creation poems, the Hexaëmera, of the early Fathers.[2] However, in external details, ornament, and technique the poem is deeply influenced by Homer and Virgil. And it has a unity, based on the strong sense of divine purpose and the existence of another action on a super-human plane, whose protagonists remain the same. This second action is also found in classical epic, but there the two are inter-woven and almost equal in importance. In Du Bartas the human action is reduced to a subordinate place, indeed in the early books it scarcely exists, while the superhuman action is independent and unfolds in limitless time and space. The distinction drawn by Thibaut de Maisières[3] between celestial and human subjects in Old Testament poems is therefore an important one.

Judith belongs to the latter category. In plan and methods it already approaches the Biblical epic of the seventeenth century. The most notable advance in relation to earlier poets is the intro-duction of recitals on the classical model. Unlike Petremand, Du Bartas takes full advantage of the opportunity offered by the Bible (Judith v) to give the previous history of the Jews in the mouth of Achior. More interesting is the story of Judith's early life (Judith viii), taken up as a recital at the end of the poem. In this way the chronology of the Bible is altered and the poet affirms

---

[1] A revised version, considerably altered, was published in 1579 and frequently afterwards (*Works of Du Bartas*, ed. Holmes, i. 184). Only the revised text was likely to be accessible to seventeenth-century poets. I therefore quote from an edition of 1616 (No. 40 in Holmes's bibliography, *Works*, i. 77). For the convenience of the reader, a reference to the Holmes edition is appended. The same system has been followed for the *Semaines*.

[2] See Delaruelle, *Revue d'histoire littéraire*, 1933; Thibaut de Maisières, op. cit.; Holmes, i. 111 ff. [3] Op. cit., p. 1.

a certain liberty with regard to the sacred text. Another innovation is the council of Nebuchadnezzar, which, unlike the pedestrian
account of Petremand, is developed into a Homeric assembly of
chieftains. At the council appear several characters who are not
found in the Bible, another sign of literary artifice. Du Bartas does
not hesitate to suppress ruthlessly, as well as to add to his source.

   With this freedom (perhaps partly because of it) is associated a
vivid feeling for the realism of the Bible and its modern application. Thus in the *Seconde Semaine* the Israelites at the rock of Horeb
become a group of French peasants:

> l'vn sur la moite riue
> Panché hume à longs traits l'onde fraischement viue,
> L'autre en remplit sa main, et l'autre son chapeau,
> L'autre dans vne seille en porte à son troupeau,
> L'autre en enfle son outre, et l'autre encor barboüille
> Dans le chrystal courant, ainsi qu'vne grenoüille.[1]

A comparison with the same scene in Saint-Amant[2] reveals the
extent of the evolution between the two, as well as the probability
of a direct influence. Like his predecessors Du Bartas finds in the
Bible a source of familiar sentiments and scenes which scarcely
require modification. The atmosphere of a war in which the
combatants are civilians fighting near and for their homes is
expressed in Jesse's farewell to his sons:

> La dextre tousiours forte
> De Dieu soit vostre force, enfans, et puissiez-vous
> Reuenir dés demain victorieux chez nous.[3]

It might equally well be a scene from the Wars of Religion.
Similarly in *Judith* Holofernes is dressed in modern fashion.[4] The
expression of violent hatred:

> Il en a, le meschant (crie tout l'ost Hebrieu)
> Ha, le vilain, l'Athee, il sent la main de Dieu[5]

---

[1] 1616 ed., p. 428; Holmes, iii. 282.
[2] Où ce peuple alteré non seulement s'abbreuve,
     Mais se baigne, se plonge, et, comblé de plaisir,
     Peut en mille façons contenter son desir.
     L'onde, au sortir du roc, *fraische*, bruyante et *vive* . . .
                                        (*Œuvres*, ed. Livet, ii. 220).
[3] *Seconde Semaine* (1616 ed., p. 452; Holmes, iii. 335).
[4] Or il se desboutonne, ore il tire ses bas . . .
     Que cuidant desnoüer de ses tremblottans doigts
     La subtile éguillette, il la noüe trois fois
                                        (1616 ed., p. 604; Holmes, ii. 119).
[5] *Seconde Semaine* (1616 ed., p. 460; Holmes, iii. 344).

shows a deep understanding of the spirit of the Old Testament, or perhaps rather a capacity for developing parallel sentiments. In the Preface to *Judith* Du Bartas defends himself against the charge of inciting to the murder of a tyrant. Whether he was sincere or not, the parallel between Holofernes and Henry III had clearly occurred to him and it may be added to contemporary feminism as a reason for the popularity of the Judith theme in the last quarter of the century.[1]

Du Bartas uses pagan mythology much more freely than most later poets. But he uses various precautions which after him soon become standardized. In

> Qui, *vray* Neptune, tiens le moite frain des eaux[2]

or

> *Telle qu'on peint* Venus, quand lasciuement molle
> Elle naist dans la mer, et qu'auecques les Thons
> Ià le feu de ses yeux embraze les Tritons[3]

the poet exploits the poetic associations of Neptune and Venus, and at the same time salves his conscience by asserting their falsity (which also of course weakens the poetic effect). Apart from the personified figures of Envy and Rumour, already conventional, Du Bartas includes a more complex allegory, similar to Belleau's Justice and Clemency. Repentance, Prayer, and Abstinence, introduced by Faith, plead with God to spare Nineveh.[4] As this forms part of the Jonah story it may also have influenced Coras. Du Bartas himself does not mention any general allegorical significance, but the commentary of Goulart refers to the theological interpretation of *Judith* as the victory of the Church over her enemies.[5]

Du Bartas has not the same capacity for symmetrical construction as the seventeenth-century poets, but the principal formal elements of their work are already contained in *Judith*. He differs from them above all in his feeling for Biblical atmosphere and in the way he distinguishes the essential from the unessential (from a poetic point of view) in the Biblical narrative. It is remarkable

---

[1] Cf. Holmes, i. 146.   [2] *Semaine* (1616 ed., p. 2; Holmes, ii. 195).
[3] *Seconde Semaine* (1616 ed., p. 478; Holmes, iii. 363).
[4] *Seconde Semaine* (1616 ed., p. 447; Holmes, iii. 440).
[5] In the *Argument de la Judith*. It is noteworthy that Du Bartas chose a book considered apocryphal by Protestants, perhaps because its less sacred character allowed him more freedom.

that this freedom should be found in a Protestant poet. The spirit of the Bible is more important for him than a literal attachment to the text.

Du Bartas bears clear traces of the influence of Ariosto, especially in the amorous scenes.[1] He in his turn was widely read in Italy. A translation of the *Semaine* by Ferrante Guisone first appeared in 1592. The influence of Du Bartas on Tasso's *Mondo Creato* has already been noticed,[2] though French poets imitated the *Gerusalemme Liberata* rather than the *Mondo Creato*.

In France the reputation of Du Bartas was enormous, even in the early years of the seventeenth century. Dr. Ashton, on the basis of the editions, concludes that the poet's fame reached its height about 1608, after which it began to decline, and collapsed completely after 1616.[3] The last edition in French-speaking territory was published at Geneva in 1632. After this date an extract from the *Seconde Semaine* appears in the *Jardin des Muses* of 1643,[4] and a sonnet and hymn were published in the *Recueil de Barbin* of 1692,[5] an historical survey beginning with Villon. On the evidence of the editions Dr. Ashton's conclusions are thus amply justified and the indifference of the public was no doubt shared by the best critical opinion. However, a writer's influence cannot be measured entirely by the number of reimpressions of his work, old books are still read, and Du Bartas still had admirers, even in Paris. The last works directly inspired by his example, the *Semaine* of Abel d'Argent and *La Loy de l'Eternel* of Jeangaston, appeared as late as 1629 and 1635.[6]

Among the epic poets there are several instances of the continued influence of Du Bartas. Saint-Amant in his letter to Bochart (1654) quotes him as authority for placing the capital of Egypt at Memphis.[7] Marie de Pech de Calages in the 'Discours aux Dames' prefixed to *Judith* (1660) quotes his *Judith* with approval, though she says she only read it after the completion of her own poem. Coras refers to him in the prefaces to *Jonas*[8] and *Josué*[9] (1665), in both cases with a quotation. Carel de Sainte-Garde in

---

[1] This influence is perhaps exaggerated by Cioranescu (i. 180–2).
[2] p. 35 above.
[3] *Du Bartas en Angleterre*, pp. 43–44. These conclusions are not seriously affected by Holmes's more accurate classification of the editions (*Works*, i. 67 ff.).
[4] Lachèvre, *Recueils collectifs*, ii. 260.   [5] Ib. iii. 317.
[6] For critical judgements during the century, see Holmes, i. 50 ff.
[7] *Œuvres*, ed. Livet, ii. 330.   [8] p. 23.   [9] e3.

his *Defense des Beaux Esprits* (1675) maintains against Boileau that Du Bartas was superior to Marot, who was merely a *railleur*.[1]

When we turn to the poems themselves, no doubt is possible. In the early years of the century it is not surprising that most poems published were so close to Du Bartas as to form part of a 'school'. The *Semaine* of Gamon is indeed no more than a verse commentary on the earlier work. But even after the break in the production of Biblical epic between 1620 and 1650, the direct influence of Du Bartas can be discovered in nearly every case—in general situations and structure and also very often in verbal imitation and plagiarism. In Saint-Amant and Coras this is not surprising in view of their references outside the poems. Marie de Pech, in spite of the affirmation quoted, had certainly read Du Bartas before she finished *Judith*, or altered it afterwards, since there are numerous coincidences. The only important exception is Desmarets, whose *Esther* belongs to another tradition and seems to bear no trace of this influence. It is, however, active as late as the poems of Saint-Martin (1667 and 1670), where the imitation is particularly marked, and possibly Charles Perrault's *Adam* (1697), at the very end of the century. Of course the original could not be copied slavishly: changes had to be made in order to render the verse of Du Bartas tolerable to the age of Louis XIV. These changes were always in the sense of elimination of picturesque detail, of substitution of the general for the particular, and of greater poetic dignity.[2]

The first-fruits of the influence of Du Bartas were the two poems of Didier Oriet, *La Susanne* (1581) and *Livre de l'Esther* (1584). Their first model was undoubtedly *Judith*:

> Muse donq haste toi, haste toi, et te guide
> Legere aprés Bartas, qui de sa Castalide

[1] p. 68.

[2] The detailed evidence of these borrowings is given in later chapters. Here may be included one example of the process at work:

> Auec le trait mignard d'vn bel œil il atrape
> Le boüillant iouuenceau: l'argent luy sert de trape
> Pour prendre l'vsurier.
>
> (*Semaine*, 1616 ed., p. 18; Holmes, ii. 215.)
>
> Pour prendre vn cœur avare, il se sert des thresors:
> Il inspire l'amour, pour signaler sa haine.
>
> (Saint-Martin, *La Nature naissante*, p. 30.)

The context establishes conclusively that the second passage was imitated from the first.

Fait reuiure Iudith par ce grand Vniuers
Au seucre miellé du dous chant de ses vers.[1]

However, although the external form and the limited theme of
the two poems are taken from *Judith*, in general they owe more
to the *Semaine*. At every point the Bible story is expanded with a
wealth of encyclopaedic allusion.

The plan of both poems shows a lack of mastery of technical
methods, though the epic intention is strongly marked. *Esther*
is an example of narration *ab ovo*: it goes back to the banquet and
the repudiation of Vashti and there are no chronological variations. In *Susanne* the heroine only appears in the last book (of
three), which leads to a lack of balance. Proposition and invocation are in their conventional place, but standard forms are not
yet settled. The technique of transitions is still undeveloped.
Incident follows incident with no real link. Recitals are extensively
employed. Thus the history of the Jews from Abraham to Moses
is introduced as part of Susanna's religious education, told by her
father. This device is of frequent occurrence in the seventeenth century. On the other hand, the short episodes derived from Susanna's
reading of the Scriptures, all of which deal with one theme, the
duties of a wife to her husband, demand a living acquaintance
with the Bible which is not found in later poets. The regular flow
of Alexandrines is twice broken: at the end of *Susanne* by a hymn
of thanksgiving in six-line stanzas (a common phenomenon)
and in *Esther* by a series of echoes, introduced for no reason in
the soliloquy of Vashti.[2]

Oriet does not, like Belleau and later d'Urfé, allot an active
role to pagan divinities, but classical mythology is so interwoven
in the texture of the poems that it would be impossible to detach
it without pulling the whole fabric to pieces. Often pagan and
Christian or Biblical allusions are audaciously juxtaposed. In an
apostrophe to God Himself:

Tu fis pour le secours des gens de Gabaon
Sur le Pole Phœbus, Hecate en Aialon
Garrotés arréter.[3]

Phoebus and Hecate are no more than conventional substitutes
for sun and moon, but their collision with the topography of
Palestine brings out all the latent associations they contain and

---

[1] *Susanne*, p. 1.   [2] *Esther*, p. 10.   [3] Ib., p. 37.

results in a violent contrast between two worlds. In later poets this contrast subsists but its external effects are softened.

Susanna's garden[1] has nothing Oriental about it. With its arcades, box hedges, small parterres, sculptures, and fountains it belongs entirely to Oriet's period. The impression of the whole is lost in a mass of detail—even the measurements are given. It is clear that the poet's method corresponds exactly to the method of the gardener of the period, in which concentration on beauty of detail obscures the harmony of the general effect.[2]

Gabrielle de Coignard (Madame de Mansencal), a Catholic of Toulouse, was the first woman to treat a Biblical subject in epic, and it is not surprising that she chose the story of Judith. Her *Imitation de la Victoire de Judith* appeared in 1595. Strangely enough, there is no evidence of the direct influence of Du Bartas, though it seems hardly conceivable that she can have been unacquainted with his work. The chief differences are her strict fidelity to the Bible, in particular to its chronology, and the absence of mythological allusions.

The course of the narrative follows the Book of Judith closely, beginning with the unfolding of Nebuchadnezzar's plans of conquest. The order of the Bible is nowhere changed and, as in Petremand, the opportunity for a full epic recital afforded by Achior's appearance is inadequately exploited. Of more importance for future developments is the intervention of Satan, who inspires Holofernes.[3]

The *Histoire tragique de Sennacherib, Roy des Assyriens*, by François Perrin, a priest of Autun, appeared in 1599. It is a straightforward story, with no *merveilleux*, episodes, or chronological variations. It may be compared for its provincial technique with Petremand's *Judith*, though it lacks even the occasional strength of that work—here all is flaccid and diffuse. It is interesting, however, for the subject, which abandons the conventional series and is well suited to epic; for the use of Josephus, who is quoted in the Preface; and for topical allusions, which are more precise than in earlier works:

Terre heureuse ou le Roy n'escoute le menteur,
Le traistre, le pipeur, le periure imposteur,

---

[1] *Susanne*, p. 95. Cf. p. 239 below.
[2] For Oriet see also Goujet, *Bibliothèque françoise*, xiii. 320.   [3] p. 113.

Et celuy qui ne sert (ha ordure execrable!)
Que d'vn mignon de nuict, et d'vn bouffon à table.[1]

Of course by this time such satire involved no danger.

Outside this series of poems, all of which deserve to some
extent the title of epic, the last decade of the century saw the
publication of three Biblical works which for different reasons
cannot be placed in the same category but which reveal the
continued influence of Du Bartas. As well as the first works of
Gamon[2] we have the *Calliope Chrestienne* (1596) of the Protestant
Benoît Alizet, a series of stanzas, sonnets, and short meditations
in various metres on the subjects listed in the title. It has no
central thread. The *Derniere Semaine ou Consommation du Monde* of
Michel Quillian (1596) is a Catholic version of Du Bartas, but it
contains, as the title suggests, little that can be called Biblical
narrative. Olivier Merault's *Poëme et bref discours de l'honneur où
l'homme estoit colloqué en l'estat de sa creation* (1600) is a sermon in
verse. There is no continuous narrative, and external events are
introduced only as pegs for moral and theological discourses.[3]

To these poems must be added the collections of Biblical
engravings accompanied by verse commentaries. Typical examples
are the *Figures de la Bible*, Bernard Salomon's woodcuts with verses
by Gabriel Chappuis (1582), and the *Tableaux sacrés* of Paul
Perrot de la Sale[4] (published at Frankfort-on-Main in 1594). The
latter, the work of a Protestant, contains one longer narrative
development, the Book of Ruth. The verses themselves are of
little value but they illustrate popular interest in the union of
poetry with iconography.

[1] p. 38.   [2] See Ch. V below.
[3] See Goujet, *Bibliothèque françoise*, xiv. 115.
[4] See Haag, *La France protestante*, art. 'Perrot de la Sale'.

CHAPTER IV

The Origins: II. Italy

BEFORE passing on to the Italian poems proper it will be necessary to deal with the first humanist epics on sacred subjects, Sannazaro's *De partu Virginis* (1526) and Vida's *Christiad* (1535), both written in Latin. To classify them as Italian is a little artificial. Neo-Latin poetry overflowed national boundaries (we have already seen the importance of Buchanan's tragedies) and had its own channels of communication. However, it did in fact originate in Italy and it is hardly possible to consider it apart from Italian developments.

The *De partu Virginis* is a work of the most flourishing period in the Italian Renaissance and is deeply penetrated by the spirit of classical antiquity. In the French poems we have examined there is a tension between classical, Biblical, and contemporary elements. Here the Christian foundation is completely absorbed by the pagan superstructure, from which it is scarcely distinguishable. The subaqueous caverns of the Jordan god or the poet's description of his Mergellina are the work of a man for whom classical legend was a living reality. The shepherds lose their rustic coarseness to become Lycidas and Aegon, figures of a Theocritean idyll. Even the most sacred figures take on some of the attributes of classical divinities. The descent of the angel in the Annunciation:

> Dixerat, ille altum zephyris per inane uocatis
> Carpit iter, scindit nebulas, atque aera tranat
> Ima petens, pronusque leues uix commouet alas[1]

is an early example of a widespread convention. Its dual origin, Biblical and classical, is here very apparent.

Technically Sannazaro is already close to the fully developed form of Christian epic, in spite of the paucity of his narrative material. The opening, with its proposition, invocation to the Muses, and invocation to the Virgin, is perfectly regular. The life of Jesus is introduced by means of a prophecy in the mouth of David. This method of recital in the future instead of the past is of considerable importance for later poets.

Through Colletet's translation of 1634 Sannazaro added to the

[1] Rome, 1526, A3.

impetus given by the sixteenth-century French epic, though his influence was primarily exercised on New Testament poets.

Vida's *Christiad*, although constructed in accordance with the author's own precepts, is much more cautious in its employment of mythology. Apart from a description of Hell and its monsters, imitated from Sannazaro, the Christian nature of the subject is strictly respected, at least in externals. The most interesting development is that the poem, unlike the *De partu Virginis*, enters *in medias res* with Christ's entry into Jerusalem. The earlier part of His life is recounted by Joseph to Pilate.[1]

The *Joseph* of Fracastorius (1555) is the first example of an Old Testament subject in the humanist epic. Two books only were completed at the poet's death, bringing the story to the return of the brothers with Benjamin. It seems probable therefore that the final text would have consisted of three books. The history is told straightforwardly with few marks of the imagination shown by Sannazaro and Vida. It begins *ab ovo* and there are no chronological alterations in the whole course of the poem.

In a comparison between Ariosto and the French epic poets the first and most striking feature is the difference between *ottava rima* and Alexandrine couplets. This distinction, by no means superficial, is the cause (or the consequence) of a wide divergence in narrative methods, which has an effect on deeper poetic qualities. A poem written in Alexandrines moves forward evenly with no other breaks than the major divisions (books, cantos, &c.) and the very slight pauses caused by the rhymes. The stanzas of Italian epic constitute a series of structural units each to some extent capable of independent existence. In the same way the narrative consists of a number of semi-independent plots, advancing abreast, a little at a time, with frequent changes of scene from one to another. Although the use of recitals is not excluded there is a fundamental difference between this method and classical (or French) epic, where there is a single action, interrupted by various episodes which rarely obscure the main thread.

On the other hand, there can be no doubt of the importance for French epic of Ariosto's extensive use of all the resources of

---

[1] For an analysis of Sannazaro and Vida see Saint-Marc Girardin, *Tableau*, pt. ii, ch. vi.

medieval enchantment, in which he followed Pulci and Boiardo. Witches, sorcerers, magicians, hermits, dwarfs, monsters, fairies crowd his pages. Mysterious disguises and concealments of identity furnish the basis for many incidents. Ruggiero and Marfisa are engaged in mortal combat when a voice from the tomb reveals that they are brother and sister.[1] Even when extraordinary events are derived from Homer and Virgil, they are often given a new content by means of medieval supernatural elements. Thus the pictures on the walls of Tristano's lodge[2] afford the opportunity for predictions of Italian history, a motive common enough in classical epic. Here, however, the pictures themselves have been painted by the enchanter Merlin and their magical origin is neither classical nor Christian. Merlin's cave[3] unites the descent of Aeneas to the underworld with the features of this new *merveilleux*. Of course Ariosto is not always the direct source of similar incidents in the French epic. His influence operates also through the French novel, where these romantic elements are greatly enlarged and varied, through Tasso, and in conjunction with popular beliefs, which were still current and on which a poet could still draw. Thus there was an epidemic of witchcraft trials in France at the end of the sixteenth and in the first half of the seventeenth century,[4] belief in fairies was common, astrology and alchemy still had numerous adepts (among whom was Gamon). But even when direct use was made of these popular sources, they were moulded in the forms bequeathed by Italian romance.

At the same time Ariosto did not neglect the resources of classical mythology and Christian miracle. Satan is sometimes active in human affairs, on much the same level as the enchanters: for example he engineers the battle between Charlemagne and the pagan armies in Canto xxvii. The flight of the angel, with which we are already familiar, appears in a more complex form: Michael is dispatched to give orders to the allegorical divinities of Silence and Discord,[5] thus combining two similar motives of Sannazaro. It is in this guise that the idea most commonly appears in France.[6]

The first Biblical epic in Italian was Lodovico Dolce's *La Vita*

---

[1] *Orlando Furioso*, canto xxxvi. Cf. p. 114 below.   [2] Ib., canto xxxiii.
[3] Canto iii.   [4] Cf. Busson, *La Pensée religieuse*, pp. 351 ff.   [5] Canto xiv.
[6] See also Cioranescu, *L'Arioste en France*. It has not been considered necessary to repeat the details of French reception of the *Furioso*, but particular examples of its influence will be considered in their proper place.

di Giuseppe (1561). It is also one of the earliest products of the Counter-Reformation. The poem begins in Hell with Satan's plans to destroy the family of Jacob, an introduction which was to become more and more familiar. Hell is again described in classical terms. The Devil's disguises, on the other hand,—he changes into a bird and then into an old woman—and the love-potion he prepares for Potiphar's wife clearly belong to the world of Ariosto.

The character of Joseph is marked by gentleness and even passivity. As his brothers attack him he bursts into tears and anguished prayers.[1] The Joseph of the Bible is not a militant figure but Dolce has exaggerated his weakness. In France the heroic ideal is in sharp contrast: it evolves in the direction of greater firmness and the disappearance of human frailties.

After Dolce appeared Alfano's *La Battaglia celeste tra Michele e Lucifero* (1568) and the two poems of Erasmo di Valvasone, *Le Lagrime di S. Maria Maddalena* (1587) and the *Angeleida* (1590). They are of little importance for our purpose and have been adequately analysed by Thibaut de Maisières.[2]

In the meantime the first complete edition of the *Gerusalemme Liberata* had been published in 1581. The *Mondo Creato* written about 1594 consists of lyrical digressions, linked by a tenuous narrative, and has few epic qualities. It is therefore in the *Gerusalemme* that Tasso's influence must be sought. Much of what has been said about Ariosto is equally true of Tasso: in particular he retains the whole apparatus of enchantments and magical rites. His greatest contribution is the firm religious purpose which inspires the work. The infernal council, already used by Vida, is enlarged and given impressive force. The ultimate source is no doubt the councils of the gods in Homer. In any case it is henceforth one of the most frequent epic devices and a clear mark of Tasso's influence. Similarly the flight of the angel is repeated in Gabriel's message to Goffredo, but it is further developed and receives its final shape. The guardian angel also makes an appearance.[3]

---

[1] *Vita di Giuseppe*, fo. 9 vº.
[2] *Les Poèmes inspirés du début de la Genèse.*
[3]   L'angelo, che fu già custode eletto
          Da l'alta Provvidenza al buon Raimondo
          Insin dal primo dì che pargoletto
          Sen venne a farsi peregrin del mondo ... (vii, stanza 80.)

Armida's garden, a mixture of the garden of Alcinous from Homer, Alcina's garden in Ariosto, and magical elements, is the source of another element which constantly recurs. These are examples of the features which had the widest diffusion. Particular imitations, of situation and style, are much more numerous and are found in nearly all the French poets with serious literary pretensions.

The revision of the poem as the *Gerusalemme Conquistata* (1593) is important chiefly for the elimination of pagan ornament, which reflects the ruling tendencies of ecclesiastical opinion, and for the elaborate allegorical interpretation of the whole work, which Tasso expounds in the *Giudizio sulla Conquistata* and which later inspired many similar explanations.[1]

After Tasso several Italians attempted epic poems on Biblical subjects—Gasparo Murtola's *Della creatione del mondo* (1608), Felice Passero's *Essamerone* (1608), Ansaldo Cebà's *La Reina Esther* (1615), Bartolomeo Tortoletti's *Iuditha vindex et vindicata* (1628, Italian adaptation 1648), and Antonio Abbondanti's *La Giuditta* (1630). It will be observed that these poems follow much the same line of evolution as the French, from Creation subjects to narrower developments of single books of the Old Testament. Esther and Judith are again favourite themes. Moreover, they fall roughly in the period between the two waves of epic in France (1610–50). It might therefore be concluded that they were of some importance in the formation of the French genre. However, they are in fact often influenced by Du Bartas almost as much as by Tasso.[2] They are nowhere mentioned in prefaces, nor so far as can be ascertained in other critical works,[3] and no translations were made. Internal comparisons show that they

[1] Cf. Marni, *Allegory*, passim, and Cottaz, *L'Influence des théories du Tasse*, pp. 73 ff. The general question of Tasso's influence in France has been the subject of many studies, culminating in Beall's *La Fortune du Tasse en France*. No attempt has therefore been made to go over the same ground. Particular instances of imitation will be dealt with as they occur.

[2] Especially Murtola and Passero. Cf. 'E che finalmente fra i Moderni vi sia stato il Sig. di Bertas, che l'habbia ridotta in Francese . . .' (Murtola, *Della Creatione del Mondo*, Lo stampatore a' lettori).

[3] Baillet has articles on Murtola and Cebà, but they contain little except the anecdote of a quarrel in which Murtola ended by firing at Marino with an arquebus (*Jugemens des Sçavans*, no. 1404—in editions after the first the arquebus becomes a pistol). Tortoletti's Italian translation is dedicated to Anne of Austria, with two liminary sonnets to Mazarin.

exercised no direct influence except that Desmarets may possibly have taken some features of his *Esther* from Cebà. These poems therefore represent a parallel evolution from the same sources and their interest lies in the different use they made of the same material.

Cebà's *Esther* exaggerates the loose structure of Italian romance. Episodes are multiplied and even repeated—thus three separate attempts are made on the life of Ahasuerus in place of the Bible's one. In a more sober poem like Tortoletti's *Judith* the story opens on the twentieth day of the siege (an echo of Homer's ten years), returning in Book VI to recount the earlier events. Although this is in accordance with critical principles, such a violent dislocation of Biblical chronology is without parallel in French epic.

Classical mythology is used much more freely by the Italians. The representation of physical love is allowed more latitude, as in Cebà's episode of Cenoclea and Tarquinio, scarcely different from the amorous scenes of Ariosto. A web of mystery, horror, and coincidence is woven round the Biblical framework. In Tortoletti an angel descends to inspire Judith and assumes the form of her nurse.[1] Cebà introduces Tarquin who makes his way from Rome to Persia, where he tells the stories of Lucretia, Brutus, and Horatius. But on his first appearance he is seen in full armour, closing his visor. In spite of its classical exterior this episode belongs entirely to the theme of the knight errant and his adventures.

Such sustained extravagance can only be paralleled in the *Esther* of Desmarets, which almost outdoes Cebà in invention. In general it is foreign to the spirit and methods of French Biblical poets. This difference may be compared to contemporary developments in architecture—the formal audacities and florid ornament of Italian baroque, which found hardly an echo in the severity of the French classical style.

If the Italian poets of the Seicento generally awakened little interest in France, the same cannot be said of Marino, who with his sojourn in Paris, his friendship with Chapelain and Poussin, and his wide influence among men of letters presents a special case. The *Adone* (1623) was important, apart from questions of style, for the authority it lent to mixed works like the heroic idyll of Saint-Amant and as a source of single situations and

---

[1] This is ultimately derived from Virgil (Iris and the Trojan women, *Aeneid*, bk. v). Similar examples can be found in French epic, e.g. Montchrestien.

especially descriptions. The *Strage degli Innocenti* (1632) is closer to true epic form, and the subject, unlike most New Testament themes, has some of the requisite qualities of heroic action. However, it has none of the technical innovations of Cebà and Tortoletti. The course of the poem, with its Satanic machinations and allegorical deities, follows the model of Tasso, though it is much simpler in structure. Its influence on French poets was considerably less than that of the *Adone*, but it is worth mentioning the attempt to introduce local colour in the Egyptian scene, with the pyramids, the sphinx, and the Pharos of Alexandria.

Finally, a word must be said of the Italian pastoral, in particular Sannazaro's *Arcadia*, Guarini's *Pastor Fido*, and Tasso's *Aminta*, which furnished many incidents and descriptive elements. It is, however, a formative influence on seventeenth-century literature generally and has little specific importance for the development of the Biblical epic. Its effects are to be seen chiefly in matters of detail.

We are now in a position to give a more complex answer to the question of the origins of seventeenth-century epic. Any wide literary movement must draw to some extent on the whole of previous effort. Here the threads cross each other so often and in so many directions that it is exceptionally difficult to distinguish a guiding principle. All the works and conceptions discussed contributed decisively to the heroic ideal of the period, to its diffusion and to its literary expression. However, the ultimate sources can be reduced to two—the Bible on one side, Homer and Virgil on the other. They were reflected through various inter-mediaries: the Bible through Protestantism, the Counter-Reformation, and graphic art; classical epic through Humanism; but poets never ceased to return to them, breaking a merely chronological line of development. Similarly Humanism was modified in different ways by its exponents in Italy and France: a Homeric situation, for example, varies considerably if it is borrowed directly, from Ronsard, or from Tasso. But when due allowance has been made for such considerations, it is legitimate to allot an order of importance to these secondary influences. The high value set on the epic, which was the principal reason for the effort expended, may be ascribed to the impulse set in motion by Du Bellay and

Ronsard, confirmed at intervals by the affirmations of Italian critics. Italian romance brought above all an external enrichment, an inexhaustible source of incident and ornament. For Tasso we may add consecration of poetic beauty to the religious ends of Catholicism. But the fundamental structure, the technical methods, and the spirit which imbue them are in the main those fixed by Du Bartas, at least in so far as Biblical epic is concerned. We have here a curious instance of the subterranean prolongation of a poet's influence long after the external signs of his glory have disappeared.

PART II

THE POEMS

CHAPTER V

Montchrestien and his Contemporaries

ANTOINE DE MONTCHRESTIEN (1575(or 6) – 1621)

Susane ou la Chasteté (published in *Les Tragedies*, Rouen, 1601 (?));[1]
Rouen, 1603; Rouen, 1604; Nyort, 1606; Rouen, 1627).

Text.[2] The 1604 edition is described in the title as *augmentée par
l'auteur*, but the text of *Susane* is in fact slightly abridged. The poem
has been almost entirely rewritten, several passages suppressed,
and many rhymes altered. Very few lines remain as they were in
the first edition. The 1606 Niort edition appears to have been
pirated during Montchrestien's absence in England. With the exception of a few misprints it is identical with the 1604 edition.
Finally, the 1627 edition returns to the text of 1601 and 1603. The
1604 revision is thus of the greatest value for the study of Montchrestien's style and thought in course of development.

It is not necessary to examine in detail all the alterations in the
text, but the principal tendencies can be indicated. ('A' refers to
1601, 'B' to 1604.) Montchrestien tries to eliminate errors and
archaisms of vocabulary, syntax, and style. Thus:

> O grand Dieu qui grauas *dedans* son Ame sainte (A 291)

> Eternel qui grauas *en* sa poitrine sainte (B 341).

Similarly *gourde vieillesse* (A 308) becomes *froide vieillesse* (B 356).

---

[1] For the date see Toinet, i. 10, n. 2.
[2] See Petit de Julleville's ed., pp. xxxix ff., and, for a complete discussion, Seiver's
ed. of *Aman.*

The language of the revision is more concentrated, the lines are packed tighter. Thus in Susanna's entry into the garden we find:

> Deux filles seulement elle auoit auec elle (A 333)
>
> Pompeuse d'apareil, deux filles auec elle (B 379).

Above all Montchrestien strives constantly to substitute concrete image for vague description, not always successfully. *Comme agreables flevrs* (A 294) becomes *Comme fleurs de Souci* (B 343). In a description of Night, which

> estendoit sur les plaines
> Sa grand robe de dueil . . . (A 294)
>
> estendoit sur les plaines
> Son voile tissu d'ombre . . . (B 343)

the ingenuity of the second image is hardly equal to the broad and majestic movement of the original version.[1]

These changes appear to have been made under the direct influence of Malherbe's theories. It is even possible that Malherbe himself corrected Montchrestien's first tragedy and certain that they were for some time on friendly terms.[2] The two editions are therefore living evidence of the process of evolution in French poetry.

Epic and Drama

The structure of *Susane* is curious. The poem consists of four books: Book I contains an exposition ending with a description of Susanna in the garden and the awakening desires of the elders; in Book II they make their attempt and Susanna is arrested; in Book III she is tried and condemned; and in Book IV rescued. Thus half-way through the poem the principal part of the action, from a narrative point of view, is already concluded. On the other hand, the second half with its vivid characters and peripeteia has considerable *dramatic* interest. And Montchrestien probably wished to stress God's justice rather than the wickedness of the elders. This is confirmed by the final scene, which follows a well-ordered plan: first the elders are punished, then Susanna's happiness is described, and lastly the glory of Daniel is foretold. There is thus an ascension from the wicked to the divinely inspired, which seems to confirm the religious intentions of the poet.

---

[1] Unless otherwise stated, further references are to B.
[2] Cf. Lebègue, *Tragédie de la Renaissance*, pp. 67 and 73; and *R.H.L.F.*, xli.

However, the exaggerated formal symmetry of the poem remains displeasing.

In spite of the absence of certain standard features, such as episodes, recitals, and chronological changes, there are considerable epic elements in *Susane*, but the general tone and treatment are not quite those of epic. Nearly all critics have agreed that Montchrestien's tragedies are lacking in dramatic qualities. It is not then entirely surprising that his attempt at epic should be coloured by his dramatic experience, that the poem like the plays should bear some of the marks of a compromise. Externally its two thousand lines make it about the same length as a tragedy. The title *Susane ou la Chasteté* emphasizes the theme of moral conflict as well as the poem's place in the series of plays, all of which bear similar sub-titles.

An examination of the narrative methods employed confirms this impression. After Joachim has seen Susanna and been struck by her beauty, he recounts the meeting to a friend (a confidant, it may be said). The servants bring in chairs, then there follows a pause indicated simply by *Enfin il parle ainsi* and Joachim begins his story:

> Doy-ie ou puis-ie à present te celer mon souci?[1]

The whole scene is conceived visually and would require very little modification to be made suitable for the theatre. Descriptions, instead of being expressed directly, are put into the mouths of the characters, as when Susanna

> Dit en se promenant: Que la torche celeste
> Espand d'ardens rayons or' que le chien brulant,
> Cuit aux champs la moisson d'vn regard violant![2]

The clumsiness of this device was surely possible only for a writer accustomed to working in a dramatic medium. The progress of the narrative depends to a great extent on dialogue, soliloquies, and speeches. The threat to Susanna[3] seems abrupt and unprepared when we consider the leisure which narrative verse possesses. On the stage, however, her attitude and gestures would be sufficient to convince the audience that no other means were of any use.

The crises of the poem are generally concentrated in tragic

---

[1] p. 344.   [2] p. 360.   [3] p. 380.

speeches in which Susanna expresses an invincible strength of mind, as when she is attacked in the garden:

> I'aimeray tousiours mieux, Vieillars pleins de malice,
> Mourir par vostre main et pour vostre iniustice,
> Que me prostituer si malheureusement
> Aux plaisirs deffendus de vostre embrassement[1]

or when she is condemned to death:

> Le genre de ma mort vous semble miserable.
> Il ne l'est point mon cœur si ie ne suis coupable.[2]

At other times, instead of these unvaried sentiments, we find hesitation or psychological evolution in the characters. Susanna's reply to the proposals of the elders presents a rudimentary conflict between fear of death and attachment to virtue:

> Helas! que doy-ie faire en ce diuers esmoy?
> A quoy me resoudray-ie? enclose ie me voy
> De deux maux differens, voire et si l'vn i'euite,
> L'autre m'ouure l'abisme et ie m'y precipite.[3]

The two sides are briefly stated and a firm conclusion follows.

Whole scenes, as well as narrative methods and the study of the characters, are constructed, it seems, under the influence of the theatre. In particular the trial, with its grouping of figures (the judges—Susanna and her friends—the people), vivid language, and contrasted characters, could easily be adapted for the stage. Susanna's farewell to her children is treated in much the same way as the incident of Hector and Astyanax in Montchrestien's tragedy *Hector*. Finally Montchrestien succeeds in inspiring some slight measure of pity for the elders in spite of the unrelieved horror of their actions, because, like so many tragic heroes, they are represented as the victims of a superior and irresistible force.

The question arises therefore why, in view of the dramatic possibilities of the subject, Montchrestien chose to give it epic form. He may have been influenced by considerations of propriety. The scene in the garden was hardly suitable for acting but would have been very difficult to suppress.[4] On the other hand, Montchrestien's *David* has a similar theme, handled with re-

---

[1] p. 366. [2] p. 384. [3] p. 365.
[4] The subject was very rarely used in Biblical tragedy. Loukovitch (pp. 51 ff.) quotes only one Susanna play between 1540 and 1640.

markable freedom. It is of course possible that objections to the play led to a concession to propriety in the poem. On the whole, however, it seems probable that *Susane* was simply an experiment in a form new to the poet. It is not surprising that he brought to it the method which he had practised, however imperfectly, in his tragedies.

The Bible in Montchrestien

In general Montchrestien follows the Bible with close attention, even including trivial if picturesque details like the time of day when Susanna enters the garden[1] or the removal of her veil in court.[2] Unfortunately this fidelity rarely extends to verbal coincidence, so that there is little material which could establish the version of the Bible used by Montchrestien. One such indication, however, suggests at least that he made use of a French translation:

Et dit estre innocent du sang de cette Dame[3]

is taken from Dan. xiii. 46, where both Catholic and Protestant translations read: 'Je suis innocent du sang de ceste femme.' The two trees used by Daniel to trap the elders[4] are called in the poem *lentisque* and *yeuse*.[5] The Vulgate readings are *sub schino* and *sub prino*; the Catholic (Louvain) and early Geneva translations *cerisier* and *prunier*; Castellio's unofficial Protestant translation of 1555 *lentisque* and *ilice*; and the later Geneva Bibles *lentisque* and *eouse*.[6] It seems probable therefore that he used the Protestant translation at least in this passage. It would be wrong to exaggerate the importance of a single reference like this, but it adds a little weight to the Protestant side in the controversy over the poet's religion, and confirms the influence of Protestantism in his formation.[7]

Other Sources

The Bible was not the only source: the *Judith* of Du Bartas, which dealt with an analogous subject, supplies some material. Montchrestien is superior in delicacy of analysis and perhaps in

---

[1] p. 349. Cf. Dan. xiii. 7.   [2] p. 374; Dan. xiii. 32.
[3] p. 388.   [4] Dan. xiii. 54, 58.   [5] pp. 391-2.
[6] Most Geneva Bibles carry a marginal note: 'Ou, yeuse, qui est vne espece de chesne.' In the Geneva Bible the chapter is printed separately as the *Histoire de Susanne* (with the apocryphal books).
[7] Cf. below, p. 64. Oriet's *Susanne* (pp. 137-8) also has *lentisque* and *eouse*. It is therefore possible that Montchrestien copied him.

narrative interest, though his work seems a little pallid by contrast. However, the resemblance is not confined to general outline. The education of Susanna, her needlework and Bible reading, are inspired by a similar passage in *Judith*. The general resemblances are confirmed by what appears to be a direct imitation:

> Ores son doigt conduit vne *aiguille argentine*
> Sur le caneuas rare ou sur la *toile fine*.[1]

> Tantost elle brodoit dessus quelque *drap fin* . . .
> Tantost d'vn art subtil son *aiguille argentine*
> Sur la *toile* tiroit quelque histoire diuine.[2]

A similar passage occurs in Oriet's *Susanne*,[3] but it seems clear that Du Bartas was the source of both.

Another instance of Du Bartas's influence is the use of the painter Apelles as an object of comparison:

> *Vn pinceau plus hardi* deuoit à l'vniuers
> Peindre ce que le mien *esbauche* pour la France . . .
> Si ce braue dessein peut lasser vn *Apelle*.[4]

This is from the *Semaine*:

> Mais si pas vn de ceux, dont les *hardis pinceaux* . . .
> D'vn *Appele esbaucha* la princesse d'Eryce.[5]

Meanwhile Oriet had used the same allusion but with no verbal resemblance which could suggest that Montchrestien had read him.[6] The question of Apelles is of little importance in itself but it recurs often in later poets, thus furnishing an example of the development of a conventional image.

A more complex problem is the source of the description of Susanna's garden, which occupies about a hundred lines.[7] The starting-point is the garden of Daniel xiii. The Bible, however, gives no description, though certain features are implied by the references to the fruit garden, to the gates, to Susanna's bath, to the heat, to the concealment of the elders, which suggests dense trees or shrubs, and to the two kinds of tree in the trial scene.

---

[1] p. 346.   [2] Du Bartas, 1616, p. 575; Holmes, ii. 74.
[3]   *Tantot* de son *aiguille* vne gaze emplissoit
             De quelque *fine* soie, et paroistre faisoit
             En l'ouurage acheué quelque tressainte *histoire* . . . (p. 89).
[4] p. 374.   [5] *Semaine* (1616 ed., p. 142; Holmes, ii. 370).
[6]   Apelles y nasquit (miracle de nature)
             Le premier et dernier en l'art de la peinture. (*Susanne*, p. 9.)
[7] pp. 349–52.

Out of this Montchrestien makes a place of delight, full of all kinds of trees, herbs, flowers, and fruits which offer themselves to the hand:

> Y prenant vne pomme vne autre aussi soudain
> Plus iaune que fin or s'offre dessous la main.[1]

One source which might be suggested is the Eden of the second *Semaine*. However, there are no particular resemblances and all that can be said is that both belong to the same tradition. The original source of such descriptions is the garden of Alcinous (*Odyssey*, bk. vii).[2] Some of the fruits are the same—pears, grapes, apples, ripe and unripe growing together. But the resemblances to Armida's garden are still closer. Again ripe and unripe fruits cluster together:

> Voire et de mesme branche on cueille à la mesme heure
> L'orange encores verte et l'orange ià meure.[3]

> E mentre spunta l'un, l'altro matura.[4]

Birds, especially doves, are found in Tasso and Montchrestien (but not in Homer). In both the garden is the result of a rivalry between Nature and Art:

> L'art cede à la Nature et la Nature à l'art.[5]

> Stimi, sì misto il culto è col negletto,
> Sol naturali e gli ornamenti e i siti.
> Di Natura arte par, che per diletto
> L'imitatrice sua scherzando imiti.[6]

This description had passed through many hands before it reached Montchrestien. It is therefore very difficult to decide whether these features were due to imitation of the *Gerusalemme Liberata* or of some other intermediary. In any case Tasso cannot have been the only source, as Armida's garden contains no reference to fruits offering themselves. However, these coincidences remain striking, if not conclusive, and suggest that Montchrestien read the *Gerusalemme*. He had already imitated *Aminta* in his *Bergerie*.[7]

Montchrestien's Religion: Christianity and Stoicism

It is well known that the poet was killed in 1621 while raising troops in Normandy for the Protestant assembly of La Rochelle.

---

[1] p. 350.   [2] Cf. p. 53 above.   [3] p. 350.
[4] *Gerusalemme Liberata*, xvi, stanza 10.   [5] p. 351.
[6] *Gerusalemme Liberata*, xvi, stanza 10.
[7] See Beall, *Fortune du Tasse*, p. 31.

This raises the important question whether he was himself a Protestant at the time of the composition of *Susane*. Funck-Brentano[1] concludes that he was born a Catholic and was converted to Protestantism on marriage (i.e. after the publication of his works). Petit de Julleville,[2] on the other hand, believes that he was originally a Protestant, but admits that he was mainly indifferent and in taking up arms was moved by ambition rather than faith. French Protestants have generally claimed him as one of their own.

It might be thought that internal evidence could throw some light on the problem. Unfortunately there are no direct references to contemporary events, and allusions to questions of doctrine are of little value because in a poem they have not the precision which is required in a discussion of fine theological distinctions. These references, such as they are, suggest at least a sympathy with Protestantism.[3]

> „Las ce n'est point de nous que vient la repentance!"[4]

has a decidedly Calvinistic ring. Susanna's education is confined to the study of the Decalogue and the books of the Old Testament:

> Elle estale à ses yeux l'escriture sacrée,
> Et par la mediter longuement se recrée.[5]

More could not have been included without anachronism and there is nothing here which is in any way contrary to Catholic teaching, but this insistence on Biblical education and study shows affinities with Protestantism, as does the stern moral attitude of the satire on women.[6] The use of the word *Éternel* (for *Dieu*),[7] though by no means exclusively Protestant, is often found in the Protestant Bibles and in 'reformed' phraseology generally.

The *Approbation des Docteurs*, on the other hand, suggests at least that any Protestant tendencies were not obvious to the examining theologians. The dedication of the *Tragédies* to the Prince de Condé is not very significant—he was then a boy and was brought up by Henry IV as a Catholic. But it may indicate an attachment, sentimental or ancestral, to that great Protestant family.

---

[1] *Traité de l'Œconomie Politique* (Introduction), pp. xiii ff.
[2] *Tragédies* (Introduction), pp. xxviii ff.
[3] Cf. p. 61 above.
[4] *Susane*, p. 369.
[5] p. 347.
[6] pp. 345 ff.
[7] e.g. p. 341.

The evidence therefore tends to show that Montchrestien had at least Protestant sympathies when he wrote *Susane*. But he lived at a time when changes of religion were frequent and it seems likely that he oscillated in sympathy between the two faiths. Similar hesitations are frequent among the Biblical poets of the seventeenth century. In particular it should be noted that Montchrestien, like Vauquelin de la Fresnaye, Saint-Amant, and Le Cordier, was a Norman and that Normandy was an actively Protestant province. It may be conjectured that a Protestant atmosphere was at any rate one influence which attracted him to Biblical poetry.[1]

Montchrestien's religious and moral conceptions are in fact those of his time, not those of the Bible, and this leads to new distortions or amplifications of the spirit of the original. Of these fresh elements the most important is no doubt Christianity, quite apart from the question of the poet's particular confession. Thus Susanna is assured of immortality:

> Mais aumoins ce confort tousiours vous accompagne
> Que partant de la terre elle va dans les Cieux.[2]

This may probably be regarded as an anachronism: in any case it gives a new significance to the character and conduct of the heroine. Her prayer that the elders may be pardoned[3] is an addition to the Bible, where she asks only that they should be unmasked.[4] It is made in order to conform with a Christian idea of perfection.

The place of Stoicism in Montchrestien's work has been treated by Willner, who gives an interesting analysis of the ethical doctrines which underlie the tragedies.[5] Here it will only be necessary to refer to the manifestations of Stoicism in *Susane* and perhaps to offer a slightly different interpretation. It seems likely that the subject itself was chosen because of the opportunities it affords for the representation of heroic virtue. Chastity was not indeed one of the specifically Stoic virtues, but it is closely related to them in its emphasis on the mastery of will over passion.[6] The importance

---

[1] On this problem see also Lebègue, *Tragédie de la Renaissance*, p. 68; Lachèvre, *R.H.L.F.*, xxv. 445–54. Lachèvre's argument for Catholicism is not very convincing.

[2] p. 384. [3] p. 383. [4] Dan. xiii. 42, 43.

[5] *Montchrestiens Tragödien und die stoische Lebensweisheit;* cf. also Zanta, *La Renaissance du Stoïcisme.* [6] Willner, pp. 186 ff.

of these questions for the poet is shown by the large number of moral *sententiae*, which, like earlier writers, he stresses by the use of quotation marks. Sometimes his Stoicism can be found in a state of purity, unadulterated by other ways of thought.

The insistence on the virtue of constancy seems to be derived entirely from the masters of Stoicism.[1] It is the foundation of Susanna's chastity and enables her to bear her misfortunes:

> Et si la sainte peur que i'ay de t'offencer
> A tousiours tins la bride à mon chaste penser,
> Sans que la mort cruelle ou la honte aprestée
> Ait iamais renuersé ma constance agitée . . .[2]

This un-Christian and un-Biblical pride becomes almost sublime in the scene of the judgement:

> Celle-là toutesfois qui reçoit la sentence
> A moins de peur en l'ame, au front plus de constance[3]

though here we may suspect contamination with a literary tradition (Marot's Semblançay, for example).

In general, however, Stoic conceptions are not found in isolation but in combination with other elements; and they themselves are often almost indistinguishable from Christian doctrines or from popular wisdom, as expressed in proverbs or everyday morality. In

> „L'audace des meschans peut les bons outrager;
> „Mais le Sauueur des bons sçait bien les reuanger[4]

the first line poses one of the central problems of Stoicism but the answer given in the second is Christian. When Susanna says:

> Meurs bien tost en mon ame, ô penser miserable!
> Pour allonger mes iours ie n'auray point le cœur
> De rendre vn court plaisir sus le deuoir vainqueur![5]

the poet lays stress on the Stoic elements in Christian ethics, and this is perhaps his most frequent proceeding.

In a deeper sense Montchrestien sometimes goes farther than Stoic or even Christian doctrine and suffuses harsh precepts with a sudden compassion:

> „Le doux feu de pitié mollit l'humain courage
> „Fust-il forgé de fer puis aceré de rage.[6]

---

[1] Cf. Willner, pp. 116 ff.　　　　　　　　　　　[2] *Susane*, p. 377.
[3] p. 383.　　　　　[4] p. 373.　　　　　[5] p. 365.　　　　　[6] p. 377.

Susanna's consolations to her family are couched in pure Stoic language:

> „Le sort est inflexible: il n'espargne personne,
> „Et les soupirs mortels ne sçauroient alterer
> „La rigueur de ses loix; il faut donc l'endurer,
> „Et finir sans douleur nostre courte iournée,
> „Si de son midi mesme on la trouue bornée.[1]

But the last line introduces a note of regret, expressed still more powerfully in her words to the elders:

> C'est donc fait de ma vie, et sa claire iournée
> Ains qu'estre à son midi se verra terminée?[2]

This piercing cry of distress is not quite smothered by the virtuous reaction which follows. Montchrestien's heroine is most moving when she excites not admiration only but a tragic pity.

Montchrestien still belongs to the sixteenth century by his contemporary application of the Bible, by his free use of pagan mythology, by the bourgeois solidity of his characters and settings, by his personal interventions in the action, and by the more important characteristics of his style. However, he strengthens certain tendencies which have appeared in his predecessors and will be further developed after him—in particular, the use of *merveilleux mixte* and rudimentary Oriental colouring. In two respects he introduces features which are new to the Biblical epic—the chastened language of Malherbe and the beginnings of psychological analysis.

The authors of other Biblical poems which appeared in the first two decades of the century were less equivocal figures than Montchrestien, both in their religious and literary allegiance. Gamon, d'Aubigné, and Schelandre were Protestants, Vauquelin and Anne d'Urfé Catholics.

[1] p. 385. [2] p. 365.

Christofle de Gamon (1575–1621)

La Semaine, ou Creation du Monde . . . Contre celle du Sieur du Bartas
(Lyons, 1609).[1] Other editions appeared at Geneva (1609),
Paris (1609), Lyons (1610), and Niort (1615).

Gamon also wrote: (i) *Les playes de l'Egypte et la magnifique sortie
des enfants d'Israel hors icelle;* (ii) *Les cantiques des trois enfants dans
la fournaise.* Both appeared in *Le Verger Poétique,* Lyons, 1597.[2]
(iii) *Poeme tragique,* part of *La Muse Divine,* in *Le Iardinet de
Poesie de C.D.G.,* Lyons, 1600, pp. 93 ff.

Gamon's *Poëme tragique* need not detain us long, though in
spite of its fragmentary character (it contains 540 lines) it has more
of the superficial marks of epic than his *Semaine*. It is a close
paraphrase of II Maccabees vii (the martyrdom of the seven
brothers) with the addition of invocation and proposition, classical
similes, mythological allusions, and apostrophes to the characters.
It furnishes another example of Protestant writers' predilection
for Apocryphal subjects. Gamon confirms that this was partly
because these subjects commanded less respect and permitted
more liberty, for the tone of the invocation is very sceptical:

> Soit, ô Dieu que ceci soit faux ou veritable . . .[3]

The contents and method of the *Semaine* are adequately summarized by the title-page, *La Semaine, ou Creation du Monde . . .
Contre celle du Sieur du Bartas*. It is in fact a poetical commentary on
Du Bartas rather than an epic in its own right. The arrangement
follows exactly that of the earlier *Semaine*. It is divided into seven
days and each argument of Du Bartas is expanded, demolished,
or, more rarely, corroborated. But although Gamon disagrees
violently with the religious and scientific views of Du Bartas,
he has an unbounded admiration for the poet, *vn nourrisson si
cheri des Muses*. This veneration is expressed again and again in the
preface and in the poem, praise mingled with scolding:

> Ie plain fort que ton luc de la Raizon s'eslongne,
> O Bartas, grand sonneur, honneur de la Gascongne.[4]

There is hardly a line which does not bear traces of imitation.

---

[1] References are to this edition, which is the first (cf. Toinet, ii. 39). Toinet's
view is confirmed by a comparison of the British Museum copies.
[2] Mazon in *Revue du Vivarais,* 1894, p. 342. This work is very rare and I have not
been able to read it.   [3] *Iardinet de poesie,* p. 93.   [4] *Semaine,* p. 146.

The mainspring of the poem is thus polemical:

> O grand Dieu donne-moy que je puisse sans peur,
> Combattre corps à corps le mensonge et l'erreur.[1]

Such militant language is continued in the imagery as well as the thought:

> Ayants Christ pour guidon, pour gendarmes les Anges![2]

This is the spirit of a combative faith, the spirit of d'Aubigné, and reflects clearly the temper of civil war, scarcely ended.[3] In fact Gamon's Protestantism is much more evident than that of Du Bartas and his work is an exposition of Calvinist doctrine. Thus he affirms the right of individual judgement:

> Et veux qu'à la Raizon, ayants presté serment,
> Vostre jugement libre en juge librement[4]

and the supremacy of the Bible:

> O regle de noz dits, ô lumiere trespure,
> Source de verité, belle et sainte Escripture.[5]

The difficult doctrine of election is explained by the analogy of the sun which causes the formation of ice by withholding its rays.[6]

The scientific elements of Gamon's work have been extensively treated. Kaiser[7] argues that he was no more than a slavish follower of Du Bartas with little or no scientific originality. Schmidt, on the other hand, calls the *Semaine* 'une réaction du véritable esprit scientifique contre le bartasisme'.[8] This is true in the sense that he subjects every statement of Du Bartas to a critical examination which is often penetrating. Thus he makes several attacks on the illusions of astrology:

> C'est se rendre complice à l'erreur monstrueux,
> De donner du prezage à l'Astre aux longs cheueux.[9]

But the greater part of his scientific theory belongs to the sixteenth century or even earlier. His universe is uncompromisingly centred on the earth:

> Par ce large Vniuers qu'en sa main il enserre,
> Dont l'entour est le Ciel, et le centre la Terre,[10]

---

[1] *Semaine*, p. 2. [2] Ib., p. 24.

[3]   Que le calme Printems de la Paix renaissante,
        Apres le long Hyuer d'vne guerre sanglante . . . (Ib., p. 26.)

[4] Ib., p. 2. [5] Ib., p. 7. [6] Ib., p. 24.

[7] *Über die Schöpfungsgedichte des Chr. de Gamon*, passim.

[8] *La poésie scientifique*, p. 311. [9] *Semaine*, p. 45. [10] Ib., p. 5.

and even in defending Copernicus he denies the possibility of the earth's motion.[1] He also appears to have been a practising alchemist and wrote two poems on the subject.[2] This is reflected in the imagery of the *Semaine*:

> Comme au creux alambic la vapeur qui contourne
> Par le chaud esleuée, en la chape séjourne . . .
> Puis par le bec courbé, toute en liqueur vtile,
> Dedans le receptoir goute à goute distile.[3]

Some mention should be made of *Les trois premiers de sept tableaux de penitence*, published in 1609 under the pseudonym Daniel d'Ancheres. They were in fact the work of the Protestant dramatist, Jean de Schelandre, and were dedicated to James I. The episodes chosen are Adam after his ejection from Eden, David after the death of Uriah, and repentant Nineveh after the arrival of Jonah. All these subjects are of importance for the later history of the epic. However, the work has no true epic qualities, though its poetry is not negligible.

It seems that it was completed later and published posthumously in 1636.[4]

AGRIPPA D'AUBIGNÉ (1552–1630)

La Création (first published in *Œuvres complètes*, ed. Réaume et de Caussade, Paris, 1873–92, vol. iii, pp. 325–444).

The poem is divided into fifteen *chants*, each of about 200–250 lines. It appears to have been written between 1620 and 1630.[5] It is a didactic, not an epic poem, a description of creation, not a history of the Creation. The Bible narrative is of little importance and d'Aubigné takes the works, not the word, of God as his source. There is no element of time, which in one way or another must be a vital factor in true epic. For all these reasons d'Aubigné's *Création* is of little importance for our purpose. However, it seemed necessary at least to mention a work closely related to the Biblical epic, and written by a poet with such magnificent epic

---

[1] *Semaine*, p. 109.

[2] 'Ce Poëte donna dans les reveries de l'Alchimie ou de la Pierre philosophale; et tout ce qu'il a écrit s'en ressent' (Goujet, *Bibliothèque françoise*, xiv. 135). Cf. also Schmidt, op. cit., pp. 333 ff. [3] *Semaine*, p. 40.

[4] See Haraszti's introduction to *Tyr et Sidon*, p. xxii; Cohen, *Les Écrivains français en Hollande*, p. 133.

[5] See Kaiser (pp. 39–40) and Schmidt (pp. 303 ff.).

gifts. It has been severely treated by modern critics and after Chant X does indeed degenerate into a rhymed medical treatise. But it is not true that d'Aubigné merely gives long catalogues of unrelated objects. For example the book on plants (Chant V) proceeds by subdivision of a general idea and so conveys the impression of an infinite burgeoning and flowering. Everywhere the multiplicity and diversity of nature are made apparent, and though the work is inferior to the *Tragiques*, the homely energy of the poet's style like that of a popular preacher often penetrates and illuminates arid abstraction. Both these qualities belong to the preceding generation, and their disappearance seriously impoverishes the epic writers of the seventeenth century.

JEAN VAUQUELIN DE LA FRESNAYE (1536–1607)

L'Israëlide (fragment published in *L'Art Poetique*, Caen, 1605).

The poem appears to have been begun before 1570; it is mentioned by Le Fevre de la Boderie in his *Encyclie des secrets de l'Eternité*.[1] Civil war and his public duties prevented Vauquelin from completing it and all that survives is a fragment of fifty lines in the *Art poetique*,[2] quoted by the author as an example of proposition and invocation. The subject was to be the life of David and, it seems, particularly his rivalry with Saul. The allegorical significance of the story is stressed, but otherwise it is impossible to deduce from the fragment what the completed poem would have been like. It clearly belongs to the sixteenth century in style and outlook as well as in date of composition.[3]

ANNE D'URFÉ (1555–1621)

(i) *Hymne de Saincte Susanne* (published in *Le Premier Livre des Hymnes de Messire Anne d'Urfé*, Lyons, 1608, pp. 185–224).

(ii) *Judic* (1599?–1620?).

Three books only of *Judic* were written and are still in manuscript.[4] A short passage (112 lines), containing an infernal council imitated from Tasso, has been published by Ronzy.[5]

---

[1] Anvers, 1570, p. 26.   [2] Bk. ii, lines 135–84.   [3] Cf. p. 37 above.
[4] Bibliothèque Nationale: Fonds français 12487, fols. 149–68.
[5] 'Une imitation du Tasse: Le conseil infernal dans la *Judith* d'Anne d'Urfé', *L'Italie classique et moderne*, No. 1, Grenoble, 1908, pp. 8–9. Ten lines of the opening are reprinted in Badolle, *Anne d'Urfé, l'homme — le poète*.

According to Ronzy the date of the poem lies between 1599 and 1620.

Anne d'Urfé's *Hymne de Saincte Susanne* is anacreontic rather than heroic in tone, but it has at least some of the external characteristics of epic. The unpublished *Judic* consists of three books (called *discours*) each of about five hundred lines. The first contains the diabolical inspiration of Nebuchadnezzar and the unfolding of his ambitious project; the second is wholly occupied by a review of the Assyrian army; the third shows the advance of Holofernes, the first alarms and preparations in Bethulia. The poem was left unfinished at this point. The heroine has not yet appeared and the Biblical elements are of small importance compared with the elaborate additions. Judging from the proportion between these three books and the rest of the story, it is possible to conclude that the poet planned a work in twelve books on the classical model. Although it cannot have exercised any influence on later poets, it is interesting as the first surviving attempt to produce a full-scale classical epic with a Biblical subject.

The influence of the Pléiade is still very strong. *Le Premier Livre des Hymnes* is preceded by a sonnet, in which Ronsard expresses high admiration for the author:

> Poursuy doncques VRFÉ; car, ou ie me deçoy,
> Ou France ne verra de long temps apres toy,
> Aucun qui ioigne mieux les Armes et les Muses.[1]

The style is plainly marked by the Pléiade tradition. At the same time d'Urfé interested himself in Tasso. He had already written a *Hierosolime delivrée*, which has not been preserved.[2] The infernal council of *Judic* is little more than a translation from the *Gerusalemme Liberata*.[3] On the whole the minor mythological allusions seem to come from the Pléiade, the larger pieces of machinery —Alecto's disguise, the angel's flight, the allegorical figures—from Tasso.

D'Urfé presents an extreme instance of the penetration of Biblical poetry by classical mythology. At the same time the pathos of Susanna's position is less strongly marked than in other poets, the emotion of the prayers is less intense and the wickedness of the elders less apparent. The poet's personal history

---

[1] Cf. Vaganay, *R.H.L.F.*, xxiii. 562–3.
[2] Beall, *La Fortune du Tasse*, p. 48.   [3] See Ronzy, loc. cit.

makes his paganism more difficult to explain. Abandoning the world, his political future, and most of his possessions at the age of forty-five, he became a priest and devoted himself to works of charity and the composition of Christian verse. This, here in exaggerated form, is the problem of the Biblical epic in general. D'Urfé has left no critical work or preface which would serve to explain the contradiction, but it is permissible to assume that he would have had recourse to the pillage theory.[1] Here the stolen ornaments are in such profusion that the original edifice is scarcely visible.

By 1610 the eagerness for great literary undertakings appeared to have expended itself. The principal works of Vauquelin and Anne d'Urfé were never completed, Gamon was content to follow in the traces of Du Bartas, d'Aubigné's *Création* lay in manuscript for more than two hundred years. All were survivals of an earlier period, either because of their age (Vauquelin and d'Aubigné) or their provincial background (Gamon and d'Urfé). However, it is possible to observe during this first decade of the century the fixing of two tendencies, the Protestant derived from Du Bartas and the Catholic from the Pléiade and Tasso, whose influence is spreading rapidly. Both are still under the spell of humanism, both mix classical fable with Biblical history, but for the Catholic writers antiquity is a living atmosphere rather than an ornament. The Protestants, on the other hand, still inspired by the militant spirit of the Wars of Religion, have a deeper feeling for the Bible and treat it organically, not superficially. Montchrestien presents a synthesis of the two methods of approach.

[1] Cf. pp. 13, 34 above.

CHAPTER VI

The Period of Preparation, 1620–50

BETWEEN Gamon's *Semaine* (1609) and Saint-Amant's *Moyse sauvé* (1653) hardly a single poem on an Old Testament subject was published (apart from verse translations). This long interval demands an explanation. Of course there is a danger in the isolation of the Biblical epic, which must be considered as part of the literary epic as a whole. However, an examination of all the examples of the genre reveals the same phenomenon. Taking as a basis Toinet's lists with necessary additions—his choice is sometimes arbitrary, but this does not affect the broad accuracy of the observations—we find in the first quarter of the century (1601–25) 45 poems; in the second (1626–50) 17; in the third (1651–75) 44; and in the fourth (1676–1700) 14. There are thus two waves of epic production and the period now under consideration is the trough between them. If individual importance rather than mere quantity is taken as the criterion, the same conclusion emerges. In the first decade, apart from Montchrestien and Gamon, appear the *Franciade* of Pierre de Laudun, the *Néréide* of Deimier, the *Mariade* of La Pujade, all poems with at any rate epic pretensions. It is unnecessary to insist on the great efflorescence between 1650 and 1670—*La Pucelle*, *Alaric*, *Clovis*, *Saint Louis*, *Saint Paul* are only the most celebrated. Between the two the only work of comparable reputation is the *Jésus crucifié* of Frenicle (1636), and even this is often more lyrical or meditative than heroic.

Reasons for this diminution of interest in epic poetry may be sought primarily in general social and literary conditions. The enthusiasm created by the appearance of the *Franciade* and the *Semaine* was already on the wane at the turn of the century and by about 1620 seemed to have withered away (a process which can be traced with some precision in the editions of Du Bartas). The influence of the civil wars, for some time a source of direct inspiration, was largely dissipated in the period of relative tranquillity which followed. The energies of Protestantism were almost exhausted, the Counter-Reformation had not yet borne full fruit. The efforts of literary circles were directed towards the purification of language and the restoration of the social amenities which had suffered from long disorder. The characteristic productions of the time were the poems of Malherbe and Théophile and perhaps especially the *Bergeries* of Racan, with their mixture of courtly refinement and escape into a world of rustic calm. In the circumstances it is not surprising that works of wider scope were neglected. A period of preparation and organization was required before they could again be attempted.

However, the rupture is by no means so complete as appears at first sight. D'Aubigné was still at work on his *Création* between 1620 and 1630. The last *Franciade* (that of Jacques Corbin) appeared in 1634, the last *Semaine* (by Abel d'Argent, a Protestant of Sedan) in 1629, reprinted in 1630 and 1632. Corbin's poem is the history of Saint Francis and has little more than an external connexion with Ronsard, but the title demonstrates the persistence of a tradition. Abel d'Argent's *Semaine* applies the plan and method of Du Bartas to the New Testament. In 1635 appeared *La Loy de l'Eternel* by Jeangaston (or Jangaston) of Orthez, another Protestant imitation of Du Bartas. It is a verse commentary on the Decalogue, of vast proportions. Like Gamon, Jeangaston covers a very wide range of Biblical material, but his work obviously has no epic properties.

From 1636 to 1639 Antoine Millieu, S.J., rector of the Collège de la Trinité of Lyons, published his *Moyses Viator seu imago militantis Ecclesiae*, a Latin epic in twenty-eight books. It follows the Bible laboriously from the return of Moses to Egypt until his death, with no chronological alterations. According to Vissac[1] he may have suggested Saint-Amant's famous lines:

> Et là, près des rempars que l'œil peut transpercer,
> Les poissons esbahis le regardent passer.[2]

The picture is indeed similar in outline:

> Hinc inde attoniti liquido stant marmore pisces,[3]

but there are no more precise resemblances. It is unlikely that Millieu exercised any general influence on the *Moyse sauvé*, since the structure and content of the two poems are different. Millieu's main subject, the wanderings of Moses, are reduced by Saint-Amant to an episode, and the hiding and rescue of the hero do not

---

[1] *Poésie latine au siècle de Louis XIV*, p. 74.
[2] ed. Livet, ii. 214.   [3] *Moyses Viator*, i. 162.

appear at all in the *Moyses Viator*. On the other hand, the poem is of interest as the first epic which took the history of Moses as its theme and its publication coincides approximately with the conception of the *Moyse sauvé*. As the title indicates, the poem is founded on an elaborate allegory in which the Israelites symbolize the Church Militant. Thus the crossing of the Red Sea represents the sacrament of baptism. Millieu's position as head of a Jesuit college lends weight to this illustration of the growing attention of Catholics to Biblical studies and their connexion with literature, as well as the ecclesiastical tendency to exaggerate the place of allegory in poetry.

The forties were marked by a revival of the Biblical tragedy, beginning with the *Saül* of Du Ryer (1642). There is the same gap in the Biblical tragedy as in the epic, though Lancaster's lists show that in tragedy it extends approximately from 1614 to 1642. The difference may be attributed to the longer period of gestation required by the epic. The principal themes of both forms are the same—Judith, Esther, Saul. In tragedy too the influence of feminism was of the first importance.[1]

The works of poets like Abel d'Argent and Corbin were faint echoes from an already distant past. Millieu was an obscure provincial and his use of Latin excluded him from the main stream of poetic evolution. Marino's *Adone* and *Strage*, however, brought the epic once more into the forefront of literary preoccupations and, whether or not under his influence, the leaders among the young poets began to devote themselves to the task of composing epic poems. Chapelain first planned the *Pucelle* about 1625 and began to write it soon after 1630.[2] Saint-Amant wrote the first version of his *Joseph* about 1630 and began work on *Moyse sauvé* before 1638.[3] This long gestation must be taken into account in the chronology of the epic. In spite of a gap of forty years, the last survivors of the old epic have not yet disappeared when the first representatives of the new begin their labours.

The religious, social, political, and general literary developments of this period, although they cannot be said to have furnished the primary impulse, produced considerable modifications in the form, spirit, and evolution of the epic. Leaving aside those

---

[1] Cf. Lancaster, *History of French Dramatic Literature*, part ii, ii. 667 ff.
[2] See Kerviler, *Étude sur le poème de la Pucel e*, p. xxxix; Collas, *Chapelain*, p. 205.
[3] Cf. p. 82 below.

factors which influenced literature in all its forms, the most important for Biblical poetry was probably the change in relationships between Catholics and Protestants after the fall of La Rochelle (1628). In 1634 La Milletière, a recent convert to Catholicism, published his first project for the reunion of the two Churches[1] and during the following twenty years wrote dozens of pamphlets and treatises on the same theme. There was perhaps never any real chance of success, but the effort is symptomatic of a new tolerance. For a short time it appeared that Catholics and Protestants could live peacefully together, co-operating in the public service and the arts, where men like Turenne, Conrart, and Bochart occupied honourable positions. Outside the ranks of official polemists the bitterness of controversy had subsided. Protestants were no doubt subjected to a constant pressure, social and political, which led to many conversions. But these converts naturally brought to their new faith much of the spirit of the old.

At the same time the period marked the zenith of the Catholic revival in France. New or reformed orders—Carmelites, Oratory, the Benedictine Congregation of Saint-Maur, the Jesuits—carried out a profound renewal of Christian studies and education, which gave rise to a more lively interest in Biblical problems among both clergy and laity. It would be tempting to seek in Jansenism one source of the Biblical epic. However, in spite of the interest of Port-Royal in religious and even profane literature (Arnauld d'Andilly's advice to Chapelain on the composition of *La Pucelle*, for example),[2] in spite of the famous Bible translation and Arnauld d'Andilly's Josephus, there is no evidence of any direct influence. None of our poets (with the possible exception of Perrault) seems to have been a Jansenist, though other religious movements are well represented. Nicole is said to have launched the success of Pierre de Saint-Louis's *Magdeleine au Desert*, which was a source of amusement to him and his friends.[3] This gives a clue to the attitude of the Jansenists. They were protected from extravagant literary enterprises by their austere mediocrity and reasonableness as well as by what would now be called a sense of humour.

---

[1] *De universi orbis christiani pace et concordia. Per eminentissimum cardinalem ducem Richelium constituenda*, Parisiis, 1634.

[2] See Kerviler, *Étude*, p. xix; Collas, *Chapelain*, p. 208.

[3] See Follard's notice in *L'Éliade*; Gautier, *Les Grotesques*, Paris, 1861, p. 140.

In science the deductive method of Descartes contrasts strongly with the empirical multiplicity which has been observed in Du Bartas, Gamon, and d'Aubigné. Of more particular importance is the attempt of Mersenne to find a new synthesis of scientific discovery and Christian teaching. The *Vérité des Sciences* appeared in 1625, the *Questions theologiques*, with their geometrical proof of the existence of God, in 1634. In the *Quaestiones celeberrimae in Genesim* (1623) a similar method is applied to Biblical difficulties, which reveals a growing need for rational explanation and contrasts with the unhesitating acceptance of the sixteenth century.

In politics the most striking development was the growth of centralization. As the heroic poem was closely bound up with questions of government and kingship, it was inevitably affected by these changes and the resulting modifications were not all superficial. The Fronde is of less importance. It seems that the conduct of its leaders was influenced by the current heroic ideal rather than inversely. It is difficult to find any direct reflection in the poems, though turbulent love-affairs between heroes and Amazons are frequent.

In this connexion feminism and the ideal of the *femme forte* gained notably in popularity. It is difficult to say whether this was due to the important part played by women in the religious movement, to social progress, or to the circumstances of Anne of Austria's regency. The dedication to the queen of the works of Du Bosc, Le Moyne, and Tortoletti illustrates the importance of the last.[1] By 1650 the active, heroic woman, like Queen Christina, the Grande Mademoiselle, or Marie de Gonzague, had become a typical figure in political life.

In her *Égalité des Hommes et des Femmes* (1622) Marie de Gournay quotes Judith, with Joan of Arc, as the supreme example of feminine virtue and heroism. Two texts are of greater significance. The first is *La Femme Héroïque* of Père Du Bosc, published in 1645, ten years before Chapelain's exaltation of feminine courage in his preface to *La Pucelle*. The first volume is dedicated to Anne of Austria, the second to Henrietta Maria. The book consists of a series of comparisons between famous women and great heroes, chosen indifferently from the Bible or from classical antiquity, though the two are never combined. Among the Biblical examples are the mother of the Maccabees and Abraham (sacrifice of chil-

[1] Cf. p. 53 above.

dren), Judith and David (defeat of a greatly superior enemy), and
Susanna and Joseph (the triumph of chastity).

Pierre Le Moyne's *Gallerie des Femmes Fortes* (1647) is also
dedicated to Anne of Austria and is preceded by a long panegyric
recounting the virtues of the Regent. It presents a series of
heroines, Jewish, Barbarian, Greek, Roman, and Christian. Of the
Jewish women only Judith is commonly treated by Biblical poets.
The others are Deborah, Jael, the mother of the Maccabees, and
Mariamne (from Josephus). To each are devoted a portrait, the
story of her achievements, a set of moral reflections, and a parallel
with a modern heroine. The engravings are of particular interest.
The Biblical and classical (though not the Christian) heroines are
all dressed in the same fashion. Deborah (engraved by Bosse after
Vignon) is a typical example. She wears a plumed helmet, a collar
and shoulder-pieces of armour, a girdle, a long robe with embroidered hem, and sandals. In her right hand is a sword, in her
left a shield. In the background we see a group of Roman soldiers.
The Biblical and classical world are thus regarded as one. The
whole book is a monument to the possession by women of qualities generally regarded as masculine, apotheosized in the great
frontispiece, engraved by Audran after Pietro da Cortona.

In literature preciosity may be mentioned for its stylistic influence. At the same time the rapid development of the novel
furnished both a substitute and a spur for epic. It seemed to the
epic poets that they might be able to combine its wide popularity
with more serious literary pretensions (the natural desire to attract
as many readers as possible is especially evident in their prefaces).

Before the great output of Biblical poems in the fifties there was
one premonitory sign, the *Joseph* and *Tobie* of Saint-Peres, which
appeared in 1648:

(i) *La Vie du Saint Patriarche Tobie, tirée de la Sainte Escriture,
conformément au Texte de la Ste Bible: Fidellement Paraphrasée,
et mise en vers François, pour seruir d'Instruction aux Peres de
famille, et d'exemple d'Obeïssance aux Enfans*, Paris, 1648.

(ii) *La Vie de Ioseph, Viceroy d'Egypte, Escrite en vers François,
conformément au Texte de la Ste Bible. Où il se voit quelle doit
estre la conduite des Princes, et quel le deuoir des Sujets*, Paris, 1648.

The name of Saint-Peres does not appear on the title-page of either work but is given in the privilege, which also supplies a biographical detail:

Il est permis au sieur de Saint Peres, Conseiller, Tresorier Payeur de la Gendarmerie de sadite Majesté . . .

He also wrote a pilgrim's guide to Notre-Dame de Liesse, first published in verse in 1647[1] and later in prose.[2] The prose version had reached its twelfth edition by 1672. An examination of these guides shows that the privilege of the 1647 edition bears exactly the same date (15 October 1646) and wording as that of *Joseph* and *Tobie*. The spelling of the name in most editions is, however, Saint Perés. The prose version includes a chapter on the glories of Picardy which in conjunction with his familiarity with the shrine suggests that he himself may have been a Picard. The work is dedicated to Madame la Princesse (de Condé). It confirms the impression of austere, even fanatical, piety given by *Joseph* and *Tobie* and shows that Saint-Peres was a Catholic.

Saint-Peres follows the Bible almost literally, with a few minor chronological alterations and one or two additions or amplifications (such as the banquets introduced in *Joseph*). The form is scarcely epic—there are no episodes or recitals, no division into books. There is no heroic action in *Joseph*, and even in *Tobie* the heroic aspects of the Bible narrative—the journey, the battle with the fish—are not fully exploited. However, some of the epic machinery is present—proposition, invocation, above all *merveilleux païen*, used as an ornament, not as an integral part of the action. The bareness of the narrative is relieved by classical similes. All these things, together with the allegorical-didactic titles, go to prove at least epic intentions.

On the whole Saint-Peres is an accidental apparition. In most respects he belongs to a much earlier period. There is probably no connexion between the appearance of his poems and the silent labours of others which were soon to be made public.

---

[1] *Le Vray Tresor de l'Histoire Saincte, sur le transport miraculeux de l'image de Nostre-Dame de Liesse*, Paris, 1647.

[2] *Histoire Miraculeuse de Nostre-Dame de Liesse*, Paris, 1657, &c.

CHAPTER VII

Saint-Amant's *Moyse Sauvé*

MARC-ANTOINE GÉRARD DE SAINT-AMANT
(1594–1661)

i. *Moyse Sauvé, Idyle Heroïque* (Paris, 1653. Seven further editions appeared between 1654 and 1664[1]).

ii. *Fragment d'un Poeme de Ioseph et de ses Freres en Egipte* in *Dernier Recueil de Diverses Poësies* (Paris, 1658).

Conception and Composition

THIS question has been discussed in considerable detail[2] and little remains to be said, though the evidence furnished by Chapelain's correspondence has hitherto been neglected.[3]

Joseph was written before the *Moyse sauvé*, as is proved by Saint-Amant's own statement in the *Advis* to *Joseph* of 1658.[4] *Il y a près de trente années* enables us to fix the date with some precision—it was written about 1630. The fragment—of about six hundred lines—follows the Bible narrative from Jacob's decision to send his sons into Egypt to the discovery of Joseph's identity. The earlier part of the poem, scarcely altered, becomes an episode of *Moyse sauvé* (Parts X and XI).

The history of the *Moyse* is complex. The first inspiration may date from 1624, when Saint-Amant mentions his Biblical studies

---

[1] For complete list see Toinet, i. 136; ii. 136. Samaran (*Journal des Débats*, 1911) produces an important document, Saint-Amant's contract with Sommaville dated 16 July 1658, which shows that at that date 890 copies of the first edition were still unsold. Of course this does not prove that the work was unpopular, since French and Dutch pirated editions had appeared in the meantime. References here are to Livet's edition, Paris, 1855, 2 vols.

[2] See especially Durand-Lapie, *Saint-Amant*, p. 441; Marni, *Allegory in the French Heroic Poem*; Vianey, *Revue des Cours et Conférences*, 1922, p. 496. Schönherr, *Saint-Amant*, may also be consulted, though his conclusions are not reliable.

[3] But cf. Adam, *Histoire*, i. 379.

[4] 'Bien long-temps avant que j'eusse fait le *Moyse*, c'est-à-dire il y a près de trente années, j'avois fait un poëme de *Joseph*, duquel ouvrage j'ay pris le commencement pour faire l'episode qui s'en voit sur la fin de l'autre . . .' (ii. 114).

in *Le Contemplateur*.[1] Durand-Lapie[2] states that the poem was begun in 1634, but he does not furnish any supporting evidence. In any case it was well under way by 18 May 1638, when Chapelain tells Balzac that Saint-Amant has just read to him three or four hundred lines.[3] Chapelain goes on to explain the original plan:

> Il le partage en trois livres de douze ou quinze cents vers chacun: le premier s'appellera le matin, le second, le midi, et le troisième, le soir, et tout l'ouvrage ne doit avoir qu'un seul jour d'étendue.[4]

There was an interval of fifteen years between this letter and the publication of the poem, but the final version did not greatly exceed the original plan in length—instead of three books of twelve to fifteen hundred lines each, we have twelve of about four hundred lines each. The original division, however, is still clearly visible, in the descriptions of morning in Part I, of noon in Part VI, of evening in Part X, and of nightfall in Part XII, all of which are particularly stressed in the table of contents for each part. There can be little doubt that they mark the limits of the three original books. It will be noticed that morning occupies six parts, afternoon and evening three each, a logical arrangement. Though these divisions do not correspond to any imperative necessity in the story, except perhaps that an atmosphere of serenity develops after the appearance of the Princess in the evening, they have a unity of their own and the breaks coincide with genuine breaks in the action. The twelve parts of the published poem, on the other hand, rarely have an organic unity and appear to have been divided entirely on a quantitative basis.[5]

Saint-Amant himself in his preface gives some information about the progress of the work:

> ... il y a quelques années que j'entrepris cet ouvrage. J'y ay travaillé à diverses reprises; j'ay esté des sept ou huit ans, tout de suitte, sans y faire un seul vers ...[6]

He goes on to compare himself to the owner of a garden who

---

[1]   Je ly ces sacrez Testamens
       Où Dieu, d'une encre solemnelle,
       Fait luire ses hauts mandemens. (i. 38.)

[2] *Saint-Amant*, p. 447.   [3] *Opuscules critiques*, p. 388.   [4] Ib.

[5] The parts are of almost exactly equal length (seven take up 14 pages each in Livet's edition, three 15, one 16, and one 18) and the divisions between them do not always correspond with breaks in the narrative. For example Part II ends as God is about to address Jacob, Part VII in the middle of the battle with the wasps which attack the cradle.   [6] ii. 139.

alters the whole layout and makes it unrecognizable, implying that the poem has been completely rewritten. This revision took place after Saint-Amant's return to France from Sweden in May 1651.[1] It does not now seem possible to discover all the details of these changes, but we may assume that the principal modifications were the division into twelve books on the model of Virgil, which appears to have been carried out in haste, and the introduction of part of the Joseph poem in order to add weight. References to external events are not of much assistance. The description of Queen Christina falling into a river when visiting warships[2] is probably connected with Saint-Amant's visit to Sweden in 1650 and may refer to an incident which took place in 1648.[3] But such an allusion was easy to interpolate and proves nothing in regard to the context. The references to John Casimir and Marie-Louise of Poland are clearly later than 1649, the date of their marriage. In particular the character of the Princess Termuth may have been adapted to that of Marie-Louise,[4] a process which was not one of simple interpolation. As the sterility of Termuth and the grief it caused her are described in detail, we may perhaps conclude that these passages were written between 1645, the date of the queen's first marriage, and 1650, when Saint-Amant wrote his stanzas on her first pregnancy[5] (she was then aged thirty-eight).

The *Moyse sauvé* is thus the result of a long period of preparation, followed by a hasty revision, from which the poem appears to have lost rather than gained. However, although the revision resulted in the ungainly plan, the superfluous Joseph episode, several additions and, no doubt, many alterations of detail, its importance should not be exaggerated—the essential framework

---

[1] Epistle to the Queen of Poland, which precedes the first edition of *Moyse* (omitted by Livet). See also Durand-Lapie, pp. 438, 441.

[2] ii. 243.   [3] Grauert, *Königinn Christina*, i. 275–6.

[4] For example:

> Cette chaste princesse, au monde infortunée
> De vivre sous le joug d'un ingrat hymenée,
> Et dolente de voir, en son espoir destruit,
> Que la fleur de ses ans ne laissoit point de fruit (ii. 292)
> Loin de la vaine pompe et du bruit de la cour (ii. 294)

which bear a close resemblance to Marie-Louise's unhappy marriage with Sigismund Ladislas and her retired life at Warsaw. It is true that the barrenness of Pharaoh's daughter was authorized by a passage from Philo Judaeus, but the parallel with the Queen of Poland cannot have remained unnoticed. For her relations with Saint-Amant cf. Tallemant des Réaux, *Historiettes*, cxlix–cliii (ed. Mongrédien, iii. 185 ff.).   [5] *Œuvres*, ii. 93.

remains unaltered and there is no proof of any considerable change
of style.

Saint-Amant also began a poem on Samson of which he wrote
four or five hundred lines, but discouraged by their loss he
abandoned the project.[1]

Saint-Amant's Historical Sources: The Bible, Josephus and Philo Judaeus

The Bible story of the rescue of Moses is a bare outline. So,
indeed, are the stories of Jacob and Joseph. To expand them into
a long heroic poem it was necessary not only to use all the conventional devices of ornament and periphrasis but also to find a
source of new incident. For this Saint-Amant turned to the Jewish
historians, Josephus and Philo,[2] as he acknowledges in the Preface.[3]

For Josephus, Saint-Amant used Génébrard's translation.[4] This
is plain from a reference in the letter to Bochart (ii. 333) where he
quotes a sentence from Josephus and gives the page number,
which corresponds to all the editions of Génébrard between 1609
and 1639.[5]

There is no such conclusive proof that Saint-Amant read Philo
in a French translation. But the fact that he used a translation of
Josephus is at least an indication that his knowledge of Greek
writers was derived solely from translation, and confirms his own
statement that he knew little Latin and Greek.[6] As there was a
French translation of the works of Philo, which seems, from the
number of editions, to have circulated widely, it is safe to assume
that he used it.[7] Unfortunately he has not followed Philo closely
enough to afford verbal coincidences.

The narrative of *Moyse sauvé* is divided into four sections: the
central theme, the concealment of Moses and the arrival of

---

[1] i. 15, ii. 13.

[2] Cf. p. 28 above.   [3] ii. 142.

[4] Schönherr (p. 59) assumed this from the popularity of the translation, but apparently overlooked the conclusive proof.

[5] 1609, 1616, 1627, 1631, 1639. In the edition of 1646, the last published before
the *Moyse sauvé*, the pagination is altered and it may therefore be safely excluded.
This applies equally to the 1st edition of 1578. These dates are those of the editions
in the Bibliothèque Nationale. References here are to the 1609 edition.

[6] *Advertissement* to the Collected Works (i. 12).

[7] Cf. p. 29 above. References in this chapter are to the 1619 edition.

Pharaoh's daughter; the subsequent history of Moses, revealed in Jocabel's dream; the story of Jacob and Esau, told by Merary; the story of Joseph, told by Amram to the Princess. The immediate task is to decide how far Saint-Amant followed the Bible and how far he drew upon Josephus and Philo.

The primary source of the central theme, the concealment and rescue of Moses, is a few verses of Exodus (ii. 1–10), to which may be added Exodus i for the description of Pharaoh's tyranny. In fact, however, for this central narrative, threadbare in the Bible, Josephus is of greater importance: there are even cases where Saint-Amant takes his version in preference to the Bible. Philo is less important, but furnishes a few details which are not to be found elsewhere. The easiest way to establish their respective contributions will be to point out differences between the three versions, showing which Saint-Amant followed. The reasons for his choice often illuminate his conception of religion, morality, or aesthetic suitability.

The first departure from the Bible is to be found in the reason for Pharaoh's order to kill all the male children of the Hebrews. The Bible (Exod. i. 15, 16) states the fact without inquiring into motives. Philo (233) points out soberly that female children, being of no use in war, were spared. But Josephus (56) introduces an oracle, prophesying that a Hebrew child will humble the Egyptian Empire. There can be no doubt why Saint-Amant followed Josephus and introduced the oracle—it enabled him to exploit the methods of classical epic.

In the Bible and Philo the birth of Moses is not given any supernatural significance. In Saint-Amant it is preceded by an angelic visit to Jocabel in which the birth of the saviour of the race is announced. This is taken directly from Josephus (57), but there are significant changes in Saint-Amant's account. In Josephus Amram prays for help for the oppressed Jews: God then announces the birth of Moses. Saint-Amant makes an angel appear unbidden. The purpose of this change is double. On the one hand there is the influence of the Annunciation, on the other that of the classical messenger. Both are plainly seen in

Un messager du ciel, un saint et vray Mercure (ii. 155).

The reader is invited to attach to the Christian angel his reminiscences of classical divinities, making a composite figure.

We are already in a position to estimate Saint-Amant's narrative method. All he finds in the Bible is a verse and a half:

> Or apres ces choses vn homme de la maison de Leui, alla et prist vne fille de sa lignée.
> Laquelle conçeut et enfanta vn fils.
>
> (Exod. ii. 1, 2, Frizon)

In expanding this he has made use of details in Josephus, but also of religious and literary traditions.

After the birth of Moses Saint-Amant continues to draw chiefly on Josephus. The motives of Amram and Jocabel in hiding Moses are not stated in the Bible, except that the manufacture of the cradle implies a plan to preserve him. Philo seeks a motive and finds a base one, ascribing it to their fear for themselves if the child should be discovered; later they regret their action.[1] Josephus too seeks a motive and finds it in Amram's trust in Providence,[2] though he admits also the element of personal fear. It was naturally this version that Saint-Amant followed, to be consistent with his presentation of the characters of Jocabel and Amram and with the story of the vision.

After Moses has been placed in the cradle his sister goes to see what will happen (Exod. ii. 4). The Bible, as usual, does not explain why she went and as usual Josephus and Philo attempt an explanation. According to Philo she goes of her own accord and there is an implicit contrast between her conduct and that of her parents.[3] In Josephus Jocabel, because of her concern for the fate of Moses, sends Marie to watch over him.[4] Saint-Amant again follows him closely (ii. 163).

At this point he abandons his historical sources to introduce two new characters, Elisaph and Merary. Their names are from the Bible (Elisaph, Num. i. 14, x. 20; Merary, Exod. vi. 16, 19), but there is nothing to attach their characters (which have quite different sources) to these persons. In fact Saint-Amant explicitly denies any connexion (letter to Bochart, ii. 330). From now on the central narrative is interrupted by the recitals of Merary and the dream of Jocabel. In the intervals between these interruptions are placed the vicissitudes of the cradle, the sources of which must be sought elsewhere.

Saint-Amant does not return to the Bible narrative until Part X,

---

[1] p. 233.   [2] p. 58.   [3] p. 234.   [4] p. 58.

when Pharaoh's daughter appears. For the portrait he made of her he drew mainly on an ideal of feminine perfection, which he may have attached to his patroness, Marie-Louise. But he was indebted to Josephus for the name Termuth and to Philo for a significant detail, the fact that the Princess was married and childless,[1] a debt he acknowledges in the Preface.[2]

At this point there is another break, where Amram recites to the Princess the story of Joseph. Afterwards, when she goes down to the river, there is a striking difference between the simplicity of the rescue in the Bible:

Quand elle vid le coffret en la rousiere, y enuoya vne de ses seruantes (Exod. ii. 5, Frizon)

and the luxuriant description of Saint-Amant. Much of this was due to his conception of the nature of poetry, but the initial impulse is to be found in Josephus:

Et tout soudain fit mettre en l'eauë des gens qui sçauoient bien nager (58).

The closing scene—the intervention of Marie and the arrival of Jocabel—again owes more to Josephus than to Philo. That Marie pretended to be there by accident (ii. 324) is to be found only in Josephus (58). Moses' refusal of the Egyptian nurses is also taken from Josephus (58).

The dream of Jocabel continues the story of Moses from the point where the central narrative ends. The sources are the same, but their treatment shows considerable differences. Events are condensed and unimportant incidents omitted, as was necessary if this minor narrative was to be kept in proportion. Moreover, these omissions and condensations are often arranged so as to make the atmosphere really that of a dream.

The dream opens with the story of the rejected diadem from Josephus (59). Saint-Amant does not mention the reception of Moses by the Egyptians and the favour in which he was held before the incident, nor their plots against him as he grew up. He seizes upon the episode with its typical dream symbol, the crown, and cuts away the surrounding portions.

From this point he goes on immediately to the war in Ethiopia,

[1] p. 234.   [2] ii. 143.

itself considerably condensed. For instance there is only a succinct reference:

> Il en vaincq les dragons avecques des oyseaux (ii. 194)

to the incident of Moses and the serpents in Josephus[1] and without knowledge of the source it is practically unintelligible. Another point in which he follows Josephus is the marriage of Moses to the Ethiopian princess, Tharbis. There is a reference to his marriage to an Ethiopian woman in Num. xii. 1 and Josephus was presumably enlarging on this.[2] But in neither the Bible, Josephus, nor Saint-Amant is there any account of what became of her. Saint-Amant probably included the incident because it has a certain mystery, again suited to the atmosphere of the dream.

He resumes with Moses in full flight (ii. 198) and goes on at once to his marriage with Zipporah, omitting the scene at the well, which is found in the Bible, Josephus, and Philo alike. The omission again has the effect of isolating the marriage scene, of making it dim and remote; but at the same time Saint-Amant makes certain details stand out sharply—the palms and the blood-stained altar with its pungent smell. This contrast also is typical of a dream. That Saint-Amant consciously strove to produce the effect is shown by the line

> Dans le songe il s'y donne à l'aymable Sephore (ii. 198).

In the story of the ten plagues the tendency to follow Philo rather than Josephus, noticeable after the return of Moses from Ethiopia, becomes more pronounced, but on the whole the narrative is more and more condensed, so that departures from the Bible are less necessary. The most important is the reduction of the place of most of the plagues to a series of rhetorical questions (ii. 208). Only the changing of water to blood, the three days' darkness, and the death of the Egyptian firstborn are recounted fully. This was dictated in the first place by the necessity for conciseness, but the choice of these three plagues was not fortuitous. It is explained by Saint-Amant himself:

> Pour les miracles seuls mon pinceau se veut teindre (ii. 209).

These three were taken because they alone were *merveilleux* (the final plague had also to be included as the climax).

---

[1] p. 60.   [2] p. 61.

From this point onward alterations of the Bible story are slighter still and generally concern small details only. For instance the bald statement of the Bible (Exod. xii. 36) that the Israelites 'spoiled the Egyptians' is considerably toned down by Saint-Amant:

> Il relasche Israël, et souffre à son depart
> Que de tous leurs tresors les siens luy fassent part (ii. 211).

This is no doubt to be attributed to a desire to present them in a light more favourable according to the ideas of the seventeenth century.

Saint-Amant does not attempt to reproduce the magnificent song of praise which in the Bible follows the safe passage of the Red Sea. This was not due to its unsuitability in a dream, since the long speeches of Aaron to Pharaoh are included. And when allowance is made for the need for conciseness, the neglect of this opportunity is a clear indication that the Bible has little influence on the *poetry* of *Moyse sauvé*.

For the journey through the desert the Bible is again closely followed. But the narrative is considerably compressed and again there is a selective principle at work. The incidents included— God's appearance on Sinai, the Golden Calf, the destruction of Dathan and Abiram, and finally Aaron's rod—are all capable of strong visual presentation.

Merary's recital of the history of Jacob is divided into two halves, the first ending with the vision at Bethel, the second with the reconciliation with Esau. The two are separated by the various infernal schemes for the destruction of the cradle and by Jocabel's dream. For this recital only two historical sources need be considered—the Bible and Josephus. In fact Josephus has contributed relatively little and the deviations from the Bible are mostly due to Saint-Amant's moral scruples or desire for psychological accuracy.

Josephus may have suggested Saint-Amant's account of the effect on Jacob of his meeting with Rachel at the well. In the Bible the sudden wave of emotion which overcomes him is shown only in what he does.[1] Josephus, on the other hand, tries to show the internal effect of this psychological impact;[2] so does

---

[1] Gen. xxix. 10, 11.   [2] p. 30.

Saint-Amant, but he has transformed it with the aid of precious love vocabulary:

> Cette noble pucelle, où brilloient tant de charmes (ii. 259).

A similar case is the theft of Laban's idols. In the Bible there is no explanation of the theft (unless indeed it is the desire for revenge against Laban revealed in Gen. xxxi. 15, 16). Josephus feels the need for an explanation of the fact that Rachel should want these false gods:

> Non pas qu'elle eust quelque religion enuers ces dieux: (car elle auoit esté apprise de son mary de les auoir en abomination) mais à celle fin qu'elle eust refuge à eux, et peust plus facilement obtenir pardon, si d'auenture lon les pouuoit attaindre (32).

Clearly this could not satisfy Saint-Amant, but his own attempt is more absurd still:

> Mais l'aymable Rachel, qui s'en estoit saisie,
> Ayant mis à couvert leur majesté moisie,
> Non pour les reverer, mais pour les rendre un jour
> Les innocens jouets des fruits de son amour (ii. 276).

A less convincing reason for their theft and retention could scarcely have been found, but it had for Saint-Amant the advantage of removing any idea of respect for the idols and at the same time of ascribing the theft to the virtue of maternal affection.

Finally, Saint-Amant has used Josephus' account of Jacob's presents to Esau. In the letter to Bochart he shows exactly how his mind worked in dealing with his sources. Josephus says that Jacob sent strange beasts; and this is sufficient justification for Saint-Amant to change the camels, asses, sheep, and so on of Gen. xxxii. 14 into lions and leopards. He continues (ii. 333): 'Le reste est une fantaisie de poëte comme de peintre, pour representer tousjours quelque chose de plus noble et de plus beau'. If he thought leopards and lions were more noble than sheep and camels it is probable that he was influenced by literary tradition and, in particular, the traditions of earlier epic poetry.

There are several deviations from the Bible for which Josephus offers no such justification. The Bible says that Jacob's seven years' service passed quickly:

> Iacob donc seruit sept ans pour Rachel, qui lui semblerent comme peu de iours, pource qu'il l'aimoit (Gen. xxix. 20, Geneva, 1588.)

Josephus (31) gives a similar if a less moving version. But Saint-Amant says that Jacob

> Blasmoit du temps prefix la lente cruauté.
> Un jour estoit un siecle à son impatience (ii. 264).

Since Saint-Amant left both his sources and gave a story not only different from but contradictory to that of the Bible, the force of the conventional view of a lover's duty must have been strong indeed.

In the Bible (Gen. xxx. 32) it is Jacob who suggests the scheme for dividing the sheep according to their markings. In Saint-Amant it is Laban who makes the proposal in order to prevent Jacob's departure. This also was perhaps intended to place Jacob in a more favourable light. In fact, his plan to defraud his father-in-law, presented quite nakedly in the Bible, would certainly have shocked the seventeenth-century moral sense if put with equal bluntness in a poem which had no sacred authority. By making the first proposal come from Laban, Saint-Amant succeeds in embellishing to some extent the actions of Jacob. A similar case is the omission of Laban's touching plea (Gen. xxxi. 26–30). Here again Saint-Amant did not wish to make Laban appear too magnanimous or to stress the contrast between this magnanimity and Jacob's fear. Instead he casts ridicule on Laban's search for his idols (ii. 277).

The story of Joseph, told by Amram to Pharaoh's daughter, follows the Bible far more closely. There is a good deal of expansion, but little alteration of facts. The only serious change is to be found in the baker's dream. In the Bible (Gen. xl. 16, 17) it is simple and harmless enough. But Saint-Amant (ii. 305) gives it a sinister setting and makes the birds horrible. This artificial contrast between the two dreams is less effective than the simplicity of the Bible.

The Bible therefore is the principal force in shaping the *Moyse sauvé*. But Saint-Amant is inclined to give equal authority to Josephus and Philo when it suits his purpose. They were both more interested in motives and in minor details and therefore perhaps supplied more material.[1] The Bible remains the foundation

---

[1] A curious example is Saint-Amant's justification of his statement that the Israelites had been in Egypt more than 300 years (letter to Bochart, ii. 330). He

of the story, but the spirit which informed this foundation, which determined Saint-Amant's emotional and moral attitude and the essence of his poetry, was not Biblical.

The Literary Sources

For the literary sources of Saint-Amant certain indications are given by the Preface of the *Moyse* and the letter to Bochart, in which he refers, apart from Homer and Virgil, to Statius,[1] Ariosto,[2] Sannazaro,[3] Tasso,[4] and Du Bartas.[5] Elsewhere he mentions Marino's *Sampogna* as a model for the heroic poem.[6] Of course such references do not necessarily prove close acquaintance with the works quoted. Saint-Amant was well known for his lack of scholarship, unusual in a professional poet.[7] The letter to Bochart suggests a deliberate and not very happy attempt to imitate the methods of erudition. However, he read Spanish and Italian with facility and knew Marino's work better than Chapelain, its learned apologist.[8] Most of his references to earlier poets concern particular passages, which imply direct knowledge of the texts. He was not as ignorant as he himself sometimes pretended.

Particular borrowings are discussed elsewhere when they serve to throw light on Saint-Amant's poetic talent. Here his debt to the principal sources will be summarized. He seems to have derived from Ariosto the episode of Calm and the angel,[9] though the theme was too widespread to permit an unqualified attribution. The Archangel Michael's visit to Discord and Silence in the *Orlando Furioso* is the answer to the Emperor Charles's prayer for the success of his arms: to this prayer corresponds that of Jocabel,

---

quotes Josephus as his authority, Josephus having said that the Egyptian captivity lasted 400 years. Saint-Amant does not seem to have noticed that a similar figure is given in the Bible (Exod. xii. 40). There is therefore ground for assuming that his reading of the Bible was cursory and confined to the parts which he thought directly interested him.   [1] ii. 331.   [2] ii. 330.

[3] Whom he cites as authority for the use of pagan mythology (ii. 141).

[4] For the allegory of the *Gerusalemme Liberata* (ii. 146).

[5] 'Le bon du Bartas, qui n'estoit pas un ignorant . . .' (ii. 330). Cf. p. 44 above.

[6] i. 12.

[7] Cf. Saint-Évremond's comedy, *Les Académiciens*, and Boileau's sneer in Satire I.

[8] Chapelain had quarrelled with Saint-Amant over the number of stanzas in the *Adone* and admits that he was wrong (Chapelain to Saint-Amant, November 1634, *Lettres*, ed. Larroque, i. 81). Cf. also: 'Pour son *Adone*, c'est une mer qui n'a ni fond ni rive et que jamais personne que Saint-Amand n'a pu courir entièrement' (Chapelain to Huet, 30 March 1662, ib. ii. 217).

[9] *Orlando Furioso*, xiv, stanzas 79 ff. Cf. p. 180 below.

which provokes the dispatch of the angel. There are also resemblances of detail. Saint-Amant's angel is called *le courrier divin*
(ii. 237): Michael is *il celeste corrier*. Silence, like Calm, is found in
a grotto and is surrounded by other allegorical figures, Sleep,
Indolence, Sloth, and Oblivion, corresponding to *Bonace* and
Tranquillité in Saint-Amant. Elsewhere there are only doubtful
points, belonging to conventions of which Ariosto was perhaps
the originator but which were considerably modified after him.
Examples are the employment of unicorns,[1] the city of Memphis,[2]
the magic herb,[3] the use of firearms in comparisons.[4] There is
also a general resemblance between the battle of Elisaph and the
crocodile[5] and that of Ruggiero and the orca.[6]

In spite of the reference in the Preface, Saint-Amant owes little
to Sannazaro, but one passage may be a direct imitation:

> Si de l'Estre divin que là-haut tu contemples
> J'ay servy les autels, j'ay reveré les temples . . .[7]

> niueis tibi si solennia templis
> Serta damus, si mansuras tibi ponimus aras . . .[8]

The description of the Princess's palace[9] follows in its general
lines the tradition of Tasso and the garden of Armida, but there
are few particular resemblances. The incident of the magic herb,
on the other hand, owes to Tasso the intervention of an angel,[10]
which is not found in Ariosto. A similar contamination occurs
in the flight of the two angels,[11] which might have been suggested
by Ariosto, Tasso, or any of their imitators.

Marino's influence on Saint-Amant is a question of diffused
qualities of style and technique rather than of precise incident.[12]
The Calm episode may owe a little to Marino's picture of Night
in his cave,[13] a close imitation of Ariosto. The angel's vase of

---

[1] Saint-Amant, ii. 312; *Furioso*, vi, stanza 69.
[2] Saint-Amant, ii. 152; 'Memfi per le piramidi famoso' (*Furioso*, xv, stanza 61).
But Memphis appears again in Du Bartas and Marino.
[3] Saint-Amant, ii. 186; *Furioso*, xix, stanza 22.
[4] Saint-Amant, ii. 321; *Furioso*, ix, stanza 29; xxii, stanza 21.
[5] Saint-Amant, ii. 181.   [6] *Furioso*, x, stanzas 100 ff.
[7] Saint-Amant, ii. 192.
[8] *De partu Virginis*, bk. i (1526 ed., A1 v°).
[9] Saint-Amant, ii. 292 ff.
[10] Saint-Amant, ii. 187; *Gerusalemme Liberata*, xi, stanza 72.
[11] Saint-Amant, ii. 236.
[12] Cf. p. 54 above; on Saint-Amant and Marino see also Adam, *Théophile de Viau*,
pp. 444–8.   [13] *Strage*, i, stanzas 165 ff.

tears[1] may be derived from a similar vase, full of the tears of unhappy lovers, with which Cupid tempers his arrow in the *Adone*.[2] More interesting is the flight to Egypt in the *Strage degli Innocenti*[3] with its references to Memphis, pyramids, crocodiles, sphinx, and mummies. Of these Saint-Amant employs the first four: his attempts to introduce geographical colouring may have been suggested by a reading of Marino.

Apart from the pastoral tradition Saint-Amant hardly seems to have drawn on Ronsard. In Book I of the *Franciade* a fight between a vulture, an eagle, and a falcon takes on a supernatural significance.[4] The incident resembles that of the eagle and the vulture in the *Moyse*.[5] There is nothing, however, to prove direct imitation. A closer resemblance is that between the Princess's chariot[6] and the equipage of Hyante.[7] A verbal coincidence is found here, in Ronsard:

> Ses iuments par le vuide
> *A bonds legers* s'eslançoient en auant:

in Saint-Amant:

> Foulant *à bonds legers*, dans l'aise et dans l'orgueil . . .

A single phrase and a general identity of situation are not sufficient to prove direct influence, and in general the differences here are more instructive than the resemblances. They illustrate the progress of the heroic style. Ronsard's coach becomes a chariot in Saint-Amant, his mares become unicorns. Hyante holding the reins and whip is replaced by *une amazone à gouverner leurs resnes*. Ronsard's horses go to graze, Saint-Amant's unicorns are not mentioned, once their task is complete. On the whole Ronsard is in a lower key, his description lacks the ornate embellishments of Saint-Amant.

This summary of borrowings is not complete, but it goes to show that Saint-Amant turned to his more important predecessors for occasional details only and that his treatment of the theme was highly original. The case of Du Bartas does not perhaps essentially alter this conclusion but it furnishes several examples of indubitable and sustained imitation, which extends to style as well as situation. Again, however, the changes made by Saint-Amant are probably more significant than the verbal transferences.

---

[1] Saint-Amant, ii. 235.   [2] Canto i. 78.
[3] i, stanzas 190–3, 208. Cf. p. 55 above.   [4] ed. Laumonier, iii. 21–22.   [5] ii. 318.
[6] ii. 312.   [7] *Franciade*, bk. iv, ed. Laumonier, iii. 128.

The labours of Israel are treated in the same way by both poets,[1] especially in the use of the word *firmament*. The description of the deluge[2] was almost certainly inspired by Du Bartas—there are no exact coincidences, but the choice of detail is the same.

In the history of the plagues there are more numerous resemblances, both in situation and expression:

> Car, si l'Egiptien, dans la faim qui le presse . . .[3]
>
> Si l'importune faim les Payens du lict chasse . . .[4]

There can be little doubt about the fact of imitation, especially as both are in contradiction with Exod. x. 23. The passage of the Angel of Death affords another example.[5]

The crossing of the Red Sea reveals the hand of Du Bartas even more plainly; first of all in the complaints of the Israelites:

> *Jacob*, qui de sa paix sent troubler la bonace . . .
> *Vomit avec aigreur* ce langage insensé . . .
> Sommes-nous des poissons, sommes-nous des *oyseaux*,
> Pour *franchir* aisement ou ces *monts* ou ces eaux?
> *O folle ambition!*[6]
>
> *Iacob*, qui craint rechoir sous la main vengeresse . . .
> *Desgorge tout son fiel* contre son conducteur,
> *O lasche Ambition!* . . .
> *Oiseaux, franchirons*-nous le front iette-fumee
> De ces *monts* droit-coupez? . . .[7]

A still closer parallel to these interrogations appears in *Judith*:

> *Sommes-nous des poissons pour* les *eaux* trauerser
> D'vne si large mer? *sommes-nous des oiseaux*
> *Pour franchir* tout d'vn vol ces montagnes hautaines?[8]

The crossing itself, one of Saint-Amant's best-known descriptions, owes much to the same source:

> Là passent à pié *sec* les bœufs et les moutons,
> Où nagueres flottoyent les dauphins et les *thons*;
> Là l'*enfant* esveillé . . .[9]
>
> Et l'*enfant* marche au *sec* où s'esbattoyent les *Thons*.[10]

---

[1] Saint-Amant, ii. 153; Du Bartas (1616 ed.), p. 404; Holmes, iii. 258.
[2] Saint-Amant, ii. 190; Du Bartas, pp. 58–59; Holmes, iii. 97.
[3] Saint-Amant, ii. 209.   [4] Du Bartas, p. 416; Holmes, iii. 271.
[5] Saint-Amant, ii. 210; Du Bartas, p. 417; Holmes, iii. 271.
[6] Saint-Amant, ii. 212.   [7] Du Bartas, p. 419; Holmes, iii. 273–4.
[8] Du Bartas, p. 546; Holmes, ii. 33.   [9] Saint-Amant, ii. 214.
[10] Du Bartas, p. 420; Holmes, iii. 275.

The vivid picture of Pharaoh brandishing his sword to the end also bears a striking resemblance to Du Bartas; taken in conjunction with the rest, it offers adequate proof of imitation:

> Pharaon seul demeure, et seul il ose encore
> De son glaive haussé, qu'à nu le soleil dore,
> Menacer Israël . . .[1]

> . . . tant seulement son bras
> Qui brandit esleué le meurtrier coutelas
> Contre le peuple esleu . . .[2]

Du Bartas like Saint-Amant takes from Josephus the detail of the floating weapons.

The rebellion of Korah is inserted, as in the *Semaine*, immediately after the episode of the Golden Calf, whereas in the Bible it comes much later.[3] This reveals the extent of Saint-Amant's obligation even more clearly than the verbal imitation, which is again found here:

> *L'encensoir à la main* cet insolent *s'y treuue*;
> *Sa faction* s'y rend . . .[4]

> Lendemain ce mutin deuant la sainte tente
> *L'encensoir en la main* . . .
> *Sa faction s'y trouue* . . .[5]

Finally Saint-Amant's liking for scientific curiosities may have been suggested in part by Du Bartas. In particular, the *Semaine* contains a description of the ichneumon and its fights with the crocodile.[6] There is, however, a deep gulf between Saint-Amant's dilettantism and the passionate universality of scientific interests seen in Du Bartas.

All these borrowings show a return to much earlier sources and there is no evidence that Saint-Amant had read his immediate predecessors in the Biblical epic (with the possible exception of Millieu).[7] A single phrase presents a parallel with Montchrestien:

> Et que le roy des feux, d'un rayon vif et pur,
> Eut refait le matin *d'or, de pourpre et d'azur*[8]

> Et faisoient esclater leur reluisante plume
> *D'or de pourpre et d'azur* que le Soleil allume.[9]

---

[1] Saint-Amant, ii. 217.
[2] Du Bartas, p. 422; Holmes, iii. 277.   [3] Num. xvi.
[4] Saint-Amant, ii. 227.   [5] Du Bartas, p. 434; Holmes, iii. 289.
[6] Du Bartas, p. 155; Holmes, ii. 385. Cf. Saint-Amant, ii. 184.
[7] Cf. p. 75 above.   [8] Saint-Amant, ii. 160.
[9] *Tragedies*, 1604 ed., p. 350.

But there may easily be a common or intermediate source. The complexity of the origins again makes it difficult to trace an unbroken line of evolution.

The Heroic Idyll

Saint-Amant explains in the Preface why he chose the title of heroic idyll:

> Quelques uns qui croyoient que je donnerois le titre de Poëme heroïque à cet ouvrage s'estonneront peut-estre d'abord que je ne luy donne que celuy d'Idyle, lequel est à peine connu en notre langue, et qui n'est employé d'ordinaire qu'à de petites matieres narratives et fabuleuses, comme on le peut voir dans les Grecs et dans les Italiens; mais quand ils auront veu de quelle nature est le dessein que je traitte, et qu'ils sçauront que j'en ay consulté nostre illustre academie, j'espere qu'ils en seront satisfaits (ii. 140).

He goes on to say:

> Le luth y eclatte plus que la trompette; le lyrique en fait la meilleure partie . . . ,

which shows that at any rate his general idea of the form did not differ from that usually accepted. This is confirmed by a passage of the Preface to the 1629 edition of his works, that is, nearly twenty-five years before the remarks quoted:

> Et particulierement j'ay pris quelque plaisir à de certains petits essais de poëmes heroïques, dont parmy les modernes le Cavalier Marin nous a donné les premiers exemples dans son livre intitulé *La Sampogna*. Ce sont des descriptions de quelques aventures celebres dans la Fable ancienne, qui s'appellent en grec *Idilios*, à ce que j'ay ouy dire (i. 12–13).

It appears then that Saint-Amant had been attracted to the idyll several years before the *Moyse* was thought of, that even then he had considered it to be primarily a narrative poem, dealing with fabulous (that is, mythological) subjects. It will be noticed that in the earlier passage Saint-Amant gives only the Greek word, not the French. It may be assumed, therefore, that its use spread in the interval, though even in the later passage Saint-Amant declares it to be rare. By the time of Boileau's *Art Poétique* (1674) it seems to have been firmly established in its present sense.[1]

---

[1] But cf. 'Petit Poëme esgayé qui contient des descriptions ou narrations de quelques adventures agreables' (Furetière, 1690). This definition is not unlike Saint-Amant's.

The reference to the Academy is easily explained: we have seen that Chapelain knew all about the poem long before its completion and that Saint-Amant had read extracts to him.[1] In his letters Chapelain particularly emphasizes the title, which had therefore been chosen very early in the history of the poem.[2] He corrects Balzac's belief that the poem is an epic. It is, he says, an idyll, which is called heroic by its author. Taking this in conjunction with Saint-Amant's preface, we may conjecture that Chapelain was the leader of those who advised the title 'idyll'.[3]

It appears, however, from the Preface and the letter to Bochart that Saint-Amant seeks the glory of the epic poet without his responsibility, and especially after the publication of the poem is anxious to show that it is essentially heroic. But whatever extraneous reasons may have contributed to the choice of the word 'idyll', it is not to be assumed that the title has no justification. The idyllic elements (in our sense and in Saint-Amant's) occupy a large place in the poem and it will be necessary to separate them from the purely epic elements and to see how far the title is applicable.

Taking as a broad distinction Saint-Amant's own lute and trumpet,[4] it may be said that the main story (the rescue of Moses) is idyllic, both in setting and material. It is, however, given an epic character by the series of battles which are represented as a struggle between the forces of Heaven and Hell. The continuation of the life of Moses (Jocabel's dream) is more heroic, like the story of Joseph, which though it has nothing to do with war is a recital of wandering, adventure, and passionate love with the final effect depending on peripeteia. On the other hand, the story of Jacob is pure idyll, especially the second part, which describes the love of the shepherd Jacob for the shepherdess Rachel. In the main story Elisaph is a shepherd and Merary a fisherman. This appearance of a shepherd as Miriam's lover transforms the Biblical narrative into an idyll on the classical

---

[1] Cf. p. 82 above.

[2] 'Le poème épique dont on vous a parlé est un idylle que le Gros appelle héroïque, à cause qu'il y veut décrire les actions de Moïse sous le titre de *Moïse sauvé*' (Chapelain to Balzac, 18 May 1638, *Opuscules*, p. 387). 'Saint-Amant s'est sanctifié par l'entreprise de son *Moïse* dont il fait un idylle héroïque tout rempli de descriptions, et belles en vérité . . .' (Chapelain to Balzac, 3 Jan. 1639, *Opuscules*, p. 399).

[3] Guillaume Colletet was also consulted (see his *Discours du poëme bucolique*, Paris, 1657, p. 44).   [4] Cf. p. 97 above.

model. The shepherd, however, is a central figure of the Bible as
well as of the idyll, so that in making Elisaph a shepherd Saint-
Amant creates the opportunity for the development of a classical
idyll without necessarily disturbing the Biblical atmosphere of the
poem. This is clearer still in the story of Jacob and Rachel. Here
Saint-Amant found his idyll ready made and only requiring a
classical form. There is yet another such subject in his source, the
life of Moses in Midian, where he guards Jethro's flocks.

The first appearance of Elisaph and Marie shows clearly to
which class of shepherd they belong. Elisaph

> Avoit d'une coustume et licite et fidelle,
> Amené son troupeau tondre l'herbe auprès d'elle;
> Et ces chastes amans, sous un palmier assis,
> S'entre-communiquoyent leurs intimes soucis (ii. 167).

The flock of sheep is a stage property. The lovers sitting under a
tree are certainly without Biblical parallel, whereas they are common in the Renaissance pastoral. It is true that in the interest
of local colour Saint-Amant has substituted a palm-tree for the
oaks of the Lignon.

What most obviously belongs to the pastoral convention, however, is the description of Jacob cutting Rachel's name on tree-
trunks.[1] Elisaph too carves a picture of Marie on a tree-trunk.[2]
This curious repetition (at a very short interval) may be attributed to the parallelism between the two stories. The subject is
so common in the pastoral that it may be said to be almost
universal.[3]

Yet much in the shepherds of the poem transcends the exact
imitation of other pastoral poets. This is partly due to the Bible,

---

[1] ii. 262.   [2] ii. 247.

[3] The ultimate source may be Virgil:

> Imo haec in viridi nuper quae cortice fagi
> Carmina descripsi et modulans alterna notavi,
> Experiar (*Eclogues*, v. 13–15).

It is to be found later in Sannazaro: 'Troueremo molti alberi, nei quali io in vn
tempo quando il sangue mi era più caldo, con la mia falce scrissi il nome di quella,
che sopra tutti li greggi amai' (*Arcadia*, Prosa v); in Tasso:

> Lo scrisse in mille piante, e con le piante
> Crebbero i versi . . . (*Aminta*, i. 1);

in Ronsard (*Le Voyage de Tours*, ed. Laumonier, i. 168):

> Et auecq'vn poinçon ie veux desur l'escorce
> Engrauer de ton nom les six lettres à force.

In *L'Astrée* there is the episode in which Andrimarte joins 'J'ayme' to the name
of Silviane (ed. Vaganay, Lyons, 1925–8, iii. 655).

which Saint-Amant was obliged to follow fairly closely. Thus
Jacob's trick, by which he steals Laban's sheep, could not be
imagined in a French or Italian pastoral. Both the method used
and its dishonesty would have appeared sordid. It is true that
Virgil's shepherds are often rascals who neglect their flocks and
steal their neighbour's. But this is rather a sign of their conventionally carefree existence: Jacob's cunning is nearer to reality.
Biblical influence is again seen in the description of Laban:

> Ton oncle maternel, le genereux Laban,
> Qui paroist comme un cedre au faiste du Liban,
> Qui voit de ses troupeaux couvrir ses vastes plaines,
> Qui voit de ses moissons ses granges tousjours pleines . . . (ii. 174).

What is remarkable is the wholly Biblical tone of this assessment
of wealth, emphasized by the comparison to a cedar of Lebanon.
The lines have something of the amplitude of *Booz endormi*. At the
same time, such pride in wealth is frequent in Virgil and passes into
the pastoral,[1] so that Saint-Amant is able to use the Bible here to
renew rather than to alter the conventions of the genre.

The shepherd's is not the only trade employed in the idyll.
Saint-Amant makes Merary a fisherman and takes the opportunity
to introduce descriptions of fishing, also a frequent subject of
the Renaissance idyll with its own conventions. A whole episode
is devoted to Merary's instruction of Elisaph and Marie in its
secrets.[2] The hook is the conventional mark of the fisherman as
the crook is of the shepherd.[3] But it soon becomes clear that this
introductory passage was intended as a means of binding to the

---

[1]   Despectus tibi sum, nec qui sim quaeris, Alexi,
        Quam dives pecoris, nivei quam lactis abundans.
        Mille meae Siculis errant in montibus agnae (*Eclogues*, ii. 19–21).

There is perhaps a closer parallel in Racan:

        De vingt paires de bœufs il seillonne la plaine,
        Tous les ans ses acquests augmentent son domaine:
        Dans les champs d'alentour on ne void auiourd'huy
        Que cheures et brebis qui sortent de chez luy (*Les Bergeries*, i. 3).

[2]   Merary, dont les mains à la pesche exercées,
        Pendant leur belle course, avecques l'hameçon,
        Avoient trompé le temps en trompant le poisson, . . . (ii. 250).

[3] A few examples will suffice to prove this:

    Seco tendeva insidie con le reti
    A' pesci ed agli augelli . . . (Tasso, *Aminta*, i. 2).

    E con l'hamo tentar ne l'onda i pesci (Guarini, *Pastor Fido*, i. 4).

    Tirer auecq' la ligne en tremblant emporté
    Le credule poisson prins a l'haim apasté (Ronsard, *Elegie*, ed. Laumonier, i. 338).

pastoral tradition a description which was to profit from the
poet's personal experience. He goes on to introduce himself as a
fisherman.[1] Doubts as to the genuineness of this declaration do not
survive the examination of the description itself:

> Il s'y secoue en vain, de sa cheute on s'approche,
> On y court, on le prend, du fer on le descroche;
> Il s'eschappe des doigts, tombe, sautelle, fuit,
> Fait voir mille soleils en l'escaille qui luit,
> Bat l'herbe de sa queue, et, sur la plaine verte,
> D'une bouche sans cry, de temps en temps ouverte,
> Baille sans respirer, comme né sans poumon,
> Et laisse à qui l'estraint un reste de limon (ii. 251).

It is evident that Saint-Amant's interest in fishing is very different
from his interest in shepherds.

In the pastoral these elements are incidental to the study of love.
The full influence of the idyllic tradition appears in the rescue of
Marie from drowning. This incident, though Saint-Amant says it
was suggested by a similar accident to Queen Christina, recalls
L'Astrée, where Céladon throws himself into the Lignon and is
believed to be drowned. After Elisaph has saved Marie by pulling
her out of the river by the hair he makes long and rather ridiculous
excuses, which she graciously accepts (ii. 244). There is a similar
scene in Tasso's *Aminta* where Aminta, wishing to untie Silvia's
hair which binds her to a tree, asks first for pardon.[2]

The *Moyse sauvé* is thus to a great extent an idyll in the seventeenth-century sense of the term. We have noticed, however,
signs of another idyll, different in approach from the pastoral,
and based on the trivial details of rural life. This corresponds to
a later view of the genre rather than to the definition given by
Saint-Amant—the lute has little part in it. Typical examples are
Goldsmith's *Deserted Village*, Goethe's *Hermann und Dorothea*, and
Lamartine's *Jocelyn*,[3] in which the daily round of work and play is
studied with elaborate care. Of course in such works one kind of
conventional countryman is replaced by another: and as in the
Renaissance pastoral he perhaps represents an attempt to escape
from the responsibilities of civilized life. This is not to suggest
that Saint-Amant is wholly original in this respect, an eighteenth-
century or Romantic poet born too early. Rather he reveals,
together with the influence of the Bible, the survival of a native

[1] ii. 250.   [2] iii. 1.   [3] Called *épopée intime* by its author.

tradition of idyll, which set out to portray French peasants, not
poetic shepherds. It is seen in Ronsard and Pibrac, as well as in
the paintings of the Le Nain brothers. In Saint-Amant the relations between parents and children, and children themselves,
furnish the principal material for this familiar idyll. Thus at the
beginning of the poem he describes in detail the hesitation and
anguish of Jocabel as she leaves Moses in the cradle.[1] Though the
Bible gives the opportunity for this description, it cannot be said
to have inspired it directly: it bears little resemblance to Biblical
portrayal of mothers in distress, like Rachel weeping for her
children. It is therefore—since other literary sources seem to be
lacking—from his own observation or imagination that Saint-
Amant drew such a scene. Almost at the end of the poem we find
a similar note of family affection.[2] The success of this description
is due not only to the idyllic element and the happy use of the
idea of the family returning at the end of the day but to its combination with an epic note, which is almost a parody (the triumphant cradle) and the religious significance which is given by the
last lines.

The celebrated description of the children in the crossing of the
Red Sea is not in the Bible and indeed may be considered, as it
was by Boileau, completely out of place in a heroic scene. It is
one more proof of the originality of Saint-Amant's delight in
children and their ways:

> Là l'enfant esveillé, courant sous la licence
> Que permet à son âge une libre innocence,
> Va, revient, tourne, saute, et par maint cri joyeux
> Temoignant le plaisir que reçoivent ses yeux,
> D'un estrange caillou, qu'à ses pieds il rencontre,
> Fait au premier venu la precieuse montre,
> Ramasse une cocquille, et, d'aise transporté,
> La presente à sa mere avec naïveté (ii. 214).

It would be exaggerated to attribute this attachment to children

---

[1] ii. 160.

[2]
> L'une porte en ses bras le saint et cher enfant,
> L'autre charge les siens du berceau triomfant,
> Et toutes deux enfin vont en ce beau spectacle
> Resjouir et charmer le rustique habitacle. . . .
> Puis, à genoux fleschis, toutes ces nobles ames,
> Couronnant ces amours par de plus hautes flames,
> Montrerent leur vray zele, et d'un ton solennel
> Pour Moyse sauvé benirent l'Eternel (ii. 327–8).

and family scenes to the poet's temperament, though it may have played a part. To the religious motive and the logical sense of detail we have noticed may be added a consciousness of poetic talent suited to these minute descriptions.

What is good in the *Moyse sauvé* is due for the most part to the poet's idiosyncrasies—his imagination with its visual orientation, his gift for trivial observation and for the study of familiar sentiments, and on the other hand his search for original material, his affection for the exotic and the bizarre. He is capable of creating rapid narrative and even occasionally of true nobility of thought and feeling. Unfortunately he lacked the critical sense, the constructive powers, and the sustained eloquence required by the epic form. With them he might have been if not a French Tasso or Milton—the high seriousness, the authentic religious mission are absent—at any rate a French Ariosto.

His place in the history of the Biblical epic is of the first importance. In spite of Boileau's gibe, the frequent editions in France and Holland reveal the early popularity of the work. The outburst of activity which followed was largely the result of his example and every poem bears the traces, superficial or profound, of his direct influence. However, the extravagances of the *Moyse*— the liberties taken with the Bible, the crocodiles and hornets, the disguises and magic, the exotic ornament—make it a characteristic product of the baroque spirit in French literature. It was equally opposed to the religious austerity of Jansenism or Gallicanism and the literary purity of classicism. We shall find that only a minority of later poets, the most interesting, continue the Italianate features of Saint-Amant. The majority choose fidelity to the Scriptures and the sacrifice of literary ornament.

CHAPTER VIII

The Fundamentalists

THE larger group of poets who reacted against Saint-Amant's florid splendour is characterized by its primarily religious inspiration, beside which desire for literary fame and care for literary form occupy a subordinate place. However, it also represents a return to a more strictly French attitude, untouched by Marinism, to the sober tradition of Du Bartas (in *Judith*) and Montchrestien.

The first of these poems was the *Providence* of Sainte-Garde Bernouin, published in 1660. The form of the sub-titles, *Saül puni* and *Suzanne délivrée*, already suggests imitation of *Moyse sauvé*.

SAINTE-GARDE BERNOUIN

La Providence ou les deux exemples. I. *Saül puni*. II. *Suzanne deliurée* (Paris, 1660).

Attribution

It has been generally assumed that the author is Jacques Carel, sieur de Sainte-Garde (*circa* 1620–84),[1] the author of *Childebrand* (1666) and one of Boileau's victims. The problem has been discussed in some detail by Toinet,[2] who agrees with the tradition. Against this there are considerable differences in style and method between *La Providence*, which is little more than the bare Biblical narrative with restrained ornament, and *Childebrand*, full of florid episodes copied from Italian romance. But the following considera-

[1] These dates are from Frère, *Manuel du bibliographe normand*. The date of death is confirmed by Goujet, *Bibliothèque françoise*, xviii. 172 ff. Carel de Sainte-Garde was born at Rouen, was ordained priest, and was in Spain from 1661 to 1666 in the suite of the Archbishop of Embrun, the French ambassador (Goujet).

[2] ii. 164–7. Toinet's arguments may be summarized as follows: (i) The only other work signed Sainte-Garde Bernouin, *La Paix de Casal* (Paris, 1660), is dedicated to La Chambre. It was the latter's son who introduced Carel de Sainte-Garde to Chapelain. (ii) The author of *La Paix de Casal* states in the Preface that three *chants* of the poem had been lost. In his letters Chapelain often reproaches Carel with carelessness. (iii) After 1660 Bernouin disappears and we find only Carel de Sainte-Garde or Sainte-Garde.

tions, in conjunction with Toinet's arguments, make the identification very probable. Again we find in the Epistle to Providence prefixed to *Saül puni* a reference to lost manuscripts and the poet's carelessness. A later work, *Reflexions academiques sur les orateurs et sur les poëtes* (Paris, 1676), contains a defence of Homer and Virgil and a study of verse forms suitable to the epic. It is signed Sainte-Garde and is certainly by Carel.[1] It bears a close resemblance to the *Advis aux Lecteurs* of *La Providence*, which is marked by a preoccupation with the aesthetics of verse, to the exclusion of wider aspects. The *Reflexions* also contain a translation of Seneca's discourse on Providence with commentary[2] and a statement of principle which though general applies exactly to the theme of *Saül puni*.[3]

Composition

In the Epistle to Providence Sainte-Garde Bernouin says: 'Dauantage, depuis six ans qu'il y a que ie l'acheuay . . . .' The poem was therefore completed by about 1654. The lapse of time, together with the difference between a Biblical and a medieval subject, go far to account for the divergences between *La Providence* and *Childebrand*. The date confirms the conjecture that the initial impulse was due to the *Moyse sauvé*.

The Poems

The two poems are related by the common theme of the workings of Providence, emphasized at the beginning of *Suzanne délivrée*, where the poet shows hope succeeding to the fear inspired by *Saül puni*. We thus see two contrasting halves of a kind of diptych. The form is original, but it is clearly dictated by a religious purpose and is far removed from classical epic. Indeed there are few signs of epic intention. There is no proposition or invocation and no division into books. The use of the *merveilleux* rarely oversteps the limits set by the Bible. *Saül puni* contains a long lyrical digression (David's lament for Jonathan). On the other hand, the style is heroic and Sainte-Garde does not content himself with mere paraphrase. Biblical events are compressed or enlarged and *Suzanne délivrée* is adorned with extensive descriptions.

[1] He is described in the title as 'Aumônier ordinaire du Roy'.

[2] *Reflexions*, p. 34.

[3] 'La bienseance veut en second lieu, que l'on ne fasse point paroitre un grand criminel dans un ouvrage accompli, que l'on n'en fasse voir aussi la punition' (ib., p. 165).

BERNARD LESFARGUES (1600–?)[1]

David, poeme heroïque, (i) Paris, 1660;[2] (ii) Paris, 1687.[3]

The details of Lesfargues's life are fairly well known.[4] Born at Toulouse, he became an advocate and a protégé of Séguier, to whom *David* is dedicated. He was also an unwearying translator and the author of a curious Latin apology[5] which gives his side of a dispute with Priezac (presumably Daniel) at the Chancellor's house. Tallemant shows that he was above all a ridiculous figure, but the statement that he had renounced his pretensions to eloquence[6] was premature, having been written before the appearance of *David*.

Three letters[7] written by Lesfargues to Séguier in 1640 add a detail to this picture. He seems to have been sent by the Chancellor to Moulins, and submits reports on an outbreak of rioting. It is not clear whether he was there as an official reporter or as a private spy of Séguier.[8]

The Preface to *David* reveals Lesfargues as one of the most uncompromising representatives of a fundamentalist position. He admits that fiction is necessary to poetry—a generally accepted axiom[9]—but declines to employ it himself.[10] He is thus led to reject the canons of art:

. . . ie ne crois pas que tu trouues estrange que ie me sois éloigné des reigles de cét art qui apprend à feindre et à mentir impunément.[11]

---

[1] *Biographie Universelle.*

[2] References are to this edition.

[3] This is identical with the 1660 edition (even the errata are the same) and is a reissue, not a new edition. Toinet (i. 185) is therefore wrong in observing with surprise that 'il a été imprimé deux fois !'

[4] See Tallemant des Réaux, ccclxii and ccclxiii (ed. Mongrédien, vi. 194 and 197 ff.).

[5] Bernardi Lesfargues *Apologia pro se Triboniano a censura sospiti nuncupata*, Parisiis, 1660. The subject of the dispute was the law of dowries and the opinions of Tribonian.

[6] Tallemant, vi. 199.

[7] Bibliothèque Nationale, MSS., fonds français 17374. The first letter (fo. 13) is dated 18 July 1640. It begins: 'Suiuant le commandement qu'il vous pleut de me faire de vous donner aduis de tout ce qui se passeroit d'important pour le seruice de Sa Majesté dans la Prouince de Bourbonnois . . .' The second (fo. 17) of 21 July 1640 and the third of 11 August 1640 (fo. 39) also deal exclusively with the riots and estimates of the conduct of the governor and other officials involved.

[8] Bourgoin (*Valentin Conrart*, p. 118) includes Lesfargues in a list of Protestants. However, no evidence is quoted and on the whole it seems unlikely.

[9] Cf. pp. 10–11 above.

[10] Advis au Lecteur, e2.   [11] Ib., e1 v°.

He repeats this expression of contempt in the body of the poem, where he attacks those who

Affectent la rigueur des preceptes de l'art[1]

and declares his intention of following the Bible story without regard to poetic form. However, with this reservation he is convinced like other poets that his work satisfies the requirements of epic:

Ce n'est pas, Lecteur, que si ie le voulois deffendre de la iurisdiction d'vne authorité vsurpée, il ne me fust aysé de faire voir qu'à la reserue seulement d'vne fiction fabuleuse, il a tous les autres incidens qui peuuent entrer en la façon des Poëmes Heroïques.[2]

Examination of the poem itself bears out the declarations of principle. Its duration coincides exactly with David's life, except that it is prolonged to include the deaths of Joab and Shimei.[3] Otherwise there are no changes in chronology and no essential alterations, additions, or subtractions. This literal fidelity to the Bible and the accumulation of unnecessary detail render the structure profusely anecdotic.

The debt of Lesfargues to literary sources is limited, at least as far as resemblances of detail are concerned. It seems to the reader that he rarely lifted his eyes from the Bible in front of him. The influence of classical epic may be discovered principally in a preoccupation with the burial of the dead and the dishonour of exposed corpses.[4] Du Bartas does not seem to have exercised such an extensive influence as on other poets, but there are striking coincidences. Thus the identity of

Est l'effort d'vn Heros[5]

C'est l'effort d'vn heros[6]

meaningless in itself, occurs at the same point of the narrative in Saul's remonstrance to David for his temerity in challenging

---

[1] *David*, p. 4.   [2] e2.   [3] I Kings ii. 28 ff.
[4] For example:

On les vid exposez sans honneur, sans tombeau,
A la sanglante faim de l'auide corbeau (p. 142).

This is not in the Bible, though Biblical parallels might be found (e.g. Prov. xxx. 17). It bears a closer resemblance to the fate of Palinurus (*Aeneid*, v. 871)

[5] p. 28.
[6] Du Bartas, 1616 ed., p. 455; Holmes, iii. 339.

Goliath. More convincing is a passage from David's story of the lion and the bear:

> Ie me souuiens encor, que quand sur vn *coupeau*
> I'auois loin du bercail fait grimper *mon troupeau*; . . .
> *M'emportoient le mouton* plus tendrement aimé[1]

> Ont peu tuer vn Ours, qui le long d'vn *coupeau*
> *Emportoit vn mouton*, l'honneur de *mon troupeau*.[2]

However, the sheep and the flock are found in the Bible,[3] leaving only *coupeau* and the choice of the rhyme as common features. It is therefore probable but not quite certain that Lesfargues had read Du Bartas.

HÉLIE LE CORDIER (1615–?)

L'Illustre Souffrant, ou Iob. Poëme (Paris, 1667).

Le Cordier was a Norman, born near Pont-l'Évêque,[4] and a physician.[5] *L'Illustre Souffrant* is dedicated to Hugues de Lionne, *Le Pont-l'Evesque* (1662) to Mademoiselle de Montpensier. Both are preceded by liminary poems offered by Richelet, Colletet, Du Pelletier, and others. Le Verdier's conjecture that he was attached to the household of *la Grande Mademoiselle*, where he met these important persons, is thus very probable.

The poem is not an epic even in a wide sense but it has epic elements, and the poet's intention is clearly revealed in the Preface, when he compares dramatic and epic poetry, placing his own work in the latter category. The poem follows the chapters of the Bible as far as chapter xiv and is thus incomplete. It may further be divided into three parts—the external events of Job's history in Alexandrines, philosophical reflections, also in Alexandrines, and lyrical stanzas. Of these only the first has epic qualities. The opening is regular, with proposition and double invocation of God and Job himself. There follows the scene of Satan in Heaven, taken from the Bible, which is closely related to the epic tradition of the Olympian council. The hero, like Saint-Amant's Moses,

---

[1] p. 29.   [2] Du Bartas, p. 456; Holmes, iii. 339.

[3] I Sam. xvii. 34. Cf. also Littré, article 'Coupeau', showing that the rhyme was a commonplace.

[4] For Le Cordier's life see Viollet-le-Duc, *Bibliothèque poétique*, i. 529; Boisard, *Notices biographiques sur les hommes du Calvados*; Le Verdier's notice to *Le Pont-l'Evesque*, Rouen, 1906.

[5] *D.M.* follows his name on the title-page.

remains entirely passive, but Le Cordier claims that his heroic patience places him above the active figures of history.[1] The poem assumes an epic character principally in the conduct of the struggle between good and evil on two planes, Satan in Hell and Job on earth. However, the conflict is never resolved. It ends with a lyrical outburst of Job, and the result of Satan's wager is not given.

Le Cordier's attitude to the Bible is that of Lesfargues—a fidelity to the text which refuses to compromise with the canons of literature. He says in his Preface:

Si quelques-vns veulent que le Poëme, comme on le veut entendre aujourd'huy, se doit commencer par le milieu, et veut d'autres regles que ie n'observe pas icy, ... l'on ne manie pas l'Escriture Sainte comme l'on voudroit (a10 v°).

But he differs from Lesfargues, Sainte-Garde, and other fundamentalist poets in that he tries to follow the style as well as the content of the Bible.[2]

In *Le Pont-l'Evesque* Le Cordier refers to 'l'incomparable Sainct-Amant . . . ce rare et diuin Genie', an indication of his continued popularity in the provinces. In spite of this admiration and his relations with other well-known poets, Le Cordier is almost untouched by contemporary fashion (except in his choice of subject and title). However, in spite of some interesting passages, his verse is generally flat and his Biblical qualities must perhaps be attributed as much to lack of technical skill as to genuine originality.

JULIEN-GATIEN MORILLON (1632 or 1633–94)

Joseph, ou l'esclave fidele. Poëme (Turin [Tours], 1679; Breda [Tours], 1705[3]).

Joseph appeared without the author's name, but the attribution is well attested. Anonymity and the false place-names were probably due to the intervention of Morillon's ecclesiastical superiors. According to the prefatory 'Le Libraire au Lecteur', the poem was published without the author's knowledge.

Morillon was born at Tours and entered the Benedictine

---

[1] *Job*, p. 2. [2] Cf. p. 213 below.
[3] This is a genuine second edition.

Congregation of Saint-Maur in 1651 (or 1652). He died in the abbey of Saint Melaine at Rennes.[1]

The Poems

Morillon was also the author of *Job*, Paris, 1668, and *Tobie*, Paris, 1674. These are not epic poems. *Job* consists of lyric stanzas bound together by a sketchy narrative framework, *Tobie* of extracts from the Bible followed by a verse paraphrase. *Joseph*, on the other hand, is a regular epic in six books.

Morillon's own view of his poetic mission is set forth in the *Avertissement* to *Tobie*. He insists on the moral object of poetry and finds the material for it in Scripture:

Or y a-t'il rien de plus relevé et de plus admirable que les veritez saintes contenuës dans l'Ecriture? et ne faut-il pas avoüer qu'au prix d'elles, tout ce qu'il y a de grand et de magnifique sur la terre n'est que vanité et bassesse?

But he does not embark upon controversial discussions of critical rules, nor does he lay down how far divergence from the original text is permissible.

The poem is accompanied by a number of footnotes, which no doubt reveal the monk and permit an exact assessment of the sources. It is noteworthy that numerous extra-Biblical sources are quoted—classical authors, the Fathers, Josephus, modern theologians (in particular Tostado's commentary on Genesis), Tasso (the *Aminta*), and d'Avity's geographical works.[2] Biblical references are, as might be expected, invariably made to the Vulgate. Morillon's erudition was of course much superior to that of lay poets, who were likely to content themselves with Josephus, but this list throws light on the general sources of additions to the Bible and of Oriental history and geography.

Purely literary sources occupy an unimportant place beside the long list of theological and historical authorities. The reference

[1] The principal source is Housseau's biographies of Touraine, Bibliothèque Nationale, MSS., Collection de Touraine 23 (fols. 186 v°–187). See also Carré de Busserolle, *Dictionnaire . . . d'Indre-et-Loire et de l'ancienne Province de Touraine*; Marolles, *Mémoires*, ed. Goujet, iii. 323; Toinet, i. 261–7; *Histoire littéraire de la Congrégation de Saint-Maur*, p. 150.

[2] Pierre d'Avity, seigneur de Montmartin, was the author of three descriptions of the world: *Les Empires . . . et Principautez du monde . . .*, Saint-Omer, 1614; *Nouveau Théâtre du Monde . . .*, Paris, 1655; *Le Monde ou la Description generale de ses quatre parties . . .*, 5 vols., Paris, 1637. Morillon probably refers to the last and most complete.

to Tasso's *Aminta*[1] concerns the source of a description of bees
and there are no signs of any extensive influence. A similar foot-
note shows that Morillon had read Saint-Amant:

> Comme le sacrè Texte ne m'apprend point le nom de la femme de
> Putiphar, je luy donne celuy d'Osirie, aprés le Sieur de Saint Amant
> dans son Moïse sauvè.[2]

Apart from this detail, however, there is no evidence of serious
imitation.[3]

Morillon illustrates clearly the evolution of the Biblical epic
after Saint-Amant. The principal changes are simplicity of plot,
which avoids on the one hand fanciful episodes, on the other the
involved detail caused by too close adherence to the Bible; a
tendency to prefer the moral to the marvellous, that is the human
to the supernatural; and modesty of style.

---

[1] p. 70.   [2] p. 67.

[3] There is one verbal coincidence:

> Hélas! qu'attendez-vous (dit JOSEPH tout en larmes) (Morillon, p. 89)

> Il me desplaist, amy, dit Joseph presqu'en larmes (Saint-Amant, ii. 305).

This occurs at the same point in the narrative and is not in the Bible.

CHAPTER IX

The Baroque Poets

AT the same time, Saint-Amant's example was more closely followed by a group of writers who had not the scruples of the fundamentalists. They were moved principally, no doubt, by literary ambition, but, as we shall see, their different approach reflects a wholly different aesthetic conception.

MARIE DE PECH DE CALAGES (1632–61)

Iudith, ou la Délivrance de Bethulie, Poeme Saint (Tolose, 1660).

The life of the poetess is recounted in the monograph of Lahondès.[1] A collection of local biographies in manuscript includes a note which adds nothing to our knowledge of her life but shows that she enjoyed a certain local reputation.[2]

The poem is prefaced by a prose dedication and a set of stanzas to the new queen, the Infanta Marie-Thérèse, who received these attentions with favour and rewarded them with a gift of money. The conclusion seems to have been hurried so that it might be presented in time for the marriage.[3] There follows a *Discours aux Dames*, which explains the intentions of the poetess. She is at once proud of the success of women in letters, which she hopes to share, and timid because of her provincial origin:

Si i'avois eu la gloire d'aprocher quelque-fois Mademoiselle d'Escudery, et ses semblables, ie serois moins pardonnable dans mes deffauts, puis qu'il est bien difficile de s'aprocher du feu sans en ressentir la chaleur: Mais le Ciel m'a fait naistre dans vne Region esloignée de ces grands Astres qui ne m'ont iamais esclairée que de leur reputation (a4).

She excuses the imperfections of the work by her family cares and lack of serious conversation. However, the reference to Mademoiselle de Scudéry illustrates the impulsion given to feminism

---

[1] *Une Poétesse épique toulousaine.* See also Toinet, i. 186, ii. 152.
[2] Bibliothèque Nationale, MSS., Collection de Languedoc (Bénédictins) 100, fol. 252.   [3] See Lahondès, op. cit.

by a great reputation. The subject itself, the dedication to the Queen, the Preface addressed only to women readers, all go to prove that *Judith* was inspired at least partly by the conception of the heroic woman, which had occupied so prominent a place in the forties and early fifties.[1] It was still strong in provincial centres after its full force had begun to dwindle in the capital.

The appeal to women readers had other consequences. As in the poems we have just considered, great stress is laid on the religious purpose, but this purpose appears both more militant and less serious. In the dedication Marie de Pech calls on the Queen to exterminate the enemies of God in France and ensure the triumph of the Church. The *Stances à la Reyne* encourage the royal pair to undertake a new crusade against the Turks:

> Et qu'enfin Lovis et l'INFANTE
> Puissent porter vn iour leurs glorieux destins
> Sur le Trône des Constantins
> Pour rendre la Croix triomphante.

In the *Discours aux Dames* Judith is identified with the Blessed Virgin, thus introducing a prefiguration of the New Testament which was not centred on the Messiah Himself. The parallel was, it is true, generally admitted: it is none the less interesting that it should be put forward as the key to the poem.

It is not surprising, therefore, that the attitude to the Bible should differ widely from that of a Lesfargues or even a Morillon. Marie de Pech begins by affirming her fidelity to the text:

> Ie ne me suis iamais escartée du grand chemin de peur de m'esgarer, i'ay tousiours trauaillé sur la Sainte Escriture, selon la traduction de l'Eglise (a4).

This principle, however, is nullified by what follows:

> Et si i'ay meslé quelque peu d'inuention dans mon Poëme, ie l'ay fait pour donner quelques petits agréemens à ceux à qui possible la seule Histoire sembleroit trop serieuse pour leur diuertissement (a4 v°).

Thus fiction is admitted, in itself an offence against the severest standards of Christian poetry. Moreover, it is not justified by attachment to the rules, by poetic necessity. The amusement of the reader is the only guide. It might be tempting to connect this doctrine, equally foreign to literary theorists and to Christian

---

[1] Cf. p. 78 above.

apologists,[1] with the similar views stated soon afterwards by Molière in the *Critique de l'École des Femmes*: as part of a general evolution towards the idea of art as pure pleasure. However, though Marie de Pech may have felt something of the sort, she was not capable of expressing it as a critical doctrine. The reference to Madeleine de Scudéry supplies a more convincing clue. *Judith* was written with an eye on the great public of novel-readers and conformed to their standards.

Otherwise the *Discours aux Dames* is taken up by details of composition and history. *Judith* was originally planned as a short narrative poem:

> Quoy que i'eusse borné mon dessein à quatre ou cinq cens vers seulement, la grandeur de mon sujet et ma propre inclination m'ont engagée dans vne plus longue carriere (a4).

It now consists of nine parts and about five thousand lines.

Biblical atmosphere is sacrificed completely to the spirit of the novel in Abra's recital. The mother of Manasses dies in bearing him. The father, overcome with grief, refuses to see the child, who is brought up by a shepherd, Abra's father. One day Manasses, now a boy of twelve, wanders along the banks of the Jordan, declaiming aloud the verses which he has composed.[2] Looking for shade from the burning sun, he enters a wood, where he finds tied to a tree a horse, richly caparisoned but all in black. There is nothing supernatural here, but the scene at once gives an impression of enchantment and mystery. A little farther on he comes upon an old man, also in black, asleep at the foot of a tree. At this moment a deadly snake appears from the undergrowth and threatens the life of the sleeper. The child kills the snake after a long struggle and is, of course, recognized by his father. The sources of this fantasy are complex but reasonably clear. The details of the fight have probably been directly suggested by the crocodile episode in the *Moyse sauvé*, though there are Italian parallels such as the fight between Ruggiero and the orca. The mysterious horse in the wood is derived from Italian romance,[3] and the sleeper is related to the figures of fairy-tale. The recognition may be compared to the episode of Ruggiero and Marfisa in the *Orlando Furioso*, where the two warriors turn out to be brother and

---

[1] Cf. p. 8 above.   [2] p. 56.
[3] Cf. Erminia and her horse in a wood (also by the banks of the Jordan), *Gerusalemme Liberata*, vii, stanzas 1 ff.

sister:[1] the parallel is not very close, but the atmosphere is the same. However, it is the novel which abounds in scenes of this kind, and if Marie de Pech drew on the Italian epic it was perhaps indirectly. Changelings and noble children growing up with poor foster-parents were almost a constant ingredient of fiction.[2] The situation bears a particular resemblance to the youth of Artamène: Marie de Pech says of Manasses:

> Ses moindres actions marquoient son origine,
> Et quoy qu'il ignorat sa haute extraction
> Nous remarquions en luy beaucoup d'ambition.[3]

In *Le Grand Cyrus* we find

> Ce ieune Prince, qui sans se connoistre agissoit en Roy.[4]

The scene in the wood resembles the meeting between Artamène and Harpage.[5] The old man's grief for his dead wife, which lasts twelve years (and black as the outward sign of mourning) are without parallel in the Bible but in full harmony with the traditions of the novel.

Of other literary sources the most important is Du Bartas. It has been seen that Marie de Pech claims that she read Du Bartas only when her own poem was far advanced and that any resemblances were fortuitous.[6] The first statement may be true, the second is certainly false. The whole economy and structure of the two works are indeed different. On the other hand, the early life of Judith is in each the object of a recital. Judith's distaste for marriage[7] and the tapestry in the tent,[8] with its illustrations of Assyrian history, are common to both. So far the explanation of accidental resemblance might easily be maintained, but detailed coincidences prove deliberate imitation. Thus the proposition runs:

> Ie chante la valeur d'vne sainte Heroïne,
> Qui *sauua* son Païs . . .
> La *vaillante* Iudith, cette *veûve* fidele,[9]

---

[1] Canto xxxvi. Cf. p. 51 above.
[2] Cf. Magendie, *Le Roman au XVIIᵉ siècle*, p. 42.   [3] p. 55.
[4] *Le Grand Cyrus*, bk. ii, p. 219 (1650 ed.).
[5] Ib., p. 231.   [6] Cf. p. 44 above.
[7] Pech de Calages, pp. 51 ff.; Du Bartas, p. 576; Holmes, ii. 76.
[8] Pech de Calages, p. 124; Du Bartas, p. 590; Holmes, ii. 99.
[9] Pech de Calages, p. 3.

Ie chante les vertus d'vne *vaillante vefue*,
Qui pour *sauuer* Iacob . . .[1]

The enumeration of the Assyrian army follows Du Bartas almost
word for word. A few lines will suffice to demonstrate this:

Les Perses belliqueux sur leurs cottes de maille
Estalent de fin or vne superbe écaille . . .
Le Mede blanc de fard et plus rouge de honte
Tâche de faire voir à celuy qui le dompte
Que si l'iniuste Sort le liure à son Vainqueur
Il manque de pouuoir, sans qu'il manque de cœur.[2]

Là le Perse, orgueilleux d'auoir en main l'Empire,
Fait les escailles d'or de ses armes reluire,
Deçà le Mede veut monstrer, qu'à faute d'heur
Le sceptre il a perdu, non à faute de cœur.[3]

The differences are even more illuminating than the resemblances.
Thus in both poems the effects of thirst on the people of Bethulia
are represented by the classical device of enumeration. But where
Du Bartas omits no hideous detail, Marie de Pech makes it a picture
of affection, which is almost soothing:

L'Amant songe bien moins à la soif qui le presse
Qu'il ne songe à la soif de l'obiet qui le blesse, . . .
L'espouse pour l'espoux sent les mesmes alarmes:
Pour étancher sa soif elle n'a que des larmes . . .
Mais l'obiet le plus triste et plus tendre à la veuë
C'est de voir en tout lieu mainte mere esperduë,
Qui poussant vers les Cieux de sanglots estouffans
Demandent vn peu d'eau pour leurs pauures enfans.[4]

Ici la triste mere auecques sa saliue
Son enfant demi mort sur la couchete auiue.
L'amie ioint ici son dernier souflement,
Au souflement dernier de son tres cher amant.[5]

Du Bartas wrote at a time when such things were at least a possibility to be reckoned with. In Marie de Pech we see, apart from
a personal aversion towards scenes of horror, greater security and
growing fastidiousness of taste.

One or two cases of general imitation from Saint-Amant have

---

[1] Du Bartas, p. 527; Holmes, ii. 5.   [2] Pech de Calages, p. 33.
[3] Du Bartas, p. 555; Holmes, ii. 47.   [4] Pech de Calages, pp. 37–38.
[5] Du Bartas, p. 563; Holmes, ii. 58.

already been observed. They are confirmed by verbal borrowings, for example in the passage of the Red Sea:

> La Mer ouurant son sein s'écarte et leur fait place,
> Faisant des deux costez deux murailles de glace;[1]

or the attributes of God

> Qui de l'Eternité fait son beau Diademe.[2]

The theme of *La Solitude* is taken up once again:

> Beaux lieux, poursuiuit-il, sacrée solitude,
> Chers et muets témoins de ma solicitude,
> Aprenez à parler pour publier vn iour,
> Ce que peut sur nos cœurs vn veritable amour.[3]

Even more than Saint-Amant's poem, this passage foreshadows the Romantic view of nature, though it contains an element of the conventional idyll.

Marie de Pech differs from most of her contemporaries by her militant spirit, her free approach to the Bible, the Italianate magnificence of minor ornament. All this, however, is derived at least immediately from a French source, the novel, and mingles with the purist tradition springing from Du Bartas.

JACQUES DE CORAS (*circa* 1630–77)[4]

i. *Ionas, ou Ninive penitente. Poëme sacré* (Paris, 1663; 2nd edition, Paris, 1665).

ii. *Samson poëme sacré* (Paris, 1665).

iii. *Iosué ou la conqueste de Canaan. Poëme sacré* (Paris, 1665).

iv. *David ou la vertu couronée. Poëme sacré* (Paris, 1665).

All four poems also appeared in one volume, dedicated to Séguier: *Œuvres poëtiques de I. D. Coras* (Paris, 1665).[5]

Coras was born at Toulouse of a well-known Protestant family. He became a pastor, but was converted to Catholicism between

---

[1] Pech de Calages, p. 13. Cf. Saint-Amant, ii. 214.
[2] Pech de Calages, p. 134. Cf. 'Qui l'eternité seule a pour son diadême' (Saint-Amant, ii. 179). [3] p. 80.
[4] See Tamizey de Larroque, *Lettres inédites de Jacques de Coras* (notice); Haag, *La France protestante*; Goujet, *Bibliothèque françoise*, xvii. 439 ff. For details of Coras's life as a pastor see *Bulletin de la Société de l'Histoir du Protestantisme français*, xv. 520 and xxiii. 561–2. [5] The four poems with general title-page and dedication.

1663 and 1665. *Jonas* is dedicated to Turenne,[1] which shows that Coras was still a Protestant in 1663. In 1665 appeared a pamphlet describing his conversion.[2] The publication of the poems thus coincides exactly with the period of conversion.

In the poems themselves the traces of this crisis are slight. *Jonas* though deeply marked by theological concepts generally avoids the controversial issues between Catholicism and Protestantism. In the epistle to the king which precedes *Josué* Coras applies the events of the poem to the struggle against the Protestant heretics. In *David* there is a clear expression of the poet's new faith. He celebrates the battles of Arques and Ivry, but goes on to call Henry IV *soûmis aux Autels* and says that Louis XIII 'Abbatra le grand FORT d'vne secte hérétique'.[3] But the preparation and background of these poems must clearly be ascribed to Protestantism.

Composition and Order of the Poems

The privilege of *Jonas* is dated 9 November 1662 : it is thus the first of the poems to be completed. Tamizey de Larroque[4] notes that in the 1665 edition the date of the privilege and the *achevé d'imprimer* remains the same. He concludes that only the title-page was reprinted with the intention of tricking the public into the belief that a genuine second edition had appeared. This is in fact unjust : an examination of the two editions reveals that the pagination, typography, and ornaments are all different. Moreover, there is one change in the body of the poem itself. In the 1663 edition the proposition is followed by an invocation to Turenne,[5] which praises his exploits in battle and his loyalty to the king. In the 1665 edition we find instead an invocation to the Virgin, followed by Anne of Austria, very Catholic in tone, and ending :

> Et par les saints efforts de son zele héroïque,
> Dresse plus d'vn trophée à la Foy Catholique.[6]

In the Preface of *Jonas* Coras says that it is to be followed by another and much superior poem : 'C'est le Dauid auquel ie trauaille depuis vn an, et dont j'ay déja fait les six premiers Liures.'[7] We can thus assume that *David* was begun in 1661 or 1662.

However, in 1665 it is *Josué* and *Samson* which appear together,

---

[1] In the 1665 edition Turenne is replaced by *la Sainte Vierge*.
[2] *La Conversion de Iacques de Coras. Dediée à Nosseigneurs du clergé de France*, Paris, 1665.
[3] *David*, pp. 141–2. [4] *Lettres inédites de Coras*, p. 7, n. 3.
[5] p. 2. [6] p. 30.
[7] *Jonas*, p. 27 (all references are to the 2nd ed., unless otherwise stated).

with identical privileges dated 19 May 1664. Coras seems to have worked on both more or less simultaneously: 'Entre tous les sujets qui se sont présentez à mon esprit, j'ay choisi l'Histoire de Iosué et celle de Samson',[1] though *Samson* was printed first.[2]

He apologizes for his failure to publish *David* as promised. It is, he explains, the *chef-d'œuvre* for which the other three poems are only a preparation and an apprenticeship: 'autant de degrés pour éleuer Dauid sur le Trône d'Israël'.[3] *David* finally appears with a privilege dated 6 September 1665. A fairly clear picture of the order of composition now emerges: (i) *Jonas*; (ii) six books of *David* (1661–2); (iii) *Samson* and *Josué*; (iv) final text of *David* (1664–5).

The published version of *David* is in seven books instead of six. No doubt Coras was sincere in believing it to be his master-piece, but we may conjecture that in delaying its publication he was influenced by a desire to modify passages reflecting his former faith.[4]

It is noteworthy that Coras goes outside the accepted group of epic subjects, to which only *David* belongs. Saint-Amant, we have seen, had begun a poem on Samson, but Joshua and Jonah had not previously been treated in heroic form. It may be supposed that the wide knowledge of the Bible which Coras would have acquired as a Protestant minister led him to explore new paths rather than content himself with literary fashion.

The Poems

For Coras, as for Saint-Amant, Josephus is a source sometimes more important than the Bible itself. The debt is acknowledged in the prefaces to *Jonas* and *Josué*, where Coras says that he has followed Josephus in preference to the Bible because he is more concise. Frequently supplementary details are derived from Josephus in order to eke out a slender narrative. For example, Jonah is vomited by the whale on the shores of the Black Sea, a fact not included in the Bible.[5] The influence extends to the imagery, as in the comparison of the Hebrews to barley:

Ce Peuple méprisé du reste des humains,
Creû non moins vil entr'eux, que l'orge entre les grains.[6]

[1] *Josué*, a5 v°.
[2] *Achevés*: *Samson*, 18 July 1665; *Josué*, 1 October 1665; *David*, 25 October 1665.
[3] *Josué*, a5. [4] Cf. Arques and Ivry above. [5] *Jonas*, p. 114; Josephus, ix. 11.
[6] *Samson*, p. 30. Cf. '. . . de tous les bleds l'orge est de moindre pris: et entre toutes les nations d'Asie on n'en trouueroit point de plus abiecte, que sont auiourd'huy les Hebrieux . . .' (Josephus, v. 8; Génébrard, 1609 ed., p. 170).

Such additions could not be reproved, but sometimes Coras
follows Josephus where he is in contradiction with the Bible.
In Judges Manoah's motives are wholly noble when his wife tells
him the story of the angel: in Josephus he is immediately filled
with jealousy. Coras adopts the latter version.[1] The story of the
Levite and his concubine[2] is entirely recast by Coras in accordance
with Josephus. The reason is obvious—Josephus had toned down
the hideous story of the Bible and made it almost innocuous.
Coras followed him not because he was more concise (as is
claimed in the preface) but because his version is more consonant
with seventeenth-century morality.

The relationship of Coras to Italian romance is a matter of
general resemblances, which are probably derived from an intermediate source or even a widespread tradition. The god of the
Jordan in *Josué*[3] may have been imitated from Sannazaro.[4] Of
more profound significance, because it consists of general atmosphere rather than particular imitation, is the mysterious appearance of a horseman followed by two virgins.[5] Neither Biblical nor
classical, the incident is clearly derived from Italy (or from the
novel).

The imitation of Ronsard in *David* has already been discussed.[6]
The borrowings from Du Bartas are more extensive. The storm
and the swallowing of Jonah are imitated from the *Seconde Semaine*,
both in general—the conduct of the pilot, the sailors taking down
the sails, their regrets for their wives, Jonah's prayer in the whale's
belly—and in particular:

> Il sent qu'il est *couuert* d'vne loge *mouuante*,
> Et qu'vn poisson horrible est sa *prison viuante*[7]

> ma maison est *mouuante*,
> Et vif ie suis *couuert* d'vne *tombe viuante*.[8]

The combat of David and Goliath also bears conclusive marks of
imitation, for example:

> De rage en expirant il *mange le terrain*,
> Et *mord son propre bras* qui *traître à sa colére*,
> A souffert qu'il ployât sous vn tel aduersaire.[9]

[1] *Samson*, p. 46; Judges xiii; Josephus, v. 10.
[2] *Samson*, pp. 17 ff.; Judges xix; Josephus, v. 2.   [3] *Josué*, p. 34.
[4] *De partu Virginis*, bk. iii. Cf. p. 49 above.   [5] *David*, p. 44; cf. p. 114 above.
[6] Cf. p. 39 above.   [7] *Jonas*, p. 108.
[8] Du Bartas, p. 447; Holmes, iii. 440.   [9] *David*, p. 102.

Goliath *mord la terre*, et de ses dents *deschire*
Ses deux mains, comme estans *traistresses à son ire*.[1]

There is, however, a great difference in the general tone of the
two poems, which illustrates the extent of evolution in the
interval. Goliath's challenge in Coras is a reasonable proposition.
Controlled pride is expressed in conventional terms. There is
even a suggestion of noble sentiment. In Du Bartas, on the other
hand, we see genuine defiance and raging arrogance.

Of all his predecessors Coras naturally owes most to Saint-
Amant. It would be tedious to pursue all the resemblances of
detail: the important point is the diffusion of the literary modes
created by Saint-Amant's poem. Many scenes in which the Bible
is transformed seem to have been suggested by similar situations
in the *Moyse*. David's encounter with a lion, half a verse in the
Bible, is developed in much the same way as the episode of Elisaph
and the crocodile.[2] The death of the king of Jericho recalls the
death of Pharaoh.[3] Elijah and Ahab form a parallel to Aaron
and Pharaoh.[4] The servility of verbal imitation in Coras may be
illustrated by an extreme example:

Et souffre que les Iuifs au temps de leur départ,
S'enrichissent des biens, dont les siens *luy* font part.[5]

Il relasche Israël, et souffre à son depart
Que de tous leurs tresors les siens *luy* fassent part.[6]

In Saint-Amant *luy* referring to Israel is perfectly correct. Coras
has copied it without even noticing that it should now be plural
to accord with *Iuifs*.

It was to be expected that Coras should have read the *David*
of Lesfargues, which appeared shortly before he began his own
poem on the same subject. The resemblances, however, reveal
haphazard borrowings rather than continuous imitation as in
the case of Saint-Amant. Thus he follows Lesfargues in making
Eliab taunt David for coming to fight, instead of (as in the Bible)
to watch the battle.[7] Resemblances of detail which prove direct

---

[1] Du Bartas, p. 461; Holmes, iii. 345.
[2] *David*, p. 42; I Sam. xvii. 34; Saint-Amant, ii. 181.
[3] *Josué*, p. 54; Saint-Amant, ii. 217.
[4] *Jonas*, p. 45; Saint-Amant, ii. 203.
[5] *David*, p. 64.   [6] Saint-Amant, ii. 211.
[7] *David* (Coras), p. 94.

imitation also occur.[1] Such an influence is of little importance in itself, but it shows the formation of the Biblical epic as a literary genre with its own traditions and methods.

According to Duchesne, 'Coras rappelait Corneille et annonçait Racine qui se cherchait encore'.[2] This seems exaggerated, except in so far as he participated in the general evolution which separates the two dramatists. It would be more accurate to say that he occupied a position between the scriptural fidelity of Lesfargues and the extravagance of Saint-Amant. His romantic additions to the Bible are clearly defined and do not set the tone for the whole narrative (as they do in Cebà, for example). They seem sufficient, however, to separate him from the fundamentalists and to place him among the poets who used the Bible as a basis for constructions of their own.

JEAN DESMARETS DE SAINT-SORLIN (1595–1676)

Esther. Poëme (Paris, 1673).

This edition is the complete poem in seven books. An earlier edition (Paris, 1670) under the pseudonym Boisval contains four books only.[3] The work seems to have been finished in haste, the last three books being very arid in comparison with the earlier part. They contain little elaboration, except for one or two fanciful recitals, there are no magnificent descriptions and few stylistic ornaments.

Desmarets was also the author, it can be said with some confidence, of the anonymous poem, *Abraham ou la vie parfaite*, which appeared after his death.[4] It is merely a narrative framework for a

---

[1] e.g.

> Et Dauid échapé de ce mortel péril,
> Forme alors le dessein d'vn volontaire exil (Coras, p. 113).

> Puis sortant de la Cour pour se voir sans peril,
> Medite le dessein d'vn volontaire exil (Lesfargues, p. 48).

[2] *Histoire des poëmes épiques*, p. 243.

[3] References are to the 1670 edition unless otherwise stated.

[4] See Brunet for the attribution to Desmarets, and Toinet (i. 268) for some ingenious and convincing arguments in support of it; also Lachèvre, *Recueils collectifs*, ii. 248. But all have overlooked a sentence in the Preface to *Esther* (1673 ed.) in which Desmarets described his works already completed: 'Le troisiéme est Abraham, ou l'estat de la vie parfaite, par une vive foi de la presence de Dieu' (a3). This seems to settle the question.

series of moral and theological reflections and is of little importance
from the point of view of epic.

The life of Desmarets has already been studied in detail.[1] He
intended to produce a series of poems covering the whole of the
Old Testament.[2] *Abraham* and *Esther* are the only surviving fragments of this ambitious project.

The place of Desmarets in the development of the epic idea
has already been examined:[3] he was the indefatigable champion
of Christian and Biblical poetry, he insisted that they offered a
far richer material than the discredited classical myths. In the
Preface to the 1673 edition he states once again his old principles,
applying them to the particular case of *Esther*. A difference from
other poets immediately attracts notice—the complete absence of
even feigned modesty. He does not try to avoid criticism by
depreciation of his book. Instead he proclaims its titles to epic
stature: its miraculous action, the high rank of the characters—
a mighty prince, two queens, and two ministers and the violence
of their conflict—and finally the suddenness of Haman's fall.

In view of the complexity of the poem itself and its wide
divergencies from the Bible, it will be preferable to give a brief
summary of its contents. Book I begins with Lucifer, who laments
the failure of his plans to destroy the Jews in the Persian Empire.
Now, to make matters worse, Artaxerxes (Ahasuerus) has married
a Jewish wife, though he does not yet know her origin. Fortu-
nately Aman, the Macedonian, remains a faithful servant and
through him the memory of the repudiated Vashti will be renewed in the king's heart. Lucifer then takes his flight to the
royal palace, where in a dream he presents Vashti and Apollo,
who persuade and command Artaxerxes to forsake his new love.
The king's resistance to these wiles is strengthened by a visit to
the apartment of Esther, who is deep in prayer. In the meantime
Aman (Haman), accompanied by his son Pharsandate, who is in
love with Vashti, enters the palace and advises the king to follow

[1] Reibetanz, *Desmarets de Saint-Sorlin*; Bremond, *Histoire littéraire du sentiment
religieux*, vi. 445 ff. (for the poet's religious activity); Caillet, *Un Visionnaire du XVIIe
siècle* (a study in mental pathology).

[2] 'Ie declare maintenant que j'ai fait la plus grande et la plus hardie entreprise qui
se fera jamais en Vers, qui est de faire des Poëmes de tous les plus grands Sujets de
l'Ancien Testament' (1673, a3). He goes on to say that four poems have already been
composed, *The Creation*, *Abel*, *Abraham* (see above), and *Joseph*. He intends to write
Moses, *David*, and *Judith*. All but *Abraham* are apparently lost.

[3] Cf. pp. 14–16 above.

the warning of the dream. Artaxerxes decides to consult the oracle of Apollo. The whole court proceeds in state to the temple, whose priestess has been commanded by Lucifer to declare that Vashti is the rightful queen. As she delivers her oracle, she is seized by a higher power and announces that Esther is the chosen one.

Most of Book II is taken up by the description of Esther's coronation with its magnificent processions and religious rites. Pharsandate, saddened by the honours showered on Vashti's rival, goes to the priestess of Apollo, Dictyne, and confesses his love. She tells him the story of Vashti's disgrace and her retirement to a palace guarded by lions, which no man may enter. Pharsandate assumes the disguise of a female slave, Artemis, and accompanies Dictyne into the forbidden precincts. They find Vashti furious at the elevation of Esther and planning vengeance on Artaxerxes. Pharsandate offers his services without revealing his identity.

In Book III Artemis-Pharsandate relates to Vashti what purports to be the early history of Aman. It begins with the defeat of Agag and the Amalekites at the hands of Saul. Agag entrusts his son Zabas to his friend Sobal, who takes the child to Greece. After many adventures (and another oracular prophecy) they arrive in Macedonia, where Zabas becomes a great chieftain. One of his descendants is Menon (later to be known as Aman). Menon consults the Delphic oracle, who predicts for him a great future in the East and for his son Pharsandate a crown and a wife of great beauty. The oracle also presents Menon with the girl Artemis who is said to be animated with the spirit of Apollo (this detail is of course invented by Pharsandate in order to influence Vashti). Menon with a large following of Greek troops then passes into Asia, where he finds Cyrus in revolt against his brother Artaxerxes. By a most involved piece of treachery he ensures the victory of Artaxerxes, sacrificing his Greek friends. To escape the stigma attached to his name he becomes Aman and is rewarded with high office. Artemis ends with hyperbolical praise of Pharsandate, who is destined to overthrow Artaxerxes and restore Vashti to the throne.

In Book IV Dictyne persuades Pharsandate that he must kill his father Aman as well as Artaxerxes. He engages two captains of the guard, Bagathan and Thares, to execute the assassinations. However, an angel warns Mardochée (Mordecai) and conducts him to a place where he can overhear the two conspirators. He is assisted by two Hebrew slaves of Thares, called Pharnabas and Iasbel. Through Esther he informs the king and the two are arrested. Pharsandate conceals his rage under a show of anger at the plot. Vashti, falsely informed that Pharsandate's guilt has been discovered, lights a funeral pyre and casts herself upon it. Here the poem ends in the 1670 edition.

In the 1673 edition the first three books and most of the fourth are preserved intact, but the end of Book IV is recast in order to ensure an orderly transition to the new material. Vashti's suicide is replaced by Mardochée's dream, in which the persecutions of Aman and the final victory of the Jews are foreshadowed.

Book V begins with Iasbel's history, related to Mardochée. Iasbel is really a girl, Thamar, who has assumed the disguise of her twin brother for love of Pharnabas. Her brother, the true Iasbel, has disappeared. From this point the book follows the Bible. Aman, enraged by Mardochée's refusal to bow the knee, persuades Artaxerxes to decree the death of all the Jews. Esther ventures into the king's presence, is pardoned, and asks for the banquet. Aman having erected a gallows is ordered by Artaxerxes to lead Mardochée in triumph through the streets.

In Book VI Esther reveals her origins and relationship to Mardochée. Aman is disgraced and executed, Mardochée installed in his place. Pharnabas and Iasbel receive the fortune of their former masters, Thares and Bagathan. The cruel edict is rescinded and the Jews prepare to exact the vengeance authorized by Artaxerxes. Mardochée divides them into companies, which he allots to different leaders, with orders for the battle. Meanwhile Pharsandate assembles ten thousand men to fight the Jews and plans to kill Artaxerxes and Esther with poisoned arrows. He then goes to Vashti's palace to tell her what has happened and encourage her with hopes of victory.

In Book VII the battle between five hundred Jews and ten thousand Persians is represented as a kind of tournament with rules. It takes place in the centre of Susa under the windows of the palace. As the struggle begins to go badly for him, Pharsandate shoots his poisoned arrows at Artaxerxes, who is watching from a balcony. Mardochée, divinely inspired, throws his cloak in front of the king, catching the arrows as they fall. At the height of the battle Thamar is reunited with her brother Iasbel, who appears suddenly to strengthen the Jewish forces. The victory of the Jews is complete. Vashti's suicide, transferred from the first edition, is now placed here. Pharsandate is tortured to death at the order of Artaxerxes, Mardochée and Esther rejoice in their triumph.

The sources of these divergencies from the Bible are partly classical. Thus Pharsandate's false recital has a parallel in the story Ulysses tells to Eumaeus.[1] Vashti's end was certainly suggested by Dido. But Desmarets drew particularly on the historians. In the Preface he says that the revolt of Cyrus is taken from Plutarch and he adds: 'Aman ... servit aussi apparemment Artaxerce contre Cyrus son Frere.'[2] In fact we find in the life of Artaxerxes the revolt of Cyrus and the role of Menon and his Greek mercenaries. Desmarets has perhaps also drawn from the same source one or two particulars of Persian customs, such as torture. There are, however, no detailed resemblances and the story of Book III appears to owe much more to Xenophon. In particular, the description of Menon's character in the *Anabasis*[3] makes it easy to understand the identification with Aman. It is chronologically possible, though it does not seem to rest on any theological or historical authority. It can safely be attributed to the rich imagination of Desmarets.

He mentions Josephus as a source of the story of Esther,[4] but in fact takes little from him. The king's regret for Vashti, which, though scarcely discernible in the Bible, fulfils an important function in the poem, may have been suggested by a passage in the *Antiquitates*.[5] The incident of the two slaves, Pharnabas and Iasbel, is based on Josephus, who, however, has only one slave, called Barnabas.[6] The alteration of the name may be due to a reminiscence of Plutarch or Xenophon.[7]

The historians furnish the raw material of the additions to the Bible but they do not explain the motives of such widespread deformation. These must be sought in a more recent tradition. It is interesting to compare the work of Desmarets with Cebà's *Esther*, which gives a similar impression of exuberant fantasy. The main prop of both poems is Vashti's revenge, which, we have seen, has no Biblical justification. It is not necessary to assume

---

[1] *Odyssey*, bk. xiv.   [2] 1673, a4.   [3] ii. 6.
[4] Preface, 1673; cf. p. 28 above.
[5] xi. 6. This is followed by Racine (*Esther*, I. i). But cf. also Book of Esther ii. 1.
[6] xi. 6.
[7] Pharnabaze was a captain in the army of Artaxerxes.

that Desmarets was inspired by Cebà here, since the idea could be deduced independently from the general situation in accordance with the logic of fiction. Moreover, the treatment of the episode differs considerably. Desmarets combines Vashti's project with the Biblical conspiracy of Thares and Bagathan. Cebà invents her revenge, introduces separately the story of Thares and Bagathan, and stages another attempt on the life of Artaxerxes (by Cenoclea and Tarquinio). There are thus three conspiracies instead of one. This repetition of almost identical episodes is characteristic of Italian epic and quite foreign to French. Like Desmarets, Cebà links Biblical and classical history by his Roman knights, Tarquin and Valerius, who make their way to Persia, and by the treason of Orontes. Cebà too makes frequent use of Plutarch. However, his borrowings rarely coincide with those of Desmarets. His poem ends with the conversion of Vashti to Judaism instead of her suicide. Here is another significant difference: Desmarets has followed Virgil, Cebà the tradition of Ariosto and Tasso (for example, the conversion of Clorinda in the *Gerusalemme Liberata*).

There are, however, more particular resemblances. The coronation in Desmarets is constructed in the same way as the wedding in Cebà. The order of procession is the same in both—the nobles followed by the women of Susa:

> Cent filles vont de rang, de Suse les plus belles.[1]
>
> Fra le più scelte dame, e le più belle.[2]

Esther takes her place beside Artaxerxes:

> Vers le Prince elle avance, et se courbe humblement. . . .
> Puis la meine avec luy se placer sur le trône[3]
>
> E con sembiante humile e cor dimesso
> A lui s'inchina, e gli s'asside appresso.[4]

The music is described in the same way:

> Des temps, en divers tons, suivent les mesmes loix[5]
>
> E per diuersi tuoni, e varie vie . . .[6]

The king is delighted by the honour shown to Esther:

> le Roy sent en son cœur
> Autant de doux transports qu'elle reçoit d'honneur[7]

[1] p. 39. [2] Cebà, Canto viii, stanza 61. [3] p. 43.
[4] Cebà, viii. 66. [5] p. 43. [6] Cebà, viii. 67. [7] p. 43.

Sente Assuero a queste voci il petto
Di dolcezza e di gioia intenerirsi.[1]

Finally, Pharsandate's appeal to Vashti resembles that of Cenoclea
to Tarquin:

Princesse, maintenant, dit-il, tu seras Reine, . . .
Epouse d'vn grand Roy, digne de ton souhait,
Qui pour l'heur de te voir à tout moment soûpire;
Pour toy, plus que pour luy, *va conquerir l'Empire*.[2]

Tu di regnar Tarquinio auampi, e brami,
Et io di dominar sfauillo, et ardo;
Tu senti stretto il cor de' miei legami,
Io sento al cor per te pungente dardo: . . .
Non *conquistiam* di Persia *i grandi imperi*?[3]

The conjunction of general situation and particular coincidence
makes direct imitation possible. However, the wedding-scene belongs to a recognized category of description and the likelihood
of a common source cannot be excluded. On the whole it seems
probable that Desmarets had at least looked through Cebà's
poem. But the question is relatively of small importance. The
essential conclusion to be drawn from the parallel is that in spite
of a few significant differences, Desmarets's work belongs to the
same tradition and derives from the same outlook.

However, as in the case of Marie de Pech, the immediate
impulse seems to have come from the French novel. The interest
in Persian atmosphere, the attention devoted to Oriental cere-
monies are almost certainly due to the vogue of *Le Grand Cyrus*.
The title itself occurs at one point:

Le Grand Cyrus à peine au trône fut placé.[4]

Whether intentionally or not, this inevitably evokes associations
with the novel. The wanderings of Aman and Pharsandate recall
those of Artamène.[5] This again is not a question of source but of
a deeper kinship. There is perhaps a closer resemblance to the
description of a ceremony in a Persian temple: in both poem and
novel, the sun's face is hidden.[6] Pharsandate's disguise in order
to approach his beloved repeats one of the most familiar situations of the novel. The case of Céladon in *L'Astrée* is perhaps the

---

[1] Cebà, viii. 71.   [2] p. 81.   [3] Cebà, ix. 128.
[4] p. 20.   [5] *Le Grand Cyrus*, bk. ii.
[6] Desmarets, p. 33; *Le Grand Cyrus*, bk. ii, p. 184 (1650 ed.).

best known.[1] Iasbel's disguise as a man exemplifies an even more frequent theme.[2] When she begins the story of her misfortunes:

> Sa valeur, son esprit, sa grace et sa prudence,
> Avoient gagné mon cœur dés ma plus tendre enfance.
> J'aimois encore un Frere, avec un chaste amour,
> Qu'un seul enfantement avec moi mit au jour,
> Iasbel; et la Nature, heureuse en cet ouvrage,
> Nous fit de mesmes mœurs, et de mesme visage.[3]

we recognize the plot of innumerable novels and comedies. The meeting of Iasbel and Thamar in the thick of battle[4] furnishes another example, though here the influence of Italian romance must also be taken into consideration. Nothing could be at once less Biblical and less classical than these incidents.

The spiritual experience of Desmarets has received sympathetic attention from Henri Bremond,[5] who divides his life after conversion into three periods—pure mysticism (1645–60), feverish activity, spying and heresy-hunting (1660–6), and old age, occupied mainly with literary polemics (1666–76). *Esther* belongs to the last period. Bremond goes on:

> Les poèmes chrétiens de sa vieillesse, la *Marie-Madeleine* (1669), indiqueraient peut-être, non pas un fléchissement de la foi, mais un sens moins sûr et moins pur des choses spirituelles. Je n'ai pas lu son *Esther* (1673).[6]

Study of the poem confirms the truth of this observation. Faith is certainly not lacking and the didactic purpose of the writer is strongly marked. There is, however, little trace of mystical communion with the divine or even of moral elevation. The spiritual reflections of the poem are concerned mainly with vituperation of the classical gods, evidently connected with the poet's critical works, and with the expression of confidence in divine succour, which is the religious counterpart of the literary use of celestial intervention. Unfortunately the source of this confidence seems to be more the discomfiture of the wicked than the assistance of the good:

---

[1] Cf. also Amadis and Palmarenne in *Le Roman des Romans*. For a full account see Magendie, *Le Roman français*, p. 178.   [2] Magendie, op. cit., p. 21.
[3] p. 62 (1673).   [4] p. 85 (1673).
[5] *Histoire littéraire du sentiment religieux*, vi. 445 ff.   [6] Ib. vi. 500, n. 1.

Mais que le Tout-puissant, des ames insensées
Sçait bien, quand il lui plaist, confondre les pensées,
Et garentir les siens par de subtils ressorts
Que sa sagesse garde en ses plus chers tresors.[1]

These lines express the frame of mind which led to the death of
Simon Morin and illustrate the spiritual decline observed by
Bremond.

A very different explanation of the work of Desmarets is contained in the medical thesis of Marie-Alice Caillet.[2] The poet,
it appears, was the victim of paranoiac delirium, the symptoms of
which were mysticism and zeal for persecution. There is, no doubt,
much truth in this contention, but it has two weaknesses: insuffi-
cient evidence is put forward, and the author quotes as proof of
madness much that belongs to the common stock of contemporary
poetry. It would certainly be possible to explain as the result of
mental derangement the extravagances which in these pages are
attributed to purely literary or aesthetic causes. The truth is that
the poet's illness only exaggerated tendencies which were already
present and which were derived from external sources.

The work of Desmarets appears then to present a strange
paradox. The champion of Christian and Biblical poetry treats the
Bible almost with frivolity and fills his poem with the pagan
divinities he scorns. Again Bremond offers an interesting observation:

. . . peut-être n'a-t-on pas assez remarqué les raisons mystiques, les
scrupules religieux qui ont présidé à cette croisade. En combattant des
fantômes jadis 'tant aimés', c'est sa propre vie intérieure qu'il veut
sauver, et par une juste récompense, le goût des choses de Dieu l'a
mis en possession de défendre le grand, le vrai goût, contre le petit.[3]

It is true that Desmarets was inspired by religious motives in his
crusade against pagan mythology; it is not true that he had ceased
to love the gods of Greece and Rome. He fights Homer and
Virgil and believes himself superior to them but he meets them
on their own ground—every innovation is judged by their standards and the aim of Desmarets is to make Biblical material
conform to their methods. Even this is not enough. The gods who
have been expelled with such clamour are admitted again by a
back door, because for Desmarets they partake of the essence of
poetry itself.

[1] p. 68 (1673).   [2] Op. cit.   [3] Op. cit. vi. 468-9.

In judging *Esther*, perhaps the most readable though not the most reasonable of the Biblical epics, it must be remembered that its author was in his late seventies when he wrote it. Its bombast and fantasy are the marks of the preceding generation and it has little in common with its immediate contemporaries.

These three poets differ widely—in origins, in talent, in religious sincerity, in treatment of the Bible, in style. They are linked, however, by their debt to the novel, by the fabulous structure of invention superimposed on the original historical material.

CHAPTER X

The Carmelites and Elijah

THE belief that the Carmelite Order was founded on Mount Carmel by the prophet Elijah himself was long cherished by its members. It was only in the seventeenth century that the critical investigation of the Bollandists began to raise doubts. From 1668 violent polemics opposed Jesuits and Carmelites, until papal intervention restored an appearance of peace (1698).[1] Henceforward the belief was generally discredited among Catholics but it was scarcely shaken in the order itself, which had attained considerable importance in France after the reforms of the great Spanish mystics and the work of Father Jean de Saint-Samson.[2] In 1682 a Carmelite father at the provincial chapter of Béziers maintained a set of Latin theses, in which the old claims were repeated and Pythagoras and St. John the Baptist were said to have belonged to the order.[3] In the meantime Father Dorothée de Saint-René had published his *Commentaire theologique sur les Livres des Rois et de l'Apocalipse* (1655), which gives the history of Elijah's life according to Carmelite tradition. After the prophet's life, based on the Book of Kings but enriched by legendary accretions, he is carried away in the chariot of fire to an earthly paradise, where he remains until the coming of Antichrist. He will then return to earth to lead the warriors of Christ. The early history of the Carmelites is recounted at length and the object of the whole work is the glory of the order. Elijah differs therefore from other Biblical heroes, in that he was still capable of inspiring fierce partisan attachment.

[JACQUELIN (?)]

Helie, poëme heroïque (Paris, 1661).

During the century two French poems were devoted to the life of the prophet. The first was *Hélie*, attributed to Jacquelin.[4]

---

[1] For a history of the legend and its representation in art, see Mâle, *L'Art religieux*, pp. 443 ff.   [2] Cf. Bremond, *Histoire littéraire*, ii. 363 ff.

[3] D'Artigny, *Mémoires*, vol. iv, article lxxi.

[4] For the attribution see Barbier, *Dictionnaire des ouvrages anonymes*.

The identity of the poet remains completely obscure. The only biographical indication is that the *Paraphrase sur les neuf leçons du Prophète Jérémie* by Jacquelin appeared in 1651 at Narbonne,[1] which suggests that he originated from the Midi. *Hélie* is preceded by the approbation of the Sorbonne doctors.

The connexion of the story with the Carmelite Order is emphasized in the Preface. The poet speaks of

ces genereux Athletes et . . . ces Illustres Amazonnes, qui combattent tous les iours sous les Estendars de ce vaillant Capitaine; et qui s'efforcent de faire reuiure en ce siecle le zele et la ferueur de ce premier Solitaire du Carmel.[2]

The athletes and amazons are the friars and nuns of the order, the captain is Elijah himself. The military terminology is characteristic of the spirit which animates this literature. There follows an ode to the blessed Virgin, *la tres-auguste Reyne du Carmel*,[3] and a set of stanzas to the prophet.[4] The tone of the ode and in particular a passage in the stanzas:

L'honneur que i'ay receu d'estre vn de vos enfans,
Et de porter sur moy vostre Sainte liurée[5]

seems to prove conclusively that the writer was himself a Carmelite. In the poem Elijah appears accompanied by a number of disciples, the first members of the order.[6] His departure from earth is prefaced by an allegorical prediction of its future history and mission.[7]

In the Preface an extreme Christian position is stated. Even ornaments of style and figures of speech are rejected as unworthy of religious poetry. The defence of the title *Poëme Heroïque* reveals ignorance of critical theory and of literary problems. The object of the poem is expressed in simple and strictly practical terms: it is to reproduce the Bible story in an agreeable way.

Hélie is interesting as an example of the sober and modest approach to the Bible, hardly modified by the superimposal of

---

[1] Cf. Toinet, ii. 157. He is also credited with the anonymous tragedy *Soliman ou l'Esclave Genereuse* (Paris, 1653). However, the author of *Soliman* is identified with a Jacquelin who was Trésorier des Bâtiments in 1648 (see Lancaster, part iii, vol. i, p. 178). Since the author of *Hélie* was certainly a Carmelite, there is some difficulty in accepting the identification. Of course he may have taken orders later, but there is nothing in the subject or style of *Soliman* to connect its author with *Hélie* or the *Paraphrase sur Jérémie*.

[2] p. 8.   [3] p. 10.   [4] p. 19.
[5] p. 22.   [6] p. 103.   [7] pp. 114–15.

Carmelite legends. It is noteworthy that the author, though he emphasizes the importance of Elijah as founder of the order, nowhere follows the hagiographical accretions of Dorothée de Saint-René. The other Carmelite poet represents in almost every respect the opposite pole of Biblical poetry.

R. P. Pierre de Saint-Louis (Jean-Louis Barthélemy) (1626–77?)

L'Éliade, ou triomphes et faits mémorables de saint Élie, Patriarche des Carmes, poème héroïque divisé en trois chants (Aix, 1827; notice by the abbé Follard, canon of Nîmes). The orthography, the grammar, and the prosody have been modernized.[1]

The poem is dedicated to the comte de Grignan, Madame de Sévigné's son-in-law.[2]

The life of Pierre de Saint-Louis is well known, thanks to Follard's notice, which had been summarized by Goujet[3] long before the publication of *L'Éliade*, and to Théophile Gautier's essay in *Les Grotesques*[4] (Gautier, however, was unaware of the existence of the 1827 edition and devoted himself entirely to *La Magdeleine au desert*[5]). He was born at Vauréas, now Valréas (Vaucluse), and entered the Carmelite Order in 1651. Follard says[6] that he died nine years after the publication of *La Magdeleine*, which gives 1677 as the approximate date of his death.

The date of the *Éliade* can be established with some certainty. Follard tells us that it was begun soon after the appearance of *La Magdeleine* and was finished shortly before his death. Thus the poem was written between 1668 and 1677.

It is divided into three *chants*, the whole containing about 2,200 lines. The first *chant* contains the life of Elijah, the second his elevation and triumph in Heaven, the third his second coming and combat with Antichrist. The plan thus corresponds approxi-

[1] There is a manuscript copy of the poem, apparently written in the second half of the eighteenth century, in the Bibliothèque Méjanes (Aix-en-Provence). It presents considerable differences from the printed version.

[2] There is no dedication in the 1827 edition, but Saint-Louis includes in the poem (p. 3) an invocation to his patron which begins: 'C'est vous, grand Adhemar . . .', addresses him as marquis, and includes: 'L'air de votre Grignan et de Roche Courbière'. He describes himself as *le fils de l'un de vos sujets*.

[3] *Bibliothèque françoise*, xvii. 259. It appears to have been first published in full in the *Mercure de France* (July 1750, pp. 8–26).

[4] Ch. iv.   [5] Lyons, 1668.   [6] *Éliade*, p. xx.

mately to that of Dorothée de Saint-René. Each *chant* is self-sufficient, there is little sense of continuity. The sharpness of each division is further emphasized by a quatrain and a set of Latin verses which close the *chant*.

It will appear from the plan that the importance of the Biblical history of Elijah is limited. The episode of the chariot of fire is treated with a certain respect for the text, but the most vivid incidents are omitted completely, like Naboth's vineyard and the prophet's resistance to the soldiers sent by Ahab (a subject very suitable for epic), or dismissed in a line, like the raising of the widow's son:

> Puis, voulant enchérir pardessus ce bienfait,
> Ressuscite son fils. Aussitôt cela fait . . .[1]

In compensation, the poet allows his imagination free rein in the addition of fresh incident and ornament. But everywhere the same rapidity may be observed. The sacrifice and confutation of the priests of Baal is entirely without dignity or reverence but it has movement; indeed it proceeds at a gallop:

> Le ciel en exauçant sa prière et ses vœux
> Fait rouler jusqu'à terre un tourbillon de feux
> Qui dévorant le bois, consumant la victime
> Mit notre grand Prophète en la plus grande estime;
> Tous ceux du faux clergé dans cet événement
> Pestent contre le ciel et grondent sourdement.[2]

This is still more evident in the second *chant*. Elijah in his chariot, scarcely pausing in Heaven, where

> On entend crier: *vive*, on entend crier: *place*,
> Quand le Prophète arrive, et lorsque son train passe[3]

is borne through space:

> Cependant les coursiers bondissans sur les nues
> Suivent au grand galop des routes inconnues.[4]

It is small wonder that the poet himself becomes alarmed and calls on his muse to stop:

> Muse, arrête-toi: veux-tu le suivre encor?
> Modère ici ton vol, et borne ton essor.[5]

[1] p. 17.   [2] p. 18.   [3] p. 40.
[4] p. 41.   [5] p. 54.

It would be futile to seek literary sources for all the extravagances of the poem. *Hélie* exercised no influence whatever—choice of detail, method, atmosphere are all different. However, two references to Italy present a certain interest. The prodigies which accompany the birth of the prophet are compared to those which heralded Alexander, Caesar (so far there is nothing remarkable), and St. Charles Borromeo.[1] This curious juxtaposition provides an instance of the importance of the Counter-Reformation in the poet's background. Elijah in Paradise is compared to Medoro with Angelica, a most improper parallel:

> Ou bien plus fortuné que n'est pas un Médor,
> Il vit heureusement avec son Angélique.
> J'entends son innocence et son âme pudique.[2]

This does not of course prove that Pierre de Saint-Louis had read the *Orlando Furioso*. It is interesting as an example of the wide diffusion of Ariosto's myths.

The principal source of the accretions is revealed, however, by a comparison with the work of Father Dorothée de Saint-René. There are indeed a few discrepancies. The *Commentaire théologique* shows Elijah transported directly to Paradise: the celestial journey seems to be the invention of Pierre de Saint-Louis. In the *Commentaire* Elijah is accompanied by Enoch in his fight against Antichrist: in the poem Enoch is omitted. The resemblances are far more numerous. The similarity in general plan has already been noted. The infant prophet cradled in flames is also found in Dorothée de Saint-René.[3] The name of his father, Sobac, not in the Bible, is given in the *Commentaire théologique*.[4] The poet argues that the absence of any reference to the prophet's childhood proves that he never did anything childish:

> Mais comme on ne dit rien de toute son enfance . . .
> On peut voir en cela, comme elle nous défend
> De croire qu'un tel homme ait pu faire l'enfant.[5]

This comes from the same source:

Ie me persuade que l'esprit infiniment sage, qui a dicté les liures Saints, nous a voulu insinuer qu'vn si grand home n'auoit iamais rien fait en enfant.[6]

---

[1] p. 8.   [2] p. 67.   [3] *Commentaire*, p. 3.
[4] Ib., p. 2; cf. *Éliade*, p. 6.   [5] *Éliade*, p. 8.   [6] *Commentaire*, p. 4.

Both works contain the story of Elijah's crucifixion and resurrection, with the neglect of the body:

> Personne ne s'empresse à donner sépulture
> Au plus précieux corps qu'eût formé la nature.[1]

Ces pitoyables restes de la cruauté sont trois iours et demy exposez, sans qu'il soit permis de leur donner la sepulture.[2]

Dorothée de Saint-René also turns Elijah into an abbot:

S. Elie visite les colleges de son institut, et reside d'ordinaire au mont Carmel.[3]

Iean Patriarche de Ierusalem, Lyra, Tostat, Denis le Chartreux, Sanctius, Salian, Corneille et Gordon tombent d'accord que S. Elie visita les principaux Colleges de son institut, auant que d'estre rauy.[4]

These coincidences do not prove, though they indicate, the immediate source of the *Éliade*. In any case, it is plain that most of the fantasies of the poem were firmly rooted in Carmelite tradition, often supported by respectable theological authority.

It would be easy to regard the poem as a piece of insanity, an excellent joke but devoid of wider significance. This is the opinion expressed by Théophile Gautier on *La Magdeleine au Desert*.[5] We have seen, however, that these strange visions are not merely the delusions of a solitary monk and we may distinguish three elements in their formation: the eccentricity of the poet himself, the influence of popular imagination, and a partisan theological training. The three are in perfect harmony. A parallel might be found in a rural church in a southern country with its coloured saints, spangled heaven, and theatrical architecture. The poem is a monument of simple piety, which must of course be considered in relation to contemporary, not medieval, feeling. Its unrestrained imagination, varied ornament, and violent movement illustrate its near kinship to the manifestations of the baroque spirit in the plastic arts.

---

[1] *Éliade*, p. 79.
[2] *Commentaire*, p. 309.
[3] Ib., p. 63.
[4] Ib., p. 85.
[5] 'Le poème du père Pierre de Saint-Louis est indubitablement l'ouvrage le plus excentrique, pour le fond et la forme, qui ait jamais paru dans aucune langue du monde, et, à ce titre, quoiqu'il soit détestable, il méritait qu'on s'en occupât' (*Les Grotesques*, ch. iv).

These two Carmelite poems draw on the same material, are inspired by the same tradition, have the same propagandist motive. None the less, they represent the two extremes of the aesthetic conceptions of their time and perhaps two opposite kinds of spiritual experience.

CHAPTER XI

The Cosmogonies: Saint-Martin and Perrault

SINCE the last faint echo of Du Bartas, the *Semaine* of Abel d'Argent, the 'celestial' epic[1] had been entirely neglected. All the followers of Saint-Amant whom we have examined had taken as their subject a particular hero from the historical portions of the Bible. Towards the end of the century two writers return to the great theme of the closing sixteenth century—the Creation itself, with all its wider poetic possibilities.

SAINT-MARTIN (SIEUR DE)

i. *La Nature naissante ou les merveilleux effets de la puissance divine dans la creation du monde achevee en six iours. En Vers François* (Paris, 1667).

ii. *Le Systeme des cieux et des elemens, ou les merveilleux effets de la puissance divine dans la Creation du Monde. En Vers François* (Paris, 1670).

Both works were republished in 1690, (i) with a new title: *L'Univers tiré du neant.* Examination of typography, pagination, and ornaments shows that the two issues of (i) are identical (apart from preliminaries). *La Nature naissante* is dedicated to Lamoignon, *Le Systeme des cieux* to Monsieur de Bellièvre, Marquis de Grignon. Saint-Martin was also the author of an *Ode présentée a Monseigneur le Peletier, controlleur general des finances*, Paris, 1684, and of a sonnet in the *Recueil Bouhours.*[2]

Apart from any conjectures which may be based on these dedications, details of Saint-Martin's life are meagre. He is described on the title-page of both works as *le sieur de Saint-Martin, mathematicien.* On the contents page of the *Systeme des cieux* (1690) we find the note:

L'Auteur demeure au haut de la ruë de la vieille Bouclerie, proche Saint Severin, chez Monsieur Crespin Fourbisseur.

Il expliquera les difficultez qui se rencontreront dans cet Ouvrage.

---

[1] Cf. p. 41 above.

[2] Lachèvre, *Recueils collectifs*, iii. 522. See also Toinet, ii. 168–72.

With the exception of *La Nature naissante* all the editions were printed at the author's expense, a fact recorded on the title-pages.

The privilege of both *La Nature naissante* and *Le Systeme des cieux* is dated 3 November 1665, which suggests that the two works may already have been completed in that year.

In the Preface to *La Nature naissante* Saint-Martin says that he owes the work to what he has learned from the Jesuits. In conjunction with the *Chant Royal à l'honneur de la Vierge* which follows the same work, this suggests that he was induced to write by motives of piety.

The Poems

Saint-Martin's original intention appears to have been a *Semaine* on the lines of Du Bartas, of which we have only the first two days. As in the case of d'Aubigné, the Biblical elements are not very strong, but it can be considered as a fragmentary epic.

La Nature naissante is headed by the first five verses of Genesis. It develops the brief story found there, examining the nature of light, darkness, and chaos, asking whether the world is eternal and why it should have been created in time. But much is included which is not even suggested by these verses—the creation of the nine orders of angels, the fall of Lucifer, the battle between the angels of light and darkness, and finally a description of Hell. Similarly, *Le Systeme des cieux* passes rapidly over the creation of the firmament and goes on to enumerate all the various meteorological phenomena—rain, snow, hail, and so on—each of which is explained in scientific terms. Their common and natural manifestations are subordinate, however, to the descriptions of comets, violent storms, armies seen in the clouds, and other prodigies drawn from ancient and recent history.

In spite of its incompleteness, the work might therefore present a certain interest as evidence of scientific progress and the changing view of the world in the course of the century. The subject of the second day touches on astronomy, in which discoveries of the first importance had been made since the earlier cosmogonies of Du Bartas and Gamon. Saint-Martin does, indeed, show frequent signs of a scientific frame of mind. He not only speaks of the earth as a globe (Du Bartas had already done so) but he revises the story of the Creation in order to conform to the modern idea:

> Et qu'au milieu des Airs la Terre suspenduë
> Fit vn globe avec l'Onde autour d'elle épanduë.[1]

Closer examination reveals, however, that Saint-Martin's conception of the universe is not fundamentally different from that of the medieval theologians. He insists that the earth is only six thousand years old.[2] In spite of Galileo the sun is made to move round the earth.[3] Matter still consists of the old four elements, earth, air, water, and fire.[4] The authorities quoted in the marginal notes belong mostly to the great body of orthodox tradition—Aristotle and Josephus, St. Bernard and St. Thomas. To these must be added modern cosmographers and memorialists—Gaffarel, Belleforest, Fracastorius, Scipion Guillet, La Chambre. There is no mention of any contemporary scientist.

The basis of the poems is thus theological, not scientific, and the theology is still mainly scholastic, as may be seen in the discussions on the nature of angels. Where Saint-Martin differs from his more educated contemporaries is in the use of popular superstitions which provide the greater part of his material. Werewolves are quoted as evidence of the existence of angels.[5] Recent history is ransacked for examples of the influence of comets.[6] Louis XIII's army besieging Montauban is seen in the clouds by the people of Caen.[7] Plagues of demons infest distant countries:

> D'invisibles Demons vne servile bande
> Infecte Baccara, la Norwegue et Groenlande,
> D'vne Isle où ces Espris font voir leur cruauté
> Le terroir n'est jamais des Humains habité:
> Par de maudits secrets et d'infames mysteres
> Les Necromanciens qui font des Caracteres
> Enferment les Demons dans de frêles Christaux . . .[8]

All these wonders are presented as ascertained truth.

The unusual features of Saint-Martin's work are largely explained by his relationship to Du Bartas.[9] Resemblances of detail are numerous. In conjunction with their context they leave no

---

[1] *Nature naissante*, p. 6.   [2] Ib.   [3] *Systeme*, p. 12.
[4] *Nature naissante*, p. 3.   [5] Ib., p. 13.   [6] *Systeme*, pp. 29 ff.
[7] Ib., p. 17.   [8] *Nature naissante*, p. 14.
[9] Cf. p. 45 above.

room for doubt.[1] The order of the poems owes much to the earlier poet. Like Du Bartas Saint-Martin goes on from the consideration of what was before the Creation to the mystery of the Trinity. The descriptions of chaos, the elements, and the firmament are closely imitated. Moreover, the method is the same. Saint-Martin makes an affirmation, quotes several objections, and answers them one by one. However, there is a difference and it is to be found in the style. Saint-Martin prunes, makes antitheses rational, eliminates concrete detail (as in the simile of the bird and the eggs), transforms the crude material into seventeenth-century verse.

In spite of his claim to be a mathematician Saint-Martin is disappointing from a scientific point of view. He shows occasional glimpses of wide reading and of a scientific attitude, but relies mostly on a collection of old wives' tales. The interest of these poems lies in the survival of the Du Bartas tradition and in the light they throw on current superstition.

CHARLES PERRAULT (1628–1703)

Adam, ou la creation de l'homme, sa chute et sa reparation. Poeme chrestien (Paris, 1697).[2]

The poem is divided into four books. The first book had already appeared with the title *La Création du Monde*, Paris, 1692 (reprinted in *Recueil de pieces curieuses*, La Haye, 1694).[3]

Adam is hardly an orthodox epic, since heroic action on the human plane is almost suppressed in order to develop the theme of divine purpose. But a large part of the poem is taken up by a prophetic dream and an angelic vision (itself an epic conven-

---

[1] For example:

Mais ainsi qu'vn oiseau, par sa chaleur puissante,
Donne aux œufs qu'il échauffe vne forme vivante (*Nature naissante*, p. 9).

Ou bien comme l'oiseau qui tasche rendre vifs,
Et ses œufs naturels, et ses œufs adoptifs,
Se tient couché sur eux et d'vne chaleur viue
Fait qu'vn rond iaune blanc en vn poulet s'auiue (Du Bartas, p. 9; Holmes, ii. 205).

Et trente deux marquez sur la docte boussole (*Systeme*, p. 38).

En marque trente deux sur sa docte boussole (Du Bartas, p. 42; Holmes, ii. 244).

[2] There is a MS., apparently an autograph, dated 1695, in the Bibliothèque Nationale. The poem was therefore completed by 1695. Fragments had been read to the Academy at various times between December 1691 and February 1693. Cf. Bonnefon, *R.H.L.F.*, 1906, p. 608; and p. 230 below.

[3] There are some stylistic corrections in the final version, but no major changes.

tion), which permits Perrault to introduce the whole of Old Testament history up to the time of Solomon. Book I contains the Creation, Book II the Fall, followed by a dream in which Adam sees the history of mankind as far as the Deluge. In Book III he is consoled by an angel who takes the tale up to Solomon. In Book IV they are joined by Eve and the angel recounts the redemption and the Day of Judgement.

In his Preface Perrault puts his finger on the principal objection to such a poem, from the critical point of view. He has been blamed, he says, because his hero is not active or at least is active only in eating an apple. The same difficulty had troubled Saint-Amant and all those poets who had chosen the less combative figures of the Bible. Perrault's reply, however, is original: instead of defending his poem by twisting the rules or by quoting precedents, he argues simply that, since most epics have had active heroes, the charm of variety justifies the change. He goes on to state his own definition of epic:

... il suffisoit que la matiere d'un Poëme Heroique fust importante, qu'elle fust narrée avec les fictions et les ornemens que demande la Poësie, et qu'il se rencontrast dans le sujet un nœud et un denouëment à peu prés comme dans les Poëmes Dramatiques.

But, more important, the whole conception is marked by a freedom and a nonchalance in strong contrast to the pedantic discussions of earlier poets and the rigorous system of Le Bossu. Perrault reduces epic theory to a few essentials, easily grasped. On the religious side he deals with his critics in the same cavalier fashion. Faced with the old objection that the subject was not suitable for poetic fiction, he begs the question unashamedly:

J'ay respondu que la Poësie pouvant parler de toutes choses, et la fiction estant de l'essence de la Poësie, on ne peut pas me faire aucun reproche là-dessus.

His position is close to that of Desmarets.

The poem itself is built in accordance with these principles. The detailed execution is generally weak. The story of the Old Testament, compressed in a thousand lines or so, is naturally shorn of nearly all significant incident. This part—more than half of the poem—is entirely cast in the future tense, which produces a monotonous and disagreeable effect. Moreover, it leads to ridiculous situations, surprising in the author of the fairy-tales and the brilliant adversary of Boileau. And there seems to be no organic reason why the angel's predictions should stop with Solomon. Adam's dream is inadmissible by contemporary critical standards, since it merely continues the main story. In spite of these defects, however, the poem stands out among similar works by the ease and simplicity of its structure. There is none of the flatness of the fundamentalists or the unwieldy complexity of the baroque poets. This structure is not an end in itself. As in Saint-Amant the use of the future tense is a means of enlarging the scope of the work. The story of Eden is made to embrace the whole of human destiny. The conception remains grandiose, however much the execution may fall short of it.

All this may seem remote from *Puss in Boots* and *Red Riding Hood*. Still, the writer of fairy-tales does appear in the treatment of animals. In the rather ludicrous picture of all the beasts lined up before Adam to receive their names and the domestic animals waiting to be domesticated the descriptions of each species have a certain charm. There is the swan:

> L'Onde claire les charme, et le Cygne en nageant
> S'applaudit d'y mirer son plumage d'argent.[1]

the stags:

> Où sans cesse déja la crainte du Veneur
> Leur fait dresser l'oreille, et leur transit le cœur:[2]

the rabbits and foxes:

> Les timides Lapins, et les Renards rusés
> Se cachent dans les troux par eux-mêmes creusés
> Pour tromper des Chasseurs la poursuite fatale,
> Par les sages détours de leur sombre dedale.[3]

We are reminded of La Fontaine, though there is none of his power of individual characterization.

The literary sources of the subject and of its general treatment are less easy to determine. The theme bears a close resemblance to that of Du Bartas, especially in the way in which the Creation story is enlarged to include the Old Testament. The description of Eden in the two poems is generally similar and there are one or

---

[1] *Adam*, p. 8.   [2] p. 9.   [3] Ib.

two particular coincidences.[1] It would be rash to conclude from such scanty detail that Perrault was influenced by Du Bartas, but the example of the *Semaine* may well have been before his eyes.

More striking is the parallel between Perrault's angel and the vision which Michael unfolds before Adam in Books XI and XII (Book X of the first edition) of *Paradise Lost*. The choice of incidents in the review of Biblical history is generally the same (though Milton goes beyond Solomon), the story is punctuated by the Angel's moralizing and Adam's questions and exclamations of wonder, above all the unreal atmosphere of a dream is sought by both,[2] and the place of the vision in the whole poem (after the Fall) is the same. Moreover, the vision is broken at the same point (after the Flood), when Adam's direct view of future events gives place to the angel's narrative. There are several possible explanations of this similarity. It might easily be due to accident or to the spontaneous generation of identical ideas. More probably there is a common source (though it does not seem to be Du Bartas[3] or Tasso's *Mondo Creato*, in which the narrative is handled differently). It is unlikely but at any rate possible that Perrault had read Milton, perhaps in the Latin translation by William Hog which had appeared in 1690.

[1]   L'Hyver n'ose y porter sa neige et ses glaçons,
        Et la terre en tout temps y donne des moissons (*Adam*, p. 15).
        Que la gresle iamais n'atterroit les moissons:
        Que la neige plumeuse, et les luisans glaçons
        N'enuieillissoient les champs (Du Bartas, p. 207; Holmes, iii. 4).
        Et là de mille oyseaux les differens ramages
        Animent les buissons et les sombres bocages (*Adam*, p. 16).
        Où cent sortes d'oiseaux iour et nuict s'esbatoyent.
                                (Du Bartas, p. 207; Holmes, iii. 4).
[2] For example Adam's vision of Cain and Abel:
        Dés que dans le sommeil ses yeux furent plongez,
        Il crut voir dans un champ deux Autels érigez,
        L'un chargé d'Animaux non encor nourris d'herbes,
        L'autre de nouveaux fruits et de nouvelles gerbes (*Adam*, p. 37).
        His eyes he opened, and beheld a field,
        Part arable and tilth, whereon were sheaves
        New-reaped, the other part sheep-walks and folds;
        I' the midst an altar as the landmark stood,
        Rustic, of grassy sord (*Paradise Lost*, xi, lines 429–33).
Cf. Hog, *Paraphrasis*, p. 323.
[3] Adam reveals the future briefly to Seth (ed. Holmes, iii. 93 ff.), but there are no resemblances of arrangement. The idea of Adam's vision seems to go back to the *Apocalypse of Moses* (see Baldwin, '*Paradise Lost* and the *Apocalypse of Moses*').

The works of Saint-Martin and Perrault yield very little if we seek a faithful reflection of contemporary scientific progress. However, the return to the cosmogony as a poetic subject (abandoned since Du Bartas and Gamon), the curiosity of the one and the disembodied abstractions of the other, perhaps too a faint breath of English influence, show that the Biblical epic, in spite of its archaisms, had evolved in accordance with the great intellectual developments of the time.

PART III

THE GENRE

CHAPTER XII

The Epic and the Bible

A STUDY of the prefaces and theoretical statements of the authors of these poems has revealed a variety of attitudes towards the treatment of Biblical material, ranging from literal fidelity to unlimited freedom. These two extremes may serve as the basis of our examination of the poems themselves, though we must not expect them to correspond exactly either to the declarations of the prefaces or to the categories of fundamentalists and others provisionally adopted here. The more exuberantly baroque poets, Desmarets and Pierre de Saint-Louis, do not indeed offer much to investigate from this point of view, since they abandon the Bible so completely. The fundamentalists, on the other hand, begin with the intention of following the text, and usually do so in the superficial arrangement of events. In most cases, however, we find them, it would seem in spite of themselves, altering their source at every point by the same means as were adopted by less scrupulous poets—omission, compression, expansion, addition, and transmutation. The principal distinction to be made here will be between those who show an understanding of the Bible and those who, whatever their intentions, do not. The latter class is by no means the less interesting.

The former belongs perhaps essentially to an earlier generation and to Protestantism, though isolated examples are found throughout the period. One of its outstanding characteristics is what may be called internal expansion. Thus Gamon's *Semaine* is preceded by a verse from the Psalms and at the beginning of each day is printed the appropriate passage from Genesis. Already in this way the subordination of literary to religious motives is clearly stressed. As in Du Bartas, the Bible is the foundation on which a vast structure of theology, science, and poetry is superimposed. The method of amplification is very different from that used by poets whose intention was in the first place literary and who treated the verses of the Bible externally as pretexts for the addition of isolated episodes or descriptions. Here each verse, each word becomes the object of a long commentary. The expansion is thus internal. For example, Chaos is described briefly in the Bible:

Et la Terre estoit sans forme et vuide, et tenebres estoyent sur le dessus de l'abisme.[1]

Gamon begins by paraphrasing the verse:

La terre enuelopée en cette onde escumeuze,
Estoit vrayement sans forme, et vuide et tenebreuze.[2]

He then analyses each member of the verse separately: *Sans forme, car* . . .; *Vuide aussi, car* . . .; *Et tenebreuze aussi, car*. . . . It will be sufficient to quote the shortest of the three:

Vuide aussi, car la Terre encor tristement vaine,
N'auoit champs, prez, ny bois, n'auoit au front la plaine,
En ses cheueux le fruit, au ventre le metal,
En son sein l'Ocean, sur son dos l'animal.

The Bible is followed in this way almost word by word.

On the other hand, it is also absorbed. Gamon finds himself unworthy to describe the wonder of the Trinity:

Populace arrestez, gardez le pied du mont,
Et, sobres atendez qu'vn tresluisant Moyse,
Redescendant instruit, plus auant vous instruise.[3]

Similar examples come constantly to his pen, drawn not only from the great heroes but also from the obscurest corners of the Old Testament. Where later poets often tend to confine themselves to their particular book (Saint-Amant is a notable example),[4] Gamon, like Du Bartas, ranges freely over the whole Bible. To him it is more than a source of narrative material.

While internal expansion of this kind seems to disappear after

---

[1] Gen. i. 2 (Geneva, 1588). [2] *Semaine*, p. 6.
[3] Ib., p. 4. [4] Cf. p. 92 above.

Gamon, there are traces of the familiarity with the Bible implied in a wide range of allusion, though never on so large a scale. In details Marie de Pech shows a certain facility of allusion to incidents outside the immediate source. Thus for the Bethulians dying of thirst she cites two parallels, the obvious one of Moses at the Rock of Horeb and the more recondite case of Ishmael in the desert.[1] The author of *Hélie*, too, like his sixteenth-century predecessors, draws his comparisons from all parts of the Bible, displaying a genuine familiarity with the text. It is perhaps this as much as anything which serves to distinguish the religious poets who regarded the Bible as a literary pretext (though Marie de Pech must be regarded as an exception).

Another feature of earlier poems which had become increasingly rare is the use of the Bible as a quarry of contemporary satirical references. Elijah's miracles, enumerated in the invocation of *Hélie*, lead to a comparison with a degenerate age and a lively attack on politicians and on modern science and philosophy (or at least on excessive confidence in their results).[2] On the other hand, the description of the festivals of Baal[3] shows a sense of pagan beauty, not to be confused with the fanciful structures of Desmarets and his like. For the moment the author suspends moral judgement and contents himself with simple enjoyment of the scene. This is most rare (the typical attitude is Saint-Amant's indignant tone in the Golden Calf episode).[4] The methods of satire and objective description, apparently contradictory, both proceed from a direct approach to the Bible, little affected by contemporary ideas.

Such cases are, however, very exceptional. The most the funda-mentalists could normally achieve was an unintelligent devotion to the letter of the text, as in the case of Lesfargues, whose guiding principle in his detailed treatment of the Bible was his attachment to 'cette adorable verité que i'ay suiuie presque iusques à la lettre'.[5] There is no doubt that he is much more faithful to the original text than any of his contemporaries, even when epic dignity or narrative efficacity have to be sacrificed. Thus he keeps in its entirety the picture of the youthful David dwarfed in a man's armour.[6] Coras, more afraid of ridicule, tones it down

---

[1] *Judith*, p. 84; Gen. xxi. 19. [2] *Hélie*, pp. 5–6.
[3] Ib., p. 18. [4] *Œuvres*, ii. 225.
[5] *David*, e2 v°. [6] p. 31. Cf. I Sam. xvii. 39.

considerably.[1] Sometimes Lesfargues imitates the Bible in making a complete change of scene or material without interruption, and this in spite of the attention which he devotes to major transitions:

> Ainsi gagnoit Dauid dans la Cour de Sion,
> De ce Prince inquiet la tendre affection;
> Lors que du Philistin la formidable armée . . . .[2]

In this last example the Biblical succession of events, whose connexion is never explicit, is for once almost captured, and very occasionally plodding fidelity is rewarded by a glimpse of the true spirit of the Bible. So Saint-Peres keeps something of the capacity for wonder at simple things, of the respect for solid wealth which is one feature of the Old Testament. He takes pleasure in enumerating

> Seruantes et valets, et bestail et chameaux,
> Or, argent monnoyé, d'autres meubles tres beaux[3]

or

> Le bled dans ses greniers à monceaux bien épais,
> Le vin dans ses celiers regorger en la tonne.[4]

Here we find in a more primitive form the note of the Biblical pastoral which is also prominent in Saint-Amant.[5] It appears again in Morillon:

> Mille nombreux troupeaux acquis par ses services
> En offrent à ses yeux les heureuses prémices,[6]

though in this case it is more conventional and its Biblical source is combined with Virgilian tradition. The respect for fertility is also Biblical:

> ASENETH en ce temps comme un arbre fécond
> Au premier de ses fruits en va joindre un second.[7]

Potiphar after buying Joseph is

> Plus guay qu'un jeune époux qui revient d'une feste.[8]

The bridegroom is a frequent symbol of joy in the Old Testament[9] and does not belong to the conventional system of Petrarchan or Renaissance imagery.

---

[1] *David*, p. 98. [2] p. 16. [3] *Tobie*, p. 27.
[4] *Joseph*, p. 18. [5] Cf. p. 100 above. [6] *Joseph*, p. 14.
[7] Ib., p. 116. Cf. Ps. cxxviii. 3.
[8] *Joseph*, p. 63. [9] Cf. especially Isa. lxii. 5.

Perrault too possesses the quality of humility towards the text. Thus God walking in the garden is represented with the familiarity and lack of surprise which characterize the original:

> Ils s'en couvroient encor lors que se fit entendre
> La voix de l'Eternel qui venoit de descendre,
> Et qui se promenant dans ce charmant sejour,
> Venoit les visiter sur le declin du jour.[1]

It is true that the scene is later attributed to a vision of Adam which has no physical reality, but this theological explanation is carefully separated from the narrative. This double attitude may indeed lead us to suspect in Perrault something of the conscious *naïveté* of later poets who have tried to recapture the atmosphere of the Bible, Hugo, Vigny, or Rilke. In any case the faint suggestion of irony shows that we have travelled far from the unquestioning piety of the sixteenth century, although the result is not dissimilar.

Apart from such rare instances the history of the Biblical epic is a history of deformation and distortion, and it is in the nature and motives of this distortion that the interest of the subject partly consists.

To the internal expansion of a Gamon corresponds the external expansion of the poets for whom the Bible is no more than a bare framework. The poet enlarges on a verse or interpolates a description of an episode with no Biblical authority and then returns to the point where the original narrative had been broken off. So in Montchrestien, instead of inspiring Daniel directly as in the Bible,[2] God sends the allegorical figure of Truth, who in turn takes on the form of an old man, Obdias. As soon as the message is delivered, Obdias resumes his divine shape and we have the familiar description of the angelic flight.[3] The method here adopted is almost a regular procedure. A verse in the Bible is seen to offer a vague resemblance (in this case the fact of divine intervention) to an incident in classical or Italian epic. It is then expanded and transformed on the model of that incident (in this case Virgil's Iris or the angelic flights of Ariosto and Tasso) until the original becomes quite unrecognizable. Similarly Coras introduces love-stories which have no justification in the Bible. Love, instead of mere greed, is the motive for Achan's crime,[4] and the presence of

---

[1] *Adam*, p. 30. [2] Dan. xiii. 45.
[3] *Susane*, p. 387. [4] *Josué*, p. 53; Joshua vii. 21.

the Israelite spies in Jericho is revealed not by chance but by
a jealous admirer of Rahab.[1] In Judges we read that 'Eglon was
a very fat man'.[2] In Coras this becomes:

> Et dans vn enbonpoint qui braue le trépas,
> N'ayme que les plaisirs, et que les bons repas.[3]

Here there is no sign of imagination, of individual character:
only the external consequences of the original are drawn. Again,
God's order to the ravens to feed Elijah, 'I have commanded the
ravens to feed thee there',[4] becomes:

> Dieu, pour luy procurer l'entiére nourriture,
> Adoucit des Corbeaux la sauuage nature.[5]

Nothing essential is altered here, but unnecessary words are added
and the miracle is shown as a rational process.

These examples are on a small scale and illustrate the detailed
working of the process of external expansion. Other poets—and
they are on the whole those who most deserve to be called
baroque—extend this expansion until it includes whole episodes
and books, usually fantastic in character. Such are particularly
Anne d'Urfé, Saint-Amant, Desmarets, and Pierre de Saint-Louis.
Not only is there usually no organic connexion between the Bible
and the attached episodes but the original narrative is reduced to
an underground trickle which appears only occasionally above the
mass of superimposed incident. The content of these additions
(in particular, the *merveilleux*) will be considered in subsequent
chapters.[6]

When, leaving extraneous interpolations, we come to examine
the changes wrought in the course of adaptation of the Biblical
material itself, we find one obvious source of distortion in the
desire to add emphasis or heighten the interest which might be
lacking in the original. Coras, for example, is not content to let
Samson's ingenuity speak for itself (as the Bible does):

> C'est alors que Samson, aux moissons Philistines,
> Porte, auec ses renars, d'*effroyables* ruines,
> Et par vn stratagême *admirable, et nouueau,*
> Il leur fait de la guerre allumer le flambeau.[7]

---

[1] *Josué*, p. 11; Joshua ii. 2.   [2] Judges iii. 17.
[3] *Samson*, p. 21.   [4] I Kings xvii. 4.   [5] *Jonas*, p. 47.
[6] Some examples have been given in Part II.
[7] *Samson*, p. 7; Judges xv. 4–5.

(We shall not be surprised to discover that, whereas in the Bible this stratagem is invented by Samson himself, in Coras it is inspired by the Holy Spirit in an antithetical discourse.) Such insistence on the virtues of the hero and the grandeur of the action is common. This straining after effect is no doubt to be considered as a baroque feature.

More often changes are made, consciously or not, in order to adapt the original version to current fashions and conventions or notions of aesthetic and moral propriety. One of the most powerful sets of literary conventions was that governing the conduct of a lover, and we have already seen how in the story of Jacob and Rachel Saint-Amant is driven to falsify the Bible rather than defy the convention.[1] Similarly, in the Bible the proposals of the elders to Susanna express desire without any suggestion of sentiment:

> Voici, les huis du iardin sont fermez, nul ne nous voit, et nous te desirons grandement. Parquoy consen à nous, et pren nostre compagnie.[2]

In Montchrestien (as also in the case of Coignard's Holofernes) this becomes a long declaration of love, full of Petrarchan conceits:

> Pardonne à tes vaincus qui demandent merci . . .
> Nous n'aimons rien que toy, prests à hair nous mesmes.[3]

Even a pious rhymer like Saint-Peres, with no literary pretensions, performs the same operation. Joseph's marriage is recorded in Genesis with the utmost simplicity:

> . . . and he gave him to wife Asenath the daughter of Poti-pherah priest of On . . . . And unto Joseph were born two sons before the years of famine came, which Asenath the daughter of Poti-pherah priest of On bare unto him.[4]

In the poem it becomes

> Aseneth, belle au corps, et plus belle en son ame,
> Conseruoit pour Ioseph en pureté sa flamme,
> Ne brusloit que pour luy, pour luy de jour en jour
> Augmentoit son honneur auecque son amour.
> Ils eurent deux enfans de leur chaste hymenée.[5]

---

[1] Cf. p. 91 above. [2] Dan. xiii. 20 (Geneva, 1568).
[3] *Susane*, p. 363. [4] Gen. xli. 45, 50. [5] *Joseph*, p. 18.

It cannot be said that the passage alters the substance of the Bible, but a unifying veil is spread over it, formed by such words as *flamme, brusloit, honneur, hymenée.* These terms are new, at least as rigid conventions. The effect is not, as in earlier poems, to present Biblical events in contemporary guise but to place them in an idealized poetic sphere.

In Jacob's seven years' service Morillon shows more respect for the original than Saint-Amant, since he tries to combine the Bible's swift passage of time with the sighs of a lover:

> Mais si les jours sont longs du côté de l'amour,
> Du côté du respect quand on les considere,
> Pour meriter RACHEL la peine en est legere.[1]

Morillon here attempts to satisfy both Biblical and contemporary conceptions of love by a finely drawn distinction. As usual such a compromise leads only to a diminution of poetic intensity.

Even more frequent are changes due to the failure of the Bible to conform to the standards of dignity befitting a heroic poem, the hero himself or his material surroundings.[2] In *Hélie* Naboth's vineyard is the object of a grandiose transformation:

> Da mihi vineam tuam, ut faciam mihi hortum olerum.[3]

> Il veut faire agrandir les Iardins du Palais,
> Faire de nouueaux plans, des terrasses nouuelles,
> Des parterres plus beaux, des fontaines plus belles.[4]

The poet, no doubt, could not imagine a king whose first pre-occupation was his kitchen garden.

When we pass from material objects to character, the same attitude is evident. In the Bible Susanna utters a cry and says her prayer aloud.[5] In Montchrestien's poem this becomes

> . . . Formoit dedans son cœur cette sainte priere.[6]

This silence was probably thought more in accordance with the dignity of the heroine and, more precisely, with the ethical principles of Stoicism, which were sufficient to outweigh the authority of the Bible. In the same way in Marie de Pech unheroic emotions, and especially tears, are suppressed or attenuated. Achior opposes invincible firmness to the rage of Holofernes.[7] We may

---

[1] *Joseph*, p. 5; Gen. xxix. 20; cf. p. 91 above.   [2] Cf. pp. 30 ff. above.
[3] III Kings xxi. 2 (Vulgate).   [4] *Hélie*, p. 138.
[5] Dan. xiii. 42, 43.   [6] *Susane*, p. 377.   [7] *Judith*, p. 17.

compare the picture of a weeping old man given by Coignard[1]
and Du Bartas.[2] It seems that Stoicism has continued to develop
during the course of the century, and with it the rigid codification
of the heroic ideal.

In a more general way the shortcomings of heroes are suppressed and replaced by more appropriate sentiments. Coras
usually avoids what might have been considered inconsistent
with epic dignity or the heroic qualities of the characters. Samson
gives himself up when the Jews promise not to kill him.[3] In
Coras he is indignant at the cowardly offer but is induced by a
prophet to accept.[4] In the Bible Joshua calls on Achan to confess
his crime, Achan confesses, and Joshua condemns him to death.[5]
In Coras Achan stubbornly refuses to confess.[6] The object of this
change seems to have been to show Achan in a still darker light
and at the same time to remove the suspicion of duplicity in
Joshua's conduct, though the effect is in reality to make the story
less convincing and the hero's character less firm. Unheroic
sentiments or actions are similarly corrected in Morillon. In the
Bible Jacob is very frightened when he hears that Esau is coming
to meet him heavily armed.[7] Morillon, like Saint-Amant,[8] shows
him full of courage and anxious only for the safety of his family:

> Il n'importe (dit-il) j'en ay plus de courage . . .
> Il ne craint rien pour luy, mais helas! il craint tout
> Pour Rachel et Joseph qu'il place à l'autre bout.[9]

Again like Saint-Amant[10] he feels that Jacob's way of increasing
his flock requires justification:

> Sa magie innocente, autant qu'elle est subtile,
> Au lieu de mille agneaux fait qu'il en a dix mille.[11]

If the poet had thought this magic perfectly innocent, he would
not have needed to lay stress on it. As so often, Biblical events are
transposed into a different scale of values.

Consistently with this ideal of dignity, much that seems crude,
barbarous, or obscene in the Bible is omitted or disguised. Marie
de Pech offers striking examples, since in her case feminine
modesty may be assumed to have reinforced the general movement

---

[1] *Judith*, p. 123.   [2] 1616 ed., p. 552; Holmes, ii. 41.
[3] Judges xv. 12.   [4] *Samson*, p. 37.   [5] Joshua vii. 18 ff.
[6] *Josué*, p. 66.   [7] Gen. xxxii. 7.   [8] *Œuvres*, ii. 280.
[9] *Joseph*, p. 22.   [10] Cf. p. 100 above.   [11] *Joseph*, p. 11.

of taste. So the burning of the crops is reduced to a pale reflection of the original narrative.[1] The savage passion of Holofernes is tamed and regulated in accordance with the reigning ideal of love. The orgy in the Assyrian camp is described only in its psychological effects: it may be compared with the corresponding passage of Gabrielle de Coignard's *Judith*, where physical coarseness is recorded without restraint.[2] Once again the contrast with the sixteenth-century poets is strongly marked.

The need to impose a new and alien dignity on primitive material is perhaps best illustrated by the example of Lesfargues, who furnishes instances of most of the types of deformation so far discussed and whose infidelities are all the more significant because no one strove harder than he to maintain literal fidelity. His genuine attempt to put the Bible before literary grace lends added interest to the transformations which occur even when he seems to be following the text step by step. He includes details, indecent by seventeenth-century standards, which were tactfully omitted by other poets, but he disguises them in a way which makes them utterly grotesque, like Saul entering the cave where David is hidden:

> Entre dans ce cachot d'vn pas precipité[3]

or David boasting of his victory:

> Par la rigueur d'vn Prince à qui du Philistin
> I'apportay triomphant le bizare butin.[4]

When Jesse sends to Saul the gift of an ass with bread, a bottle of wine, and a kid, Lesfargues chooses to speak in veiled terms:

> Vn don plus conuenable à sa condition,
> Qu'au magnifique esclat du Prince de Sion.[5]

He does not understand that Saul's magnificence was very limited. In the Bible Eliab taunts his brother David for coming to watch the battle.[6] Here it is for wishing to fight in spite of his youth.[7] This alteration is minute, but its effect is to exaggerate slightly the heroism of David. A sincere desire for exactitude has not prevented Lesfargues from trying to make the Bible more poetic.

---

[1] *Judith*, p. 27; Judith ii. 17.   [2] p. 147.
[3] *David*, p. 84. Cf. I Kings xxiv. 4 (Vulgate).
[4] *David*, p. 134. Cf. I Sam. xviii. 27.   [5] p. 15. Cf. I Sam. xvi. 20.
[6] I Sam. xvii. 28.   [7] p. 26.

Even more important than such changes, due largely to aesthetic causes, are those inspired by the need to rationalize what in the Bible is left unexplained and to find moral justification for actions which in the Bible never seem to require it. Thus in the Bible Joachim's reaction to the news of his wife's dishonour is not even mentioned. In Montchrestien he at once loses consciousness:

> D'vn si grand creue-cœur il se trouue surpris,
> Qu'il perd incontinent l'vsage des esprits.[1]

This fulfils a dual purpose: it answers a question which a modern (or at least a contemporary) reader was bound to ask, and it describes the situation of Joachim without giving him an active role which might disturb the sequence of the poem. Again, in the Bible the king of the Philistines refuses to let David fight against the Hebrews because of the distrust the nobles feel towards him,[2] but in Marie de Pech it is because of his integrity of character:

> Que lors qu'il vient donner la bataille aux Hebreux
> Il ne l'oblige point à combattre contre eux,
> Iugeant bien que son cœur estoit trop magnanime
> Pour souffrir seulement l'apparence du crime.[3]

The subtlety of this explanation reveals the difficulties of all the Biblical poets. Marie de Pech regards as treason David's willingness to take up arms against his own people and so she reverses the sense of the Bible. At the same time she keeps some respect for the text by referring to the appearance of crime.

Lesfargues again shows these tendencies in a particularly obvious form, because he seems to make the changes almost automatically. Everything must be explained rationally, even when the Bible leaves the meaning implicit in a simple statement. David's remorse for having cut Saul's coat is due to a mysterious reverence for the anointed king.[4] Lesfargues introduces irrelevant juridical considerations:

> Qu'vne honte secrette et qu'vn iuste regret
> Condamne sans excuse vn larcin indiscret.[5]

In the Bible it does not matter whether David's regret is just or not, and *larcin indiscret* is grossly inadequate as an expression of the emotions contained in the passage. Like Saint-Amant with

---

[1] *Susane*, p. 372. [2] I Sam. xxix. [3] *Judith*, p. 114.
[4] I Sam. xxiv. 6. [5] *David*, p. 84.

Jacob and Laban,[1] Lesfargues attempts to imprison the relation-ship between Saul and David, and later between David and Absalom, in the framework of a narrow rationalism. Each act is explained, but the motives are contradictory and trivial. The beauty of the Bible, where nothing is explained, its mysterious alternation of love and hate, passes by unnoticed. With this rationalism goes the need for moral justification, which often leads to serious inconsistencies. In the Bible[2] David's war against the Amalekites is inspired only by the desire for pillage, in Les-fargues it is directed against

> Cét ennemy commun dont le Ciel irrité
> A condamné le crime et la posterité.[3]

After the stern condemnation of adultery, Bathsheba's child is described as

> . . . l'aymable fruict de la sainte caresse.[4]

Such latent discrepancies are resolved in the Bible because events are regarded as the expression of the Divine Will, not as problems in human morality.

The intrusion of seventeenth-century ideas is seen more parti-cularly in the conception of humanity. The words *humain* and *barbare* are employed constantly to record praise or blame, though they bear little relation to Biblical realism. It is difficult to see more than cowardly prudence in Saul's plot to have David killed by the Philistines rather than commit the crime himself:

> Let not mine hand be upon him, but let the hand of the Philistines be upon him.[5]

Lesfargues detects noble motives even in this faithless heart:

> Il vaut mieux, dit Saül dans son cœur infidelle,
> Qu'il meure soustenant vne iuste querelle,
> Que d'vn coup qui n'eust rien de noble ny d'humain
> Le voir cheoir par mon ordre, ou perir de ma main.[6]

All the characters strike such attitudes, equally remote from the Bible and from contemporary reality (though not from the con-temporary heroic ideal).

It is interesting to observe the formation of a special vocabulary

---

[1] Cf. p. 91 above.   [2] I Sam. xxvii. 8, 9.   [3] *David*, p. 100.
[4] p. 176.   [5] I Sam. xviii. 17.   [6] p. 50.

and even a particular figure of speech to deal with situations of this sort. In Saint-Amant's *Moyse sauvé* Jacob's trick on Esau is disguised with simpering approval:

> Qu'enfin, par les ressorts d'une *douce imposture*,
> Il se vit confirmer la primogeniture.[1]
>
> Sa moitié, s'avisant d'une *agreable ruse*
> Qui portoit avec soy sa legitime excuse . . . .[2]

Coras treats Rahab's lie to the soldiers and Samuel's lie to Saul in exactly the same way. He evidently wishes to follow the text of the Bible as closely as possible, but he is not quite happy and feels the need for justification:

> A peine de Rahab l'*artifice innocent*[3]
>
> Va, répond l'Eternel, et d'vn *saint artifice*,
> Dy que dans Bethléem j'attens ton sacrifice.[4]

In the Bible all these acts are good because they are in accordance with the Divine Will, but in each of the four cases our poets try to suggest that they are good in themselves. In each case their uncertainty is conveyed by oxymoron, a figure which in its condensed violence is perhaps especially characteristic of baroque poetry. In this case we may conjecture that it expresses in microcosm the fundamental contradiction inherent in the efforts of the Biblical poets and furnishes one explanation of their failure.

We have examined in detail the treatment of the Bible in these poems and the results tend to confirm the impression that there was a fundamental incompatibility between the spirit of the century and the Hebrew Scriptures. This may perhaps be considered as a reflection of the contrast between the 'literary' and the 'primitive' epic, since Homer was misunderstood in much the same way. The deformations of the Bible are of two kinds—material and moral. The simple grandeur of Jewish history is overlaid with magnificence, Greco-Roman or French or more often timeless. Shepherds become princes, Ahab's kitchen garden is transformed into an imitation (or, more accurately, prefiguration) of Versailles, rigid class distinctions replace the easy familiarity of the tribes and their leaders. Sometimes the process is

---

[1] *Œuvres*, ii. 171. [2] Ib. ii. 172.
[3] *Josué*, p. 12. [4] *David*, p. 35.

merely one of suppression—details which clash with modern ideas of royal or heroic dignity are omitted. Even the poets who adhere most closely to the text make these changes almost automatically.

At the same time they try at every step to reconcile Biblical violence with modern ethics. The moralizing tendency is everywhere apparent (and it is in no way opposed to the desire to give pleasure, since it eliminates or disguises the features which were likely to offend the fastidious reader). In the Bible Jacob's trick on Laban, the Jews' pillage of the Egyptians, Samson's burning of the Philistine corn seem to spring from greed or desire for revenge (through which a divine purpose is fulfilled). In the many similar cases we have observed in the poems, some justification in terms of human morality is nearly always found. Sometimes the object is to preserve the hero's dignity, to conform to a code of literary or social propriety, but more often it is in deference to ideas of humanity and charity. It may be said that the morality of these poems is profoundly Christian and that this serves to account at least partly for the failure to understand the Old Testament. Of course this is not the Christianity of Calvin (we have seen how much closer the sixteenth-century poets came to the heart of the original text) but rather that of the Jesuit casuists.

With this moral bias goes naturally enough the absence of mystical experience, the sense of awe which pervades the earlier books of the Old Testament, Jacob at Bethel or Moses on Sinai. This is partly accounted for by the limitations of epic form, since direct religious emotion is difficult to express except in lyrical effusion. It may be attributed also to deficiency in the poetic gifts which are needed to render this kind of experience: however, even attempts to do so are rare. On the whole, the religious life of seventeenth-century France seems to have assumed a moral rather than a mystical aspect—the Jansenists, the Jesuits, the Oratory, with their emphasis on education, rather than the Carmelites or Quietists, represent the main current. In literature the importance of allegory, itself to some extent a consequence of ecclesiastical pressure, and the theories of Le Bossu with their insistence on moral significance exemplify the same attitude. In this respect the Biblical epic is at one with the broad movement of contemporary feeling.

In the technical methods by which these changes in the Bible are accomplished we have noticed the difference between the internal expansion of the earlier poets, the enlargement of each verse in harmony with its meaning, and the external expansion based on the addition of extraneous material. The latter is certainly better adapted to the nature of epic, but it reveals a less intimate comprehension of the Biblical text. Closely connected with it is the emphasis with which the seventeenth-century poets heighten the simple effects of their model. Again the Bible is in a way deformed, although the poet merely makes explicit what is already latent in the original. Finally, the frequent appearance of oxymoron reflects and concentrates the ever-present contradiction between the poet's own aesthetic or moral standards and the situations he found in the source which he regarded as sacred.

CHAPTER XIII

The *Merveilleux*

THE character and indeed the primary inspiration of the Biblical epic are closely bound up with the great debate over the true sources of the supernatural or magical element in modern literature.[1] The conflict between *merveilleux chrétien* and *merveilleux païen* may well be interpreted not as an academic squabble but as the confrontation of two historical systems or even two conceptions of man and the universe: on the one hand the Christianity of the Middle Ages and the Counter-Reformation, identifying aesthetic satisfaction with transcendental truth; on the other anthropocentric humanism, looking backward to antiquity for permanent canons of terrestrial beauty. Since the Biblical poets are *ex hypothesi* in the Christian camp, we should not expect to be concerned here with more than one side of the controversy. This is, however, a simplification. In fact, examples of recourse to the pagan supernatural are very numerous, though as a rule they do not amount to much more than superficial decoration. More serious, the Christian supernatural (which for convenience of analysis may be divided into (i) Old Testament or Jewish; (ii) New Testament or traditionally Christian; (iii) medieval and popular; (iv) allegorical or ill defined, sometimes known as the *merveilleux mixte*[2]) is itself usually transformed by a like process to that which we have observed at work in the treatment of the Biblical text. That is to say, a Christian wonder, derived from one of the four sources, is presented in a distorted form which accentuates every possible parallel with similar cases in the literature of antiquity. It is thus, so to speak, classicized. A study of the different categories as they appear in the poems may serve to clarify and corroborate this assertion, though the interpenetration of these categories makes any rigid distinctions untrustworthy.

In the simplest cases the *merveilleux païen* may be no more than a matter of vocabulary, for example the substitution of a classical

---

[1] See Ch. II above; also Delaporte, *Du Merveilleux*; Gillot, *Querelle*; Marni, *Allegory*. [2] Delaporte, *Du Merveilleux*, pp. 129 ff.

deity for the element or natural phenomenon he represents—
Neptune for the sea, or Ceres for crops. The sterner poets reject
these substitutions: Coras specifically condemns the metaphorical
use of pagan deities.[1] The majority, however, admit them, often
on the authority of the pillage theory. Saint-Amant's defence is
characteristic of the less rigorous attitude:

> Car, pour ce qui est des noms fabuleux dont je me suis servy,
> comme de l'Olimpe au lieu du Ciel, de l'Herebe ou de l'Averne au
> lieu de l'Enfer, . . . de Cerés ou de Cybele au lieu de la Terre, de Nep-
> tune ou de Thetis au lieu de la Mer . . . ce n'est que pour rendre les
> choses plus poetiques, et encore n'alleguay-je jamais aucune fable
> qu'avec precaution.[2]

However, this excuse, the greater poetic quality of the classical
names, gives up the centre of the Christian position. It is true that
there can be no harm in such a use of names alone. But the final
effect is the creation of a classical atmosphere which is in conflict (at least from a religious point of view) with the Christian
or Biblical atmosphere. When Heaven is called Olympus a number of associations are evoked which radically alter the visual
image formed by the reader.

How this happens can be illustrated from Montchrestien.
Susanna's garden—

> Ce lieu hanté de tous apres le chaud du iour,
> Delices du Printemps de Zephyre et d'Amour,
> Et ceint des moites bras de l'ondoyant Euphrate[3]—

could be disapproved only by the sternest partisans of Christian
poetry. None the less, Biblical Mesopotamia has been transformed
by a glimpse of something like Botticelli's 'Primavera'. Montchrestien uses such expressions far more freely than later poets.
However, few poems lack them completely. In spite of Coras's
condemnation, we find occasionally in his work verbal substitutions like *Auerne, Zephyre, Halcyons*.

The transformation is perhaps more profound still in the case
of allusions without the name of the classical deity, for then the
classical element is not merely a superficial metaphor, a substitute,

---

[1] *Jonas*, preface, p. 10 (2nd ed.). On the other hand, in the epistle to Turenne,
which precedes the first edition, he says: 'Il ne nous doit pas estre défendu d'enrichir
la Montagne de Sion des dépoüilles du Parnasse.' It seems, therefore, that his views
became more rigid during the course of his conversion.

[2] *Œuvres*, ii. 141.   [3] *Susane*, p. 342.

but has entered directly into the thought. An example is Saint-Amant's reference to the Parcae:

> Au lieu de voir couper sa jeune et chere trame.[1]

It shows a mind accustomed to think in classical terms or at least to follow those who did so.

This is not, however, the limit of the *merveilleux païen*. The gods of antiquity are sometimes, especially in the early years of the century, introduced not as symbols but as real beings. Even a Protestant like Gamon does this, though there is a difference between him and those who may be called the literary poets. It is not so much that he shows more respect for the Bible but that he has less feeling for the spirit of antiquity, as may be seen in the heavy pedantry of

> La belle Thaumantide, au jour encor absent
> N'ouuroit de ses longs doys son portail jaunissant,
> Ny du beau Cynthien la torche vagabonde
> Ne faizoit voir encor sa clairté, ny le Monde.[2]

Mythological figures are found in profusion: generally Gamon, as here, makes not one allusion but several. Later poets were less learned and exercised a stricter choice. The Pléiade, though superficially their method was the same as Gamon's, were imbued with a genuine paganism which enabled them to transform this ponderous material into lightness and gaiety. Gamon's attitude was primarily that of the lesser Humanists for whom the classics of antiquity were a repository of knowledge rather than a source of inspiration.

His Catholic contemporary, Anne d'Urfé, goes much farther. He begins *Susanne* with the machinations of Love:

> Amour, fils de Venus, armé d'arc et de traicts.[3]

This *Amour* is no mythological abstraction but a living child, Cupid himself:

> Passant pour tel sujet vn iour sous la fenestre
> Où ces Iuges estoient, Amour ce petit traistre . . .[4]

His attacks on the elders, his arrows and the wounds they inflict are treated as physical realities.[5] Susanna herself is compared to Diana,[6] a parallel which throws some light on the iconographical

---

[1] *Œuvres*, ii. 151.   [2] *Semaine*, p. 7.   [3] *Hymnes*, p. 186.
[4] Ib., p. 191.   [5] Ib., p. 192.   [6] Ib., p. 205.

development of the story and suggests a contributory cause of its popularity. We may compare Montchrestien's sub-title *Susane ou la Chasteté*. Elsewhere Susanna appears like Venus escorted by a troop of Amours:

> Car il ne faut douter que la belle Cyprine
> Sortant tout de nouueau de sa conque marine,
> N'auoit tant de beautez et d'attraictz gracieux
> Que cette belle Nymphe en logeoit dans ses yeux.
>   Les Amours la suiuoient en fretillant de l'aisle
> Comme les Passereaux suiuans vne pucelle.[1]

The Biblical Susanna is quite lost in this picture of Venus Anadyomene. The rest of Olympus occupies the scene almost as often. Thus in a few lines Susanna's charms are declared sufficient to rob Jupiter of his thunder, Neptune of his trident, Cupid of his bow, Saturn of his scythe, Mars of his armour, Vulcan of his hammer, and Pluto of his sceptre.[2] These are a few examples only of the use of classical mythology in d'Urfé's *Susanne*: in fact such allusions occur on every page. In *Judic* they are less obtrusive, though they play a large part.

Anne d'Urfé was still writing under the direct inspiration of the Pléiade,[3] and we shall not expect to find such shameless paganism in later poets, though the Ronsardian influence can be traced as late as 1648, in the *Joseph* of Saint-Peres:

> Dauanture Morphée assoupit d'vn sommeil
> Composé de Pauots, de laict, de vin vermeil,
> Le grand Roy Pharaon.[4]

Even in Saint-Amant's celebrated picture of Noon, Ceres is more than a metaphor:

> La bruyante cygale, au milieu des guerets,
> Saluoit le midy de la part de Cerès,
> Qui, joyeuse de voir sous la chaleur feconde
> Briller en ondoyant l'or de sa teste blonde,
> Montroit que dans la terre elle sentoit encor
> Cette mesme vertu travailler à d'autre or.[5]

There is here more than a veneer of classicism, the pagan earth-worship is deeply felt.

---

[1] Ib., p. 193.   [2] Ib., p. 213.   [3] Cf. p. 72 above.
[4] *Joseph*, p. 14.   [5] *Œuvres*, ii. 229–30.

It is true that Saint-Amant commits none of the gross anachronisms of d'Urfé or Saint-Peres. None the less the poem is charged with the direct and positive influence of the ancient gods and those who believed in them. Moreover, their use demolishes the main foundation of faith in Christian epic, the idea that Christianity is superior to paganism as a source of poetic delight.

We have seen that Desmarets considers mythological allusions permissible if they are put in the mouth of a pagan.[1] Coras, in spite of his attack on the *merveilleux païen*, also makes this concession,[2] and the loophole it affords is freely exploited, especially by later poets. So Marie de Pech, in the miracle of Joshua, gives the sun an active role and the whole passage assumes a Greek dress:

> A ces cris le Soleil redoublant sa lumiere,
> Remonte tout brillant au haut de sa carriere,
> Et trompant de Thetis l'attente et le desir,
> Vient combler Iosué de gloire et de plaisir.[3]

The miracle has become an arrangement between Joshua and the sun: Jehovah is scarcely mentioned. The advance of Holofernes frightens Neptune himself:

> Il fait trembler le Dieu qui produit les tempestes,
> Neptune s'épouuante et craint que Jupiter
> Vient encore vne fois son Trident disputer.[4]

This goes beyond a figurative expression for the sea. However, both these allusions occur in Achior's recital, that is, in the mouth of a pagan, so that appearances are saved. Coras cannot resist the device in *Jonas* in spite of the historical inaccuracy involved in the attribution of Greek beliefs to the Ninevites: the son of the king's mistress is disguised as Cupid[5] and the pilot of Jonah's ship appeals to Jupiter.[6] Desmarets himself makes freer use of mythology than any poet since Anne d'Urfé, mainly by the same means. The role of Apollo with his oracles and priestesses in Book I of *Esther* is similarly an historical error, since the poem is set in Persia (though Desmarets may have identified Apollo with Mithras). Desmarets turns them into demons and appendages of the Christian Hell, but he seems occasionally to regard them as mere figments of the imagination. In any case the interesting question is why he introduced the gods unnecessarily, even in defiance of

[1] p. 15 above.   [2] *Jonas*, p. 10.   [3] *Judith*, p. 15.
[4] Ib., p. 26.   [5] *Jonas*, p. 139.   [6] Ib., p. 81.

local truth. The reason must be that he believed firmly in their poetic reality.

There was another and still wider loophole. The passage quoted from Saint-Amant's Preface[1] ends: 'et encore n'alleguay-je jamais aucune fable qu'avec precaution'. *Precaution* might be taken for a vague prudence: in fact it refers specifically to a conventional method of introducing mythological allusions, the beginnings of which we have already noticed in Du Bartas.[2] The allusion is accompanied by a qualification which shows that the poet is aware of its falsity and in this way he hopes to render it innocuous. It is interesting to observe the formation of a conventional system of such precautions. Gamon often describes God as *veritable Iupin*, the true as opposed to the false Jupiter. Anne d'Urfé concludes his catalogue of Susanna's charms[3] with a belated reservation:

> Si les Dieux estoient vrais que chantent les Poëtes.

In his case it seems little more than an empty formula. Later poets generally use the words *feint*, *faux*, or *fabuleux*, as in Saint-Amant's Memphis:

> Ses temples où la noire et fausse deïté
> Attiroit des mortels la vaine pieté.[4]

Pierre de Saint-Louis compares the horses drawing Elijah's chariot to the stags

> Que la métamorphose et la fable profane
> Feignent être attelés au coche de Diane.[5]

Even the fundamentalist Lesfargues employs the same method in order to introduce Hercules:

> Mais, ô spectacle affreux! sa luisante salade
> Du fabuleux Alcide ou du feint Encelade,
> Eust accablé la teste . . . ,[6]

though in his poem such cases are rare. This use of words implying falsehood and illusion, producing at the same time a positive effect (since the image of the false deity is unmistakably evoked) and a negative effect (since it is erased or at least attenuated by the suggestion of falsehood), may be thought to correspond to the oxymoron which reflects a similar conflict in the handling of

[1] p. 163 above.   [2] p. 43 above.   [3] p. 165 above.
[4] *Œuvres*, ii. 153.   [5] *Éliade*, p. 42.   [6] *David*, p. 17.

Biblical material.[1] Again it is probably allied to the technique
of illusion which plays a prominent part in baroque architecture
and painting.

To what absurd lengths these precautions could be carried may
be seen in some special cases. Desmarets apologizes even for the
conventional and fossilized *hyménée*, giving a fanciful explanation:

> Par les Assyriens, et d'un mot confirmé,
> Le nœu du mariage estoit ainsi nommé.[2]

He shows infinite resource in the use of these precautions, that
is to say in the evasion of his own principles. An extreme example
occurs in Coras:

> Et si du faux Neptune, en ses bords éperdu,
> Ils seurent trauerser l'empire prétendu . . .[3]

Not only is the poetic force of Neptune largely dissipated (the
usual consequence of the convention) but the impression is given
that the sea they crossed did not exist at all. However, a certain
pleasure can be derived from the very complexity of the contradictions involved, as in a case from Morillon, where the invocation
of the Saviour is preceded by a rejection of the Muses:

> Eloignez-vous de moy fabuleuses beautez,
> Dont la Gréce jadis forma des Déitez.
> Muses, phantômes vains que l'erreur a fait naistre . . . .[4]

The poet cannot resist the temptation to introduce the Muses
whom he professes to scorn. The invocation, in effect double,
though one half is negative, presents a striking example of the
fascination exercised by the classical world on the Christian poets.

The various forms of Christian *merveilleux* must be considered
against this background of pagan antiquity. In some cases—the
least numerous—the wonders furnished by the Old Testament are
used directly and without alteration (apart from the general
stylistic transformation discussed in Chapter XII). So Saint-Amant
recounts the miraculous incidents of the Book of Exodus, the
changing of Moses' rod into a serpent, the Plagues of Egypt, the
crossing of the Red Sea, Aaron's rod. In these cases he follows
the Bible fairly closely and owes little or nothing to classical mytho-

---

[1] Cf. p. 159 above.   [2] *Esther* (1673), p. 62.
[3] *Josué*, p. 36.   [4] *Joseph*, p. 2.

logy. The Witch of Endor and the raising of Samuel are naturally
included by the David poets, Sainte-Garde, Lesfargues, and Coras.
However, they make little of the episode, apart from the trappings
of conventional horror. Sainte-Garde reduces the witch's charms
and incantations to the colourless

> Elle prononce bas mille noms inconnus[1]

and Lesfargues is equally vague:

> Dans son tremblant gozier roule d'horribles mots,
> Qui ne sont entendus que dans les noirs cachots.[2]

Lesfargues himself treats witchcraft with scepticism. Saul, he
says, had

> Chassé tous ces Deuins de qui les impostures
> Se meslent d'éclaircir les veritez futures.[3]

The general attitude had changed fundamentally since the time of
Du Bartas, who, in the corresponding passage, expresses fervent
belief.[4] The demons who torment Saul[5] are strictly confined to
what is found in the Bible, and this fidelity is characteristic of the
fundamentalist poets.

More adventurous writers invent miracles on the model of
genuine Biblical miracles. So in Morillon Joseph is commanded
by a voice in a dream to marry Aseneth.[6] In Coras Jesse's house
is encircled by a halo of light,[7] the hills of Ephraim bow their
heads in fear and respect.[8]

Saint-Amant's treatment of Jacob's ladder is a case by itself,
though the process involved is that observed generally in Chapter
XII, the transformation of simplicity into magnificence. In the
Bible (Gen. xxviii. 12) there is no more than the fact that Jacob
saw a ladder, with angels ascending and descending. Saint-Amant
decorates it with jewels:

> L'or, la perle, l'azur, toute la terre entiere,
> N'avoit rien que d'abjet au prix de sa matiere,
> Et toutesfois son œil creut voir en ce tresor,
> Ensemble confondus, l'azur, la perle et l'or.[9]

[1] *Saül puni*, p. 6. [2] *David*, p. 104. [3] Ib., p. 102.
[4] Holmes, iii. 354. [5] *David* (Lesfargues), pp. 13, 47.
[6] *Joseph*, p. 108. Cf. Gen. xli. 45. [7] *David*, p. 9.
[8] Ib., p. 28. [9] *Œuvres*, ii. 178.

Both this magnificence itself (which is neither Biblical nor classical) and the importance attached to the miracle of the ladder show the workings of the baroque imagination.[1] Marino's Palace of Love presents, on a larger scale, a similar decoration of precious stones and precious metals.[2]

There are other cases where the source is impossible to determine or where we must assume that Biblical and classical reminiscence are completely fused. In Montchrestien the thunder and lightning which signify the wrath of God at the unjust trial[3] suggest Jupiter as much as Jehovah. In Saint-Amant the dream of Jocabel certainly owes much to the Biblical dream. It is true that the latter is usually the vehicle of a divine message rather than of prophecy, but there are examples of prophetic dreams, like those interpreted by Joseph. On the other hand, the sustained prophetic vision belongs to the classical epic (the revelations of Anchises to Aeneas in the underworld, for example). The warning dream can also be found there (Hector's apparition before Aeneas). The comet which guides Amram and Jocabel to the chosen hiding-place was no doubt primarily inspired by the star of the Magi, but the description of the comet itself follows classical convention. Such coincidences of form between Christian miracles and classical mythology strengthen the case of those who believed that the former were suitable material for epic, and again they show to what extent Christianity in the poems with which we are dealing was impregnated with classical reminiscence and parallelism.

The second and principal source of the Christian *merveilleux* was the mass of beliefs which, though founded on the Bible, had been developed and enriched by the theologians or by ecclesiastical tradition. The most important for the epic were those which concerned angels and demons, the powers of Heaven and the powers of Hell. The importance attached to them is again simply explained: they correspond to the conflicting forces of gods and goddesses in classical epic.

Angels perform many roles. They may be the comforters and supporters of heroes in peril from earthly or infernal foes. In the *Moyse sauvé* the beasts and insects which, inspired by demons, attack the precious cradle are driven off with the help of unseen

---

[1] Cf. p. 245 below.
[2] Cf. Mango, *Le Fonti dell'Adone*, pp. 72 ff.   [3] *Susane*, p. 378.

allies.[1] In Coras, while Satan helps Goliath, Michael flies round David:[2] two fights are in progress at the same time, one on the terrestrial, one on the celestial plane. In Desmarets a mysterious figure comes to the aid of Mardochée, Pharnabas, and Iasbel attacked by Thares and Bagathan.[3] He is obviously a hybrid of Homeric deity and Biblical angel.

The messenger angel, Gabriel–Mercury, shows a similar duality of origin, one case of which has already been examined.[4] In Desmarets's *Esther* an angel is sent to reveal the plot to Mardochée (with no Biblical justification, of course). Marie de Pech (like Tortoletti) makes Judith receive her inspiration from an angel instead of directly from God, as in the Bible. This provides the opportunity for a complete episode, in which the physical appearance of the angel is described with unusual precision. Like Ronsard's Mercury, he receives the divine command and prepares for his journey from Heaven: his attributes, which do not belong to his celestial essence, are assumed in order to make his splendour visible:

> Au sortir de l'Olympe il emprunte vn beau corps
> De tout ce que les Cieux ont de riches tresors,
> Du plus pur du Soleil sa cheuelure est faite,
> D'vn rayon lumineux il couronne sa teste,
> Ses yeux sont d'vn azur subtil et delicat,
> Et son teint de l'aurore a le bel incarnat,
> Son front plus blanc que neige, et plus poli qu'yuoire,
> Esclate de grandeur, de pudeur et de gloire,
> Son port noble et Diuin est plein de Maiesté,
> Et tous ses traicts font voir son immortalité,
> Sa tunique à fonds d'or est de fleurs bigarrées,
> Qui donnent de l'éclat à ses aisles dorées.
> Vne riche ceinture en serre les beaux plis,
> Faite de Diamans, de Perles, de Rubis.[5]

It will be noted that nothing here (in strong contrast to Ronsard and his contemporaries) is concrete or individual. Even the tunic and the belt remain vague; the repetition of gold, the diamonds, pearls, and rubies are the ingredients of a stock recipe for magnificence. This lack of particular qualities is, however, exactly suited to a being who surpasses the individual imperfections of

---

[1] Saint-Amant, *Œuvres*, ii. 256. [2] *David*, p. 101.
[3] *Esther* (1673), p. 58. [4] p. 85 above. [5] *Judith*, p. 88.

humanity. And celestial splendour is to some extent achieved. The sun and the sky have been captured in the hair and eyes of the angel. The unimaginable has become accessible to the senses. This is due to the use of a common store of images[1] rather than to the individual talent of the poetess. We have here something like an angel from a baroque painting.

The angelic flight is found most often in the appearances of the messenger angel. We have examined the origins and early development of this conventional descriptive set-piece.[2] It recurs with great regularity in the poems and here one or two examples will suffice. The descent of Marie de Pech's angel may serve to typify a score of others:

> Dans les plaines de l'air il se trace vne voye . . .
> Dans cette pompe auguste il fond en Bethulie.[3]

A similar scene occurs in no less than three of Coras's poems.[4] Montchrestien varies the convention slightly by describing the upward instead of the downward flight:

> La Déesse aparue, ainsi comme l'esclair,
> Qui trauerse la vague en vn si prompt espace,
> Que l'œil humain en perd et la veuë et la trace.[5]

(The *Déesse* is the allegorical figure of Truth and so not strictly an angel, but there is no formal difference.) In such cases the Christian angel behaves like Mercury or Iris.

Angels may perform other functions which in classical epic are assigned to the gods. In Coras the angel who foretells the history of France by means of celestial portraits[6] occupies a position like that of the Sibyl in the *Aeneid*. In the same poem we are told that an angel has forged Goliath's armour,[7] an obvious echo of Homer.

---

[1] A contributory source may be sought in Tasso:

> Tra giovane e fanciullo età confine
> Prese, ed ornò di raggi il biondo crine.
> Ali bianche vestì, c'han d'or le cime,
> Infaticabilmente agili e preste (*Gerusalemme Liberata*, i, stanzas 13–14).

But the picture is amplified and more richly adorned. For similar descriptions in Godeau and Scudéry, see Delaporte, *Du Merveilleux*, pp. 249–50. A close parallel is presented by the description of Gabriel in Cowley's *Davideis* (*Poems*, ed. Waller, Cambridge, 1905, p. 304).

[2] See Ch. IV above.   [3] *Judith*, p. 88.

[4] *David*, p. 47; *Samson*, p. 45; *Jonas*, p. 54.   [5] *Susane*, p. 387.

[6] *David*, p. 134.   [7] Ib., p. 86.

They are often substitutes for the Muses, for example in Marie de Pech:

> Ainsi s'en va Iudith, suiuons là, chere Muse,
> Guide moy sur ses pas dans l'ombre tenebreuse,
> Ou plustost inuoquons l'Ange qui la conduit
> Afin qu'il daigne encor éclairer qui la suit.[1]

Here the interest lies in the separation of muse and angel. Instead of merging in a composite figure, part Christian, part classical, the two elements are dissociated and the double image is clearly visible.

So far these types of angel are Biblical or classical, or both in combination. Others seem to be of more recent origin and to belong to the Counter-Reformation or more specifically to the world of the baroque imagination. We have already seen something of the origins of the belief in a guardian angel and his earlier appearances in literature.[2] There are two guardian angels in the *Moyse sauvé*. One is attached to the poet and inspires his work:

> Ange particulier, fidelle et saint Genie
> Qui du luth que je touche animes l'harmonie,
> Qui releves ma muse et fais que son ardeur
> Aux plus humbles objets donne quelque grandeur.[3]

This is once more the angel-muse, but with a difference from the case just discussed. There is neither fusion nor dissociation of Christian and classical. Angel and muse are regarded as equally existing, but the Christian angel is a superior being, dominating the classical muse. This strange situation may have some bearing on the nature of baroque poetry. Moses also has an *ange tutelere* who protects him from evil.[4] In Marie de Pech the angel who descends to spare Isaac becomes an *ange tutelaire*,[5] perhaps under the influence of Saint-Amant.

Yet another angel in the *Moyse* is employed to gather the tears of Jocabel in a golden vase:

> . . . l'ange qui s'employe à recueillir nos pleurs
> Quand un juste sujet rend leur cours legitime . . .
> Dans un beau vase d'or ses larmes ramassa.[6]

Later the angel kneeling presents the vase to God. There is here

---

[1] *Judith*, p. 92.
[2] Cf. pp. 32, 52 above.
[3] Saint-Amant, *Œuvres*, ii. 192.
[4] Ib. ii. 231.
[5] *Judith*, p. 81.
[6] *Œuvres*, ii. 235.

a striking mixture of emotion (almost of sentimentality) and magnificence. The scene may well be due to Saint-Amant's own exuberant imagination, but in any case it is in harmony with the general tendencies of the period, with Marino in particular. Moreover, although the physical description is probably literary, the collection of tears by an angel has theological justification.[1]

The Devil and his forces also show traces of mixed origins. The elders in Montchrestien invoke the assistance of a *grand Demon des amours* who is clearly Cupid in a Biblical disguise.[2] In Coras the minions of Hell are often derived from the Bible. Dagon, the god of the Philistines, is presented not as a figment of the imagination but as a demon inspiring Delilah and adding to her beauty.[3] As in the case of Desmarets's Apollo we are here dealing with the tradition that the pagan gods were, so to speak, Christian demons.[4] Saul's madness, brought about by a demon, is described at length :[5] here a Biblical victim of possession by an evil spirit is combined with a classical prey of the Furies. The attempt of the demons to save doomed Jericho[6] seems to have been inspired solely by the example of Troy. The use of these infernal figures shows no diversity and they never inspire real horror. Satan himself is a personification of the forces of evil, who never assumes any individual qualities. Moreover, supernatural intervention is often wasted on trivial objects. Saul's envy of David is inspired by a demon,[7] which destroys the human and psychological interest of the passage with no compensating miraculous effect.

Desmarets's *Esther* begins with Lucifer's plans for the destruction of the Jews. His physical attributes are not described, but his presence seems more real for Desmarets than for other poets, as when he arrives at the palace gate :

> Il quitte les Enfers d'vn vol précipité.
> Pendant la nuit tranquille il arrive au portique
> Qui du palais d'Aman rend l'abord magnifique.[8]

The poem is thus presented as a conflict between Heaven and Hell and the theme is taken up at intervals throughout. But on his way to instruct Aman in the part he is to play, Lucifer meets the Arch-

---

[1] Cf. Bossuet, *Sermons*, Paris, Garnier, 1872, i. 567; also Delaporte, *Du Merveilleux*, p. 248.

[2] *Susane*, p. 359.

[3] *Samson*, pp. 44, 55.

[4] Cf. p. 15 above.   [5] *David*, p. 69.   [6] *Josué*, p. 50.

[7] *David*, p. 110; cf. I Sam. xviii. 8–9.   [8] p. 21.

angel Michael, who tells him that he may incite Aman and Artaxerxes
to persecute the Jews but forbids him to reveal Esther's race. He
has to submit in spite of his fury:

> Hé bien, faisons, dit-il, ce qui nous est permis.[1]

Another fundamental weakness of the Christian position is now
apparent. In the classical epic the struggle between the gods was
waged on equal terms. Here the conflict is illusory, since one
camp can only operate within the limits set by the other. Theological appearances are saved at the expense of poetic effect.

Saint-Amant makes perhaps the most extensive and varied use
of this infernal *merveilleux*. Satan himself generally remains in the
background. Once, however, he appears in person, when the
Commandments are delivered to Moses:

> Le superbe demon qui, parmy les supplices,
> Voit fremir et hurler ses enormes complices,
> Croit dejà voir le temps où, surchargé de fers,
> Il sera pour tousjours lié dans les enfers.[2]

The Satan who is a direct enemy of God is hardly to be found in
the Old Testament, and certainly the idea of his ultimate defeat and
binding is essentially Christian.

His minions, on the other hand, appear constantly as instruments of his attacks on Moses and the cradle. The angels, we have
seen, intervene to protect them, so that each struggle is conducted
on three planes: between men or animals (for example, Merary and
Elisaph against the hornets[3]); between the moral forces which they
represent allegorically; and between supernatural beings. Once
again the demons are simply the gods of classical epic translated
into Christian terms.

A particular form of the classical-Christian *merveilleux* appears
in the Homeric council of the gods. In Anne d'Urfé it is the
infernal council presided over by Satan;[4] in Coras a council of
the Trinity.[5]

The Messianic prophecy, found in many poems, shows how the
perspective of the Old Testament may be altered by knowledge of
the New. Pierre de Saint-Louis presents a variant of it in the relation, constantly emphasized, between the life of Elijah and the

---

[1] p. 22.   [2] *Œuvres*, ii. 225.   [3] Ib. ii. 253 ff.
[4] *Judic*, fo. 149v⁰. It has been analysed by Ronzy (*L'Italie classique et moderne*,
No. 1). Cf. also Delaporte, *Du Merveilleux*, p. 265.   [5] *David*, p. 2.

history of the Carmelite Order. So Elijah on Mount Carmel erects an altar to the Virgin.[1] However, it is the *Moyse sauvé* which is richest in such references. Thus God's final words to Jacob at Bethel:

> ... et qu'en toy soyent benis
> De tout le rond mortel les peuples infinis[2]

were for Saint-Amant a reference to the coming of Jesus. Very similar but more explicit is the prophecy of the Divine Voice which speaks to Jacob after the deception of the marriage-feast.[3] In this case, however, there is no Biblical justification for the prophecy. Saint-Amant has used the typically Jewish elements of the story, the rivalry between the sisters and the right of primogeniture in marriage, and has put them at the service of Christian ideas. In the same way he uses an allegorical invention, the vulture which seizes a lamb, to put a prophecy in the mouth of Marie (suggested no doubt by the fact that she afterwards becomes a prophetess).[4] Saint-Amant was certainly influenced in the introduction of these prophecies by their conformity with classical epic, with its sibyls, oracles, and prophetic dreams: he calls Marie's prophecy *cette parole, ou plustost cet oracle*. But even without employing this device he attaches the incidents and characters of the Old Testament to those of the New, simply by a comparison. Thus Aaron's rod turned into a tree is compared to a more sacred tree,[5] and the rescue of Moses from Pharaoh to the rescue of Jesus from Herod.[6] Most of these parallels were theological commonplaces and as we have seen were of considerable importance in the treatment of Old Testament themes by artists of the Counter-Reformation.[7]

The third division of the *merveilleux chrétien* is the popular legend of the Middle Ages (whether derived directly from traditional sources or from Italian romance) with its enchanters, witches, fairies, and elves. It is naturally less common than the

---

[1] *Éliade*, p. 19. [2] *Œuvres*, ii. 179.

[3] Lya, cette Lya dont doit sortir un jour
Le plus rare tesmoin de son divin amour (ii. 272).

[4] La Vierge, qui dèslors eut le don prophetique,
S'ecrie à cet objet, mais d'un air extatique:
Ainsy faut-il qu'un jour, jour grand, cruel et dous,
Un innocent agneau paye et meure pour tous! (ii. 290.)

[5] *Œuvres*, ii. 229. [6] Ib. ii. 156. [7] Cf. p. 32 above.

others, but it presents a special interest in view of the rarity (or supposed rarity) of medieval survivals in the seventeenth century. When it occurs it may perhaps be regarded as one manifestation of the baroque spirit, an offence against strict classical purity. We find it particularly in the poets who may be placed in the baroque group: Saint-Amant, Coras, Desmarets, Marie de Pech, Pierre de Saint-Louis.

Saint-Amant presents the most curious examples. There is an elf who grooms one of the Princess's horses:

> L'un fait caprioler un barbe genereux
> Dont est, selon le bruit, un lutin amoureux,
> Qui d'un soin assidu toutes les nuits le pense,
> Qui luy tresse le crin, de riches nœus l'agence,
> Et fantasque et jaloux, ne voudroit pas souffrir
> Qu'à ce travail aymé nul homme vinst s'offrir.[1]

This is in the purest tradition of Fairyland: it bears a striking resemblance to the activities of Puck in *A Midsummer Night's Dream*, or the goblin in Milton's *L'Allegro*. It may be derived from Ronsard:

> On dict qu'en Norouegue ilz se loüent à-gaiges,
> Et font, comme valetz, des maisons les mesnages.
> Ilz pensent les cheuuaux, ilz vont tirer du vin,
> Ilz font cuire le rost, ilz serençent le lin.[2]

However, the liveliness of the description is hardly compatible with a convention which has no meaning for the poet. It may be assumed that literary tradition and popular superstition are here united.

When Elisaph is wounded by the crocodile, he is healed by a magic herb shown by an angel to Merary.[3] The magic herb is part of the recognized machinery of enchantment. In particular the preparation of the remedy:

> Il broye, il mesle tout, fueille, tige, racine,
> L'epreint, en prend le suc, l'aigre playe en bacine,
> Reitere l'office . . .,[4]

---

[1] *Œuvres*, ii. 313.
[2] *Hymne des Daimons*, 251–4 (ed. Schmidt, p. 50). Cf. also Delaporte, *Du Merveilleux*, pp. 38, 100.
[3] *Œuvres*, ii. 187. [4] Ib. ii. 187–8.

though shorn of the more terrifying rites, recalls the recipes of
the witches. Coras's Witch of Endor is a mistress of the black
arts. Unlike Sainte-Garde and Lesfargues, Coras describes her
spells with some precision:

> Elle en forme vn triangle, elle en trace vn ouale.[1]

Another episode, not quite in the same tradition, is Saint-
Amant's transformation of Rachel. In the Bible (Gen. xxix. 25)
Leah is simply substituted for her sister. This did not satisfy
Saint-Amant, who makes Rachel, by a miracle, take on the form
of Leah.[2] Here we have an example of the disguise, which can
be traced from classical epic through the Italians.[3] It appears
twice in Coras: Merab assumes the form of her sister Mical,[4] and
Mopse is transformed into Salmon.[5] Both incidents seem to be
imitated from Saint-Amant. The story of Manasses and his father
in Marie de Pech[6] may be placed in the same category, though the
theme is recognition, not disguise.

We are left with what Delaporte calls the *merveilleux mixte*,
though in fact the *merveilleux chrétien* as a whole deserves this
designation, being normally a compound of Christian and classical
sources. However, allegorical figures present an extreme case of
mixed origins, partaking as they do of the nature of classical
divinities and Christian angels, springing more directly from
similar figures in ancient epic (Virgil's Rumour for example) and
perhaps connected (through Italian romance) with the allegories of
medieval poetry. We are therefore dealing here with an instance
of a perennial literary form which survives changes in fashion and
even artistic revolutions. In judging rightly the flux of history
such enduring elements are clearly of great importance. That is
not to say that, in this particular case at least, they are not adapted
to the outlook of the time in which they appear.

In these poems allegorical figures are very common, but they
appear most frequently, or in most interesting ways, in Gamon,
Anne d'Urfé, Saint-Amant, Marie de Pech, and Coras. Again, it
will be observed, the baroque poets predominate. However, an

---

[1] *David*, p. 79.   [2] *Œuvres*, ii. 269.
[3] Cf. *Odyssey*, xiii. 429; *Orlando Furioso*, Canto vii.
[4] *David*, p. 79.
[5] *Josué*, p. 56.   [6] p. 114 above.

evolution is discernible between earlier and later poets. In Gamon's *Semaine* it is Ingratitude who incites the angels to revolt:

> L'ingratitude noire,
> Enceinte de malheurs, trainant la vaine Gloire,
> Qui porte vn cueur boufi, des yeux pleins de desdain,
> Des cornes sur le front, et le sourci hautain.[1]

The concrete realism of this description is paralleled in the Impiety who at the beginning of the *Poëme tragique* persuades Antiochus to persecute the Jews. She too is a terrifying figure, and the balance between the person and the quality she represents is well maintained:

> Elle est, ce dit on, noire, elle a troubles les yeux,
> La bouche blasphemante, et le port furieux,
> Elle est fille d'Enfer, de cent fraudes coifée,
> Et fait de sacrilege ordinaire trofée.[2]

Anne d'Urfé's Rumour reminds us of the classical origin of such apparitions and of their relation to the allegories of contemporary painters and sculptors.[3] She is not entirely an abstraction, like the lifeless figures of Coras and Marie de Pech, but a living monster, covered with eyes and carrying a trumpet which swells from a hardly audible note to a great roar.[4]

Saint-Amant's Rumour belongs to the same family, but she is stripped of these physical attributes:

> Soudain la Renommée, en nouvelles feconde,
> Qui le faux et le vray seme par tout le monde,
> Qui tousjours en volant l'un et l'autre agrandit,
> Et qui, plus elle est loin, plus elle a de credit . . . .[5]

This portrait, confined entirely to moral characteristics, illustrates the progress towards classical abstraction and psychological inwardness, even in a poet like Saint-Amant who is most at home in the concrete and the physical.

However, other figures are more consonant with his natural genius. A more fully developed instance is Antipathy, who is used to begin and end the story of Jacob. She appears at the birth of Jacob and Esau[6] and vanishes with their reconciliation,[7] so that

---

[1] p. 18. [2] *Iardinet*, p. 94. [3] Cf. p. 238 below.
[4] *Judic*, fo. 163v°. Cf. *Aeneid*, bk. iv; *Orlando Furioso*, xl. 27; *Gerusalemme Liberata*, xv. 32; Ronsard, *Franciade*, ed. Laumonier, iii. 20.
[5] *Œuvres*, ii. 280. [6] Ib. ii. 168. [7] Ib. ii. 283.

the story is given a kind of allegorical unity. Sterility is more like
the Ingratitude and Impiety of Gamon:

> Chagrine, seche, noire, affreuse, languissante,
> L'œil cave, le sein plat et la voix gemissante . . . .[1]

Even here the more repulsive details are lacking.

But the most elaborate and most characteristic of such figures
is that of Calm, who is not alone but is placed with attendant
figures in an appropriate background. When the Nile and the air
are lashed to fury, in order to destroy the cradle, the attack is not
repelled in the usual way by the direct intervention of the angels.
Instead one of them is sent by God to a being called Calm, who is
ordered to subdue the storm. The Christian messenger is projected into a pagan world when he arrives on an unknown island
where Calm sits on a throne of moss and seaweed, with his sisters
Bonace and *Tranquillité*. The whole scene offers in combination most
of the types of *merveilleux* discussed. The gates of Heaven (called
Olympe) are opened:

> . . . du saint portail le bronze radieux,
> Qui fait sur de beaux gonds un bruit melodieux.[2]

The detail of the hinges, with its sound-image, is characteristic
of Saint-Amant's aptitude for drawing minute consequences.
There follows the angelic flight, but now doubled (a baroque
device), since the messenger to Calm is accompanied at first by the
angel of the vase of tears:

> Comme au plus beau des nuits, à ce qu'à l'œil il semble,
> Deux astres destachez partent du ciel ensemble,
> L'un à droit, l'autre à gauche, et d'un chemin divers
> Precipitent leur cours en ce bas univers
> Ainsy des deux courriers, qu'un beau devoir embrase,
> L'un tire vers l'Egipte avec le riche vase,
> Et l'autre va trouver, d'un vol au sien pareil,
> Le paisible demon qu'adore le sommeil.

Calm himself is found in the grotto where he has taken refuge
from the storm:

> Là, sur un trosne d'algue et de mousse et d'esp9onges,[3]

while his sisters adjust his crown of halcyon feathers.

---

[1] *Œuvres*, ii. 219.   [2] Ib. ii. 236.   [3] Ib. ii. 236–7.

The sources of this fantasy have already been indicated.[1] It comes from Ariosto and Marino, but Saint-Amant has made it his own, as well as one of the most finished examples of the baroque in French literature. Theologically speaking, it embraces all the contradictions of the Christian position. The angel's message is more like an order from Jupiter, who is *primus inter pares*, than from the omnipotent God. The whole conception of the intermediate power, Calm, is indeed absurd. Yet it is impossible to deny the poetic qualities of this strange mixture, and especially of the submarine grotto.

The foundation of the Christian and Biblical epic was the belief that the Bible offered literary themes and characters which far surpassed those of the ancient poets. Yet the Biblical writers not only adopted classical forms: nearly all hastened to introduce by means of various pretexts the pagan divinities whom they had condemned as false and even unpoetic. The most fervent champion of Christian poetry and the principles of the *Modernes*, Desmarets, went perhaps farthest along this path. It becomes increasingly clear that even the most resolutely modern poets can conceive of epic only in classical terms. There is here a paradox which seems fundamental to the outlook of the whole period.

We have seen that contemporary poets and critics generally solved the difficulty by means of the pillage theory: the children of Israel have the right to take from Egyptian temples the ornaments which will serve the glory of the true God. The religious origin of this critical doctrine and its use of architectural imagery are equally noteworthy. However, it remains unconvincing because the key of the Christian position was the inferiority of these ornaments even as ornaments. Moreover, the supernatural elements in the poems which are derived from Biblical or Christian sources are generally dressed in classical garb. The angels fulfil the functions and possess many of the attributes of Homeric gods; Hell is peopled with Harpies, Furies, Pluto, Cerberus, and Charon; God Himself is divided into abstractions, Truth, Mercy, or Justice, which again influence human affairs by the same means as Mercury or Iris. Where impregnation of Christian faith by classical reminiscence has gone so far, it is scarcely possible to speak of the theft of occasional ornament.

[1] See pp. 51, 93 above.

Some light is thrown on the question by the Oratorian Father Thomassin's *Methode d'étudier et d'enseigner chrétiennement et solidement les lettres humaines par rapport aux lettres divines et aux Écritures*. It appeared towards the end of our period (1681) and thus formulates in a clear-cut system ideas which had till then only been half expressed. The argument is based on a series of parallels which tend to prove that the classical poets derived their mythology from the Bible, either directly or through the medium of popular tradition. Homer and Virgil are worthy of the first place in a Christian education because of these parallels, as well as for the moral lessons which they inculcate. The book is ingenious and attractive (it provides an early example of the modern comparative study of religion), but the reader is faced with exactly the same problem as in the case of the Biblical poets. Why should these lessons be sought in the ancients, where, as Thomassin admits, they are mixed with so much idolatry and immorality, rather than in the purity of the Scriptures themselves?

He puts forward two answers. The first is the power of poetry: but he does not, naturally enough, develop this to its logical conclusion, the love of beauty for its own sake. The second, the force of custom, is no doubt the true reason. The authors of antiquity were so firmly established that the Church could only try to use them to the best advantage. Thomassin himself shows as deep a love of the classics as Boileau, and his religious arguments perhaps only rationalize an aesthetic attraction.

Like him the Biblical poets, especially those who had serious literary intentions but to some extent even the most devout, were fascinated by the writers of Greece and Rome. From their education and reading they derived a genuine belief in the gods and heroes of antiquity. This was not the religious faith which inspired the men of the Renaissance but a poetic substitute. Their Biblical material was weighed by classical standards and their angels and demons, their heroes and saints, were assimilated, consciously or unconsciously, to classical models. The one has no meaning without the other. The two forms of the *merveilleux* are thus two facets of the same spirit.

There has recently been a tendency to belittle the importance of antiquity in the seventeenth century. M. Henri Peyre, for example, points out with some justification that mythology and the *merveilleux païen* also play a great part in nineteenth-century literature.[1] For the Romantics and their successors, however, these were merely one source of poetic material, to be exploited along with many others. For our poets they were the stuff of poetry itself. It would perhaps be unwise to draw too broad conclusions from the Biblical epic, but, as we have endeavoured to show, in this respect at least it touches the central preoccupations of the period.

At the same time, the poetic beliefs which produced this combined Christian and classical *merveilleux* were clearly in opposition to the religious devotion which animated most of these works. The variations in balance which we have observed between the two gave rise to serious contradictions. Their solution, which presented a superb task to contemporary artists, was never fully achieved in the epic. We may find it in Corneille, Racine, and Poussin.

[1] *Qu'est-ce que le classicisme?*, p. 91.

CHAPTER XIV

Religious Attitudes

APART from this fundamental religious and aesthetic conflict between the Christian and classical sources of our civilization, the seventeenth century was a period of great theological debates, particularly between Catholics and Protestants and between Jesuits and Jansenists; of renewed activity in the monastic orders; and of profound religious experience in individuals. We should expect to find some reflection of these phenomena in our poets, and indeed we do, though in a somewhat disappointing measure. The reasons for this are partly contained in Chapter XIII: the better writers were concerned with literary rather than purely religious values. Moreover, although the earlier poets, Du Bartas and Gamon especially, were impregnated with theological argument, among the later only Coras and Morillon stand out as having received a serious theological training. Again, it would be unfair and misleading to press too far differences of doctrine, which depend so much on delicate changes of emphasis, in works whose intention was literary, or at least moralizing and narrative, rather than doctrinal. With these reservations, the poems may throw some light on religious history.

It was inevitable that they should contain both Jewish and Christian elements: the interaction of these elements has appeared to some extent in our discussion of the poets' treatment of Biblical material. However, Saint-Amant's combination of the two is of special interest and deserves separate treatment.

The conception of God revealed in the *Moyse* owes much to the Old Testament. He is a jealous God,[1] His Name cannot be uttered,[2] He is the only Omnipotent, but not the only God.[3]

Saint-Amant also attempted to present his characters historically,

---

[1] 'Sa redoutable main, jalouse de sa gloire . . .' (Saint-Amant, *Œuvres*, ii. 226).
[2] 'Nous venons t'annoncer de la part du grand Dieu,
   Du monarque eternel de qui l'Estre supreme
   Ne peut estre exprimé que par sa bouche mesme . . . ' (ii. 204).
[3] 'Dieu seroit le seul Dieu qu'au monde il choisiroit' (ii. 180).
   'Et la gloire est rendue au Dieu de tous les dieux' (ii. 224).

from the point of view of the changes brought about by the law
of Moses and the Redemption. We read in the Preface:

> Il est à considerer que mon histoire est prise sous la loi de nature . . .
> Cela estant, j'ay pû faire dire à mes personnages des choses que je
> ne leur aurois pas fait dire si ç'avoit esté sous la loy de rigueur, qui ne
> fut que plus de quatre-vingts ans après, ou sous la loy de grace, qui
> est à present.[1]

This distinction, which appears to go back at least as far as Hugh
of St. Victor in the twelfth century,[2] was eminently suitable in a
Christian poem, introducing a religious principle into the behaviour
of the characters, yet avoiding intrusive didacticism (as we have
seen, the theorists believed that the useful effects of epic could
only be attained by the means of pleasure). Unfortunately there
is little in the poem itself to show that Saint-Amant had this
principle in mind when he wrote it. Once or twice it appears in
the form of discussions on natural religion. Isaac in his farewell to
Jacob (ii. 174) gives reasons for active faith in God: there is no
question of obedience to a definite set of laws (*loi de rigueur*) nor
of redemption (*loi de grace*). The motive is a natural duty, inherent
in things themselves. Man must ascend from the creature to the
Creator. The animals praise Him in following the order which He
has made and man created in His image must do likewise. Even
in this case there is an anachronism in the introduction of the idea
of immortality. Moreover, though this division has an historical
basis, it depends on the Christian view of the world and can
hardly be employed without the enunciation of Christian principles by way of contrast.

In the same way, although the conception of God in the *Moyse*
is often Jewish, it is in general only so when the beliefs of the
characters are in question. In attempts at direct description the
conception is naturally Christian. The most complete statement
of it is to be found in the return of the angel carrying the vase
filled with tears:

> Et dans le saint Olympe, où la divine essence
> Estale sa grandeur et sa magnificence,
> Où l'on adore en Trois l'ineffable Unité,
> Où, sur un trosne pur fait par l'eternité,

[1] ii. 144–5.
[2] Curtius, *Europäische Literatur*, p. 322.

> Le seul Estre infiny, le Monarque supreme
> Luit de son propre eclat et s'abisme en soy-mesme,
> Et voit dessous ses pieds s'humilier le Sort,
> La Fortune, le Temps, la Nature et la Mort . . .[1]

It is scarcely necessary to stress the classical colouring, the use of the word *Olympe*, and the group of allegorical figures. It is largely superficial, and the essentials of the passage, the affirmation of belief in the Trinity and the 'divine essence', are purely Christian. Again, the line

> Luit de son propre eclat et s'abisme en soy-mesme

reveals perhaps a subtler analysis of the attributes of God than is to be found in the Old Testament.

The notion of immortality in the farewell of Isaac to Jacob has already been mentioned. Isaac ends with a firm declaration of his belief in the immortality of the soul:

> Il voulut infuser un rayon de sa flâme
> Dans ce premier des corps où fut la premiere ame,
> Et que par ce moyen la nostre est un flambeau
> Qui ne se peut esteindre en la nuict du tombeau.[2]

The idea of immortality of the human soul is generally foreign to the Judaism of the Old Testament. We may compare these lines with their source (Gen. xxvii. 27–29), where Isaac promises only earthly blessings.

The clash between Catholicism and Protestantism is most clearly discernible in the works of the early part of the century, and we have seen that Gamon's *Semaine* is an exposition of Calvinism.[3] After 1640 the conflict has diminished in intensity, but traces of it may still be found, especially in the two converts, Saint-Amant and Coras. Saint-Amant's own careless and gentle temperament, not inclined to any violent religious emotion, is certainly closer to Catholicism than to the Protestantism of his day. But the signs of his conversion in the poem are slight indeed. There is praise of the Virgin, to whom Jocabel is compared:

> L'honneur du genre humain, la divine Marie,
> Ensemble et mere et vierge . . . .[4]

A Protestant could have called Mary *l'honneur du genre humain*, though it is doubtful whether in fact he would have done so. But

---

[1] ii. 235.   [2] ii. 175.   [3] Cf. p. 69 above.   [4] ii. 156.

this seems the only precise evidence. There may, however, be certain signs of a Protestant attitude, if not a Protestant doctrine, in the emphasis on the Divine Will, which shapes the events of the poem. The simplest of facts is presented as the result of a divine plan: and this occurs not once but many times.[1] It was natural that a Christian poet should wish to show the hand of God in his narrative: and there is nothing contrary to the doctrines of Catholicism in this direction of events. Yet the general effect is perhaps more Protestant than Catholic because of the feeling produced in the mind that everything is in accordance with a predestined scheme, of which the characters are merely the instruments.

On the whole, then, it is impossible to say that the *Moyse* is a Catholic or a Protestant poem. Both parts of the poet's life find expression in it to a limited extent. But he was not a theologian and the poem touches theological questions only rarely. It was written during a period of truce in the conflict between the two faiths, a period in which these theological questions formed the only serious difference. And since Saint-Amant never seems to have been a very active Protestant and only became a devout Catholic in his last years, this absence of sectarian spirit is not surprising.

Coras, whose conversion took place during the composition of his poems,[2] presents a more interesting case. The view of predestination, faith, and works which emerges from the poems is still marked by his Protestant origins. Thus Saul's ruin is inscribed on tables of bronze.[3] Samson's pride is stigmatized:

> C'est ainsi que Samson ose dire, ose croire,
> Qu'il est l'auteur luy-mesme, et l'ouurier de sa gloire;
> Sans penser, comme il doit, que sa mortelle main
> Tire tout son secours d'vn pouuoir plus qu'humain.[4]

This is not specifically Protestant, but it seems to derive from

---

[1] For example, in the proposition we read that Moses
> Fut, selon le decret de l'arbitre eternel,
> Rendu par une Nymphe au doux sein maternel (ii. 152.)

The approach of the hour of rescue is described:
> Dejà le souverain, le Dieu de la nature,
> Voulant de mon heros couronner l'avanture,
> En determinoit l'heure, et dejà le soleil
> Enflamoit l'Occident de son lustre vermeil (ii. 290).

[2] Cf. p. 118 above.   [3] *David*, p. 34.   [4] *Samson*, p. 41.

a Calvinistic horror at reliance on works alone. The converted king of Nineveh expresses his penitence in a discourse which consists entirely of doctrinal arguments. He insists on the complete unworthiness of all men but claims the right to pardon through repentance:

> Ah! nous sommes, Seigneur, par nostre repentance,
> Dans le droit de prétendre à ta sainte alliance![1]

Here again a Protestant note may be detected. However, these are once more questions of emphasis rather than of tangible doctrine.

The controversies over Jansenism have likewise left no profound mark in the poems. Sainte-Garde stresses the part played by grace both in Saul:

> Saül a negligé ce que ta voix ordonne,
> Et depuis ces moments, ta grace l'abandonne[2]

and in the elders:

> C'est ainsi que parloient ces langues forcenées,
> Que la Grace diuine auoit abandonnées.[3]

In the first case, it will be noted, the loss of grace is a consequence of human demerit. These passages suggest at least that Sainte-Garde was anti-Jansenist. The same may be said of Marie de Pech, who affirms the orthodox Catholic doctrine:

> Mettons-nous en estat de meriter sa grace.[4]

On the other side, in Morillon, the abyss of original sin and human misery is illuminated only by the rays of grace:

> L'homme est né pour la peine en naissant criminel . . .
> Il est vray que ce Dieu par grace seulement
> Apporte à cét arrest quelque temperament.[5]

The insistence on sin and grace, the absence of references to free will, have perhaps a Jansenist flavour. Again, however, too much importance must not be attached to a question of emphasis. Perrault goes farther, and his *Adam* is remarkable for its recurrent allusions to the gratuitousness of divine election. Thus the choice of the apostles is made

> Sans égard au mérite, et par pure faveur.[6]

---

[1] *Jonas*, p. 168.   [2] *Saül puni*, p. 2.   [3] *Suzanne délivrée*, p. 9.
[4] *Judith*, p. 84.   [5] *Joseph*, p. 19.   [6] *Adam*, p. 78.

Again the angel tells Adam that pardon of sinners is entirely the
effect of divine mercy[1] and even introduces the notion of pre-
venient grace.[2] Pascal's reflections on confidence are echoed by
the angel's warning to Adam that sin is aggravated if the sinner
believes it greater than the mercy of God.[3] These traces of Jansenism may appear unexpected in the light of Perrault's enmity with
Boileau and the support he received from the Jesuits in the great
quarrel.[4] However, there is no doubt that Perrault and his family
sympathized with Port-Royal,[5] and *Adam* affords evidence that
his theological opinions were not far removed from those of his
brother Nicolas and the Jansenist doctors.

The activity of the orders appears naturally in the Carmelite
poems. Pierre de Saint-Louis devotes much attention to the
founding of the order. Elijah's character has three facets—the
Biblical prophet, the soldier, and the abbot. The first is scarcely
visible, being submerged by the others. Elijah is everywhere described in military terms, as the *général du Seigneur des armées*[6] or

> [Le] plus grand conquérant qui jamais ait été.[7]

His virtues appear as armour:

> Mais voyons en passant sa riche cote d'armes,
> Son casque de salut, le bouclier de sa foi.[8]

The object was probably to add to his epic stature and at the
same time to inspire respect for the first Carmelite. The author
of *Hélie* had left the foundation of the order in a vague and
allegorical form.[9] Saint-Louis, starting from the Biblical reference
to the sons of the prophets,[10] recounts in detail how Elijah re-
cruited novices and organized convents:

> Visitant ses couvents, comme un pasteur fidèle.[11]

---

[1] Ib., p. 57.
[2]   Et que sa grace enfin purement gratuite,
      Prevenant la bonne œuvre, en fait tout le merite (ib., p. 58).
[3] Ib., p. 48. Cf. *Pensées*, ed. Brunschvicg, no. 497.
[4] Gillot, *Querelle*, p. 513; Rigault, *Querelle*, pp. 229 ff.
[5] Sainte-Beuve, *Port-Royal*, iii. 41–43 and *passim*; Hallays, *Les Perrault*, p. 247.
[6] *Éliade*, p. 6.
[7] p. 39.   [8] p. 76.
[9] Cf. p. 133 above.
[10] II Kings ii. 3.
[11] *Éliade*, p. 27.

The fierce old prophet has become a figure of the Counter-Reformation:

> Ce premier Général fait souvent ses visites,
> Console, voit, instruit ces nouveaux cénobites.[1]

At the same time he lays down the principles which are to govern the new order: prayer and solitude.[2]

When we come to consider the expression of religious experience we find two tendencies: the moralizing and allegorizing (which of course has other implications than the literary ones discussed in Chapter XIII), and the mystical. The epic is not well suited to the unfolding of direct religious experience and examples of the latter are not numerous.

The place of allegory in the epic has been fully treated by Mr. Marni,[3] and here we need only remark on its connexion with the theoretical development of abstract schemes which culminates in the work of Le Bossu. Even Saint-Amant, who would not appear to be much interested in moral generalizations, such is his attachment to the concrete and particular, claims in the Preface that his poem has a hidden allegorical significance, which the reader is left to work out for himself, probably guessing meanings never intended by the author.[4] It is possible to arrive at a plausible allegorical system for the *Moyse*, as Mr. Marni has done,[5] but it seems likely that Saint-Amant's cryptic reference was designed at once to conform to the prevailing fashion and to whet the curiosity of the reader. No such suspicion is possible in the case of Coras, who in his prefaces explains in detail the allegories of *Jonas* and *Josué*. Thus Nineveh is the human soul, the people of Nineveh are the passions at work in it, Jonah the divine law, and so on. In *Josué* the land of Canaan is Heaven and the Israelites are the Christian Church (this is close to Millieu's allegory in *Moyses Viator*[6]). It is clear that Le Bossu's elaborate theories were based on what was already current practice.

At the same time, it is possible to see after the publication of his work in 1675 (though not necessarily under its influence) a less superficial use of allegory, now absorbed more completely in the structure of the poems. In Morillon's *Joseph* of 1679 the theological

---

[1] *Éliade*, p. 24.   [2] p. 22.   [3] See Bibliography, p. 266 below.
[4] *Œuvres*, ii. 146–7.   [5] *Allegory*, pp. 120 ff.
[6] Cf. p. 76 above. For a fuller treatment of Coras's allegories see Marni, *Allegory*, pp. 170 ff.

reflections are not merely decorations or commentaries, they act as props on which the framework of the poem is erected. It therefore expresses a direct theological purpose and not only a poetic allegory. The exclusion of mysticism, the preoccupation with moral problems, shows a sense of the requirements of epic and has affinities with Le Bossu's theories. All this is more strikingly apparent in Perrault's *Adam*. In spite of occasional anthropomorphic simplicity, the religious feeling of the poem is set in a refined atmosphere of philosophical, almost scientific abstraction. This note is struck at once by the invocation of the Holy Spirit, suggesting an immaterial approach. The proposition reveals a plan on a much larger scale than other epics studied here. It is not merely that the events of the poem receive an allegorical interpretation, the allegory (of sin and redemption) is the poem. Thus Adam's love for Eve prefigures the union of Christ and His Church,[1] the incident of Jacob and Esau is not inserted for its own sake but as an illustration of the workings of grace,[2] the manna in the desert is a symbol of the bread of the Last Supper.[3] Much of the first part of the poem is devoted to the prologue in Heaven, which makes plain the divine purpose. Here in fact is a poem that might have been conceived to illustrate the thesis of Le Bossu. This conclusion again may seem surprising in view of Le Bossu's friendship with Boileau and Perrault's attack on his system in the *Paralelle*.[4] Mr. Marni assumes in consequence that 'an epic by this author could not be allegorical'.[5] However, this *a priori* assumption is clearly invalidated by an examination of the poem itself. The contradiction between Perrault's theory and practice is not inexplicable. It is a special example of the inconsistency which vitiates in part the position of the Moderns and which we have already observed in Desmarets and in the general treatment of the Bible and the *merveilleux*. Perrault attacks Le Bossu's system because he is unwilling to accord to Homer the profound significance and clear plan which the system implies. But when he comes to write an epic poem himself, he is as anxious as any of the Moderns to outdo the writers of antiquity on their own ground, and the fact that Homer had been praised for his allegorical structure might well lead Perrault

---

[1] *Adam*, p. 22.   [2] p. 58.   [3] p. 65.
[4] 'Que de chiméres ce bon Pere s'est imaginées!' (*Paralelle des Anciens et des Modernes*, iii. 38.)   [5] *Allegory*, p. 189.

to think that he ought to do better. This account of his motives is conjectural: it may none the less serve to illustrate the forces at work on the side of the Moderns.

For our immediate purpose, however, it is more interesting to observe, in the last quarter of the century, the growth of an abstract and rational attitude towards religion. On the one hand this may be considered a reflection of the classical emphasis on reason. On the other, with the conception of the world and its history as a perfect intellectual design mirrored in the structure of the poems, we are approaching the deism of the eighteenth century. Thus Morillon makes no attempt to give a direct view of the Divine Majesty, visible only by its reflection in the created world:

> Ce qui frape nos yeux, l'air, la terre, les mers,
> Ce qui nous est caché dans la nuit des enfers,
> Tout ce qui n'a que l'estre, et tout ce qui respire,
> Connoist un Souverain, et sert à son Empire.[1]

There is genuine emotion here, but the thought (apart from the second line) would not seem out of place in Voltaire.

Some poets are less reticent in this respect, and occasionally we come upon a representation of the highest mysteries which is partly literary convention (derived perhaps from Du Bartas) but partly also personal experience. We see it in Gamon, who, though rarely, succeeds in conveying his great theme in language adequate to it, as in the miracle of the Burning Bush:

> Quoy? Dieu, comme Lumiere, ez personnes s'est veu:
> Le Pere au feu luizant du buisson revestu,
> Le Fils ez resplendeurs sur le mont alumées,
> Et l'Esprit sacré saint ez langues enflammées.[2]

Again Anne d'Urfé at one point attempts to describe the whole majesty of God and the mystery of the Trinity. For a moment this splendour is seen in all its purity:

> Sur vn throsne de feu faict en Eternité,
> Plus luysant qu'vn Soleil, siege la Deité,
> Supreme en Majesté, dont la splendeur entiere
> Reluit en trois flambeaux d'vne seule lumiere.[3]

The resemblance to Gamon is plain and illustrates the formation of a convention,[4] but in spite of this and the appearance soon

---

[1] *Joseph*, p. 36. [2] *Semaine*, p. 15. [3] *Hymnes*, p. 215.
[4] Cf. also Saint-Amant, p. 185 above.

after of the allegorical figures of Nature and Destiny at the feet of the Deity, genuine adoration is unmistakably present.

Later poets show themselves less willing to scale these summits, though Perrault is more successful than most in his description of God before the Creation, who

> Vivoit, et trouvoit seul dans son immensité
> Sa grandeur, son repos, et sa felicité,
> Sans desirs, sans besoins, suffisant à lui-méme . . .[1]

The use of repetition to suggest both infinity and circular self-sufficiency recalls, like the cosmogonic theme itself, the poetic heights of Du Bartas and d'Aubigné.[2] However, a comparison with them, or with Gamon and d'Urfé, confirms the growth of abstraction during the period and its particular importance in Perrault. God's immeasurable attributes are conveyed in a noble language, but His presence is not physically felt as it is in the earlier poets.

The two Carmelites again confront us with special cases. Pierre de Saint-Louis's religious spirit may be deduced from the sectarian fidelity which we have already noticed and from the florid decoration which characterizes his work. It consists partly of ardent sensuality:

> Après tous ces soldats, des filles généreuses
> De *Jésus* leur époux ardemment amoureuses.[3]

A familiar doctrine is here presented in such a way as to make it appear almost scandalous. Pierre de Saint-Louis has been compared to Crashaw,[4] and a passage like this confirms the aptness of the comparison. It is one more instance of the baroque element in his poetry. He is troubled by none of the moral scruples which beset his contemporaries. So he condemns the priests of Baal without feeling any need to justify their slaughter:

> Élie ayant gagné cette illustre bataille
> Sacrifie à la mort toute cette canaille.[5]

---

[1] *Adam*, p. 2.
[2] Cf. for example Du Bartas, *Works*, ed. Holmes, ii. 195–6, ll. 25–30 and iii. 104, ll. 151–60; d'Aubigné, *Tragiques*, ed. Garnier and Plattard, i. 42–43, ll. 35–40.
[3] *Éliade*, p. 63.
[4] Cf. Boase, *Revue des sciences humaines*, 1949, p. 181.
[5] *Éliade*, p. 19.

Even the most venerable rivals of Elijah are treated with the same contempt. A reference to Jeremiah provokes a very one-sided comparison:

> Mais que sert d'appeler ce prophète pleureux,
> Il nous en faut un autre ardent et valeureux.[1]

We are reminded of local feuds between patron saints. This furnishes the key to a characteristic of the poet which at first sight appears in contradiction to his love of the chimerical—the reflection of personal experience, which is perhaps stronger here than in any of the other poems. The most sacred events are seen as part of a ceremony in a country cathedral or abbey. The archangels are reduced to the role of canons and the god Mercury, confronted by the victorious Elijah, is compared to an incompetent preacher, hurrying away from the pulpit after his discomfiture.[2] The poem is an excellent illustration of simple, popular piety as it developed after the Counter-Reformation.

The author of *Hélie* presents, as usual, a wholly different attitude. Though the literary opinions expressed in the Preface are rudimentary, the object to be pursued in the study of Elijah's character shows some originality:

. . . m'estendre beaucoup sur sa maniere de vie retirée, sur ses sentimens interieurs, sur sa façon de perfectionner ceux qui se rangeoient sous sa discipline, et qui venoient apprendre de luy le chemin des Cieux, en apprenant celuy de la Sainteté.[3]

This aim is scarcely compatible with the canons of epic, but it reveals a serious preoccupation with a fundamental religious problem—the inner life of the characters. Such a conception is far removed from even the most sincere of the poets examined so far. The execution does not correspond to the elevation of the project, but the sustained dialogue between the prophet and God is often moving. God's anger at the wickedness of Israel[4] expressed in a violent argument with Elijah may be theologically dubious, but it is very lively. Again, Elijah's inward awareness of the divine response to his prayer, very different from the external machinery of angelic visitations, is studied as a gradual process.[5]

---

[1] *Éliade*, p. 65.
[2] Ib., p. 46.
[3] *Hélie*, p. 8.
[4] p. 9.
[5] p. 50.

Sometimes this sort of analysis rises to a mystical sense of communion with divinity, as in the prophet's beatitude:

> Là dans vn plein repos, dans vne ioye entiere,
> Son esprit s'appliquoit sans cesse à la priere;
> Ses sens tousiours fermés aux obiets du dehors,
> A peine luy laissoient l'vsage de son Corps;
> Son ame recueillie au dedans d'elle mesme,
> Y contemploit tousiours la Maiesté supréme . . .
> Elle laissoit le corps priué de sentiment,
> Les mains, les bras, les pieds sans aucun mouuement;
> Et d'vn homme viuant par vn prodige estrange,
> Elle en faisoit vn mort, ou pour mieux dire vn Ange.[1]

It is tempting to see here at least a pale reflection of the sublime
tradition of Carmelite mysticism.

[1] *Hélie*, pp. 101–2.

CHAPTER XV

Structure and Technique

WE have seen that the critics and rhetoricians of antiquity and the Renaissance had built up not only a general theory of epic but a number of detailed injunctions, based for the most part on the practice of Homer and Virgil, which taken together constitute something like a standard pattern for the epic poet to follow.[1] The interest of an investigation into the methods of the seventeenth-century poets will lie partly in the degree of their conformity to the general model, which will vary as a rule according to the primacy of literary or religious inspiration; and partly in the modifications or distortions of classical forms, even among those whose intention is mainly literary.

The classical convention may be seen at its most rigorous in the opening of the poem. The proposition and invocation were indispensable for any poet with serious literary pretensions, but the conventions of the introduction extend beyond them. The complete system can be observed in Virgil. There we find the proposition (*Arma virumque cano*); the invocation (*Musa mihi causas memora*); a brief description of the setting (*Urbs antiqua fuit*); and, as a transition to the action, the appearance of the hero's divine enemy (*Cum Iuno aeternum servans*). Some or all of these stages may be present in the modern poets.

Occasionally the proposition may be quite irregular. Thus in *Hélie* (1661) it consists of no more than a catalogue of miracles and a succession of comparisons between Elijah and other Biblical heroes, which stress the primarily religious character of the poem. This, however, is very exceptional and long before the middle of the century the normal form had become standardized, even down to the opening formula *Je chante*. Montchrestien avoids the formula:

> Ces vers vont publier comme vne chaste Dame,
> Belle parfaitement et du corps et de l'ame,
> Reçeut et repoussa les lubriques assaux
> Liurez à son honneur par deux Iuges riuaux.[2]

Later in the century it is all but universal.

[1] Cf. Ch. II above.   [2] *Susane*, p. 341.

It will be noticed that this is also an example of the modest type of proposition, recommended by Horace and later by Boileau. Montchrestien confines himself to a summary of events and justified praise of his heroine: there is no straining for effect. Later poets tend more and more to adopt the bombastic type, condemned equally by Horace and Boileau, and made ridiculous by Scudéry's famous line:

> Je chante le Vainqueur des Vainqueurs de la Terre.

The distinction is not always plain, except in extreme cases. The transition may be observed in Anne d'Urfé's *Judic*:

> J'entonne la trompete et chante icy de Mars
> Le fer, le sang, le feu, les guerres, les soldars,
> Et les rares vertus d'vne prudente Juifue
> Ardente en Charité et plaine de foy viue.[1]

The enumeration of calamities and the choice of such adjectives as *rares*, *plaine*, and especially *ardente* reveal an attempt to force the emotional content of the story, though strictly speaking there is no exaggeration.

When we come to the later baroque poets there can be no doubt. Marie de Pech, writing of Judith and Holofernes, echoes Scudéry's play on words:

> Et d'vn grand Conquerant fit sa grande Conqueste.[2]

Pierre de Saint-Louis introduces Elijah:

> Je chante les combats, triomphes et victoires
> Du plus fameux Héros qui soit dans nos histoires.[3]

Desmarets, as might be expected, goes furthest of all, and his proposition far exceeds in arrogance the fanfare of a Scudéry:

> Ie chante du grand Dieu les forces triomphantes,
> Dans le cours d'vn seul jour cent batailles sanglantes,
> Ce prodige étonnant, cet exploit sans pareil,
> Le plus grand que jamais éclaira le Soleil.[4]

In all these cases, but particularly in the last, we can see at work a conception of poetry based on astonishment (or *maraviglia*): the reader is to be forced into admiration and surprise from the very

---

[1] *Judic*, fo. 149.
[2] *Judith*, p. 3.
[3] *Éliade*, p. 1.
[4] *Esther*, p. 17.

first lines. But there is more: a strictly conventional classical form is employed, distorted in such a way as to produce a wholly different effect. We may discover here what is perhaps the fundamental characteristic of baroque art.

Saint-Amant's proposition conforms generally to this pattern, but in it yet another element makes its appearance. The opening of the poem is rigidly constructed according to epic tradition:

> . . . Je chante hautement la première avanture
> D'un heros dont la gloire estonna la nature;
> Je descris les hazards qu'il courut au berceau;
> Je dy comment Moyse, en un fresle vaisseau
> Exposé sur le Nil, et sans voile et sans rame,
> Au lieu de voir couper sa jeune et chere trame,
> Fut, selon le decret de l'arbitre eternel,
> Rendu par une Nymphe au doux sein maternel.[1]

The second line is typical of the bombast of Saint-Amant's generation, anticipating Desmarets. The rest follows the conventional model, beginning with *Je chante* and continuing with a list of some of the events of the poem. The fourth and fifth lines may well have been inspired, directly or indirectly, by

> multum ille et terris jactatus et alto.

This parallel at once shows, however, the element of parody, almost of burlesque, in the epic elements of the *Moyse*. There is a violent disproportion between the cradle and the ship of Aeneas. Again the classical form is distorted.

Similar tendencies are manifest in the invocation. A simple and single invocation of the Virgilian type can be found, for example, in Montchrestien, who addresses God in person,[2] and in Perrault's *Adam*, where the Holy Spirit alone is invoked in four unassuming lines.[3] Usually, however, the invocation is doubled: to the hero (Moses) and the poet's patroness (the Queen of Poland) in Saint-Amant; to God and the new Queen of France in Marie de Pech; or to God and Turenne in the *Jonas* of Coras. In one case (the *David* of Lesfargues) the invocation is tripled: to God, to David (no doubt an echo of Saint-Amant's Moses), and to the poet's Muse. All these examples represent a complication of the Virgilian pattern followed by Montchrestien and Perrault, but still

---

[1] *Œuvres*, ii. 151–2.   [2] *Susane*, p. 341.   [3] *Adam*, p. 2.

they correspond approximately to the variations allowed by critical opinion.[1] This can hardly be said of Pierre de Saint-Louis, who, instead of to God or Elijah, addresses himself to all the hosts of angels and seraphim:

> Séraphins tous charmans, angéliques sirènes,
> Vous dont les belles voix surpassent les humaines,
> Choristes embrasés, tous rouges et brûlans, •
> Célestes amphions, musiciens volans,
> Chantres étincelans, grand-maîtres de musique.[2]

This difference is significant: on the one hand, singleness and austerity (or limited multiplication), on the other multiplicity and exuberance. It might be compared to the difference between Poussin and Rubens (whose Heaven is also peopled with myriads of angels[3]).

We have seen that according to most critics the invocation should be repeated at the principal crises of the poem,[4] but earlier poets had used this device sparingly. Montchrestien, though he excludes the Muses from his main invocation, twice invokes a Muse in the body of the poem when he wishes to emphasize the importance of an incident or description.[5] Coras repeats his invocation (to God) at certain turning-points, though it does not become an automatic procedure as it does in Lesfargues's *David*, where it recurs with monotonous frequency, at the beginning of nearly every book and as an introduction to all the more important incidents. Finally there is another triple invocation, to a Muse, to the Virgin, and to God.[6] The proposition also is repeated three times, probably as a guide in a complex narrative. But there is a deeper reason—the tendency to multiply the simple structural elements of classical and even sixteenth-century epic. Proposition and invocation are not essentially different from their earlier counterparts. Originality is sought by repetition and arrangement in more elaborate patterns. This tendency is especially marked in Italian romance, and it is interesting to find it in a narrowly Biblical poet like Lesfargues.

The setting (*descriptio loci*) is less rigidly formalized, but it too is expanded and developed beyond the limits of its classical model.

---

[1] Cf. p. 23 above.
[2] *Éliade*, p. 2.
[3] e.g. the Munich 'Last Judgement'.
[4] Cf. p. 23 above.
[5] *Susane*, pp. 351, 377.
[6] *David* (Lesfargues), p. 321.

The more sober poets, like Morillon and Perrault, omit it, but the force of the convention can be judged from the fact that Coras employs it in each of his four poems. Examples range from Montchrestien, who indicates the setting with the utmost brevity:

En l'antique Babel que Membrot fist notable[1]

where we have an exact imitation of *Urbs antiqua fuit*, contained in the limits set by Virgil himself and not used as a pretext for digression, to Saint-Amant, whose description of the Nile and the town of Memphis occupies about thirty lines.[2] This description has now attained its full stature as an independent part of the introduction.

The appearance of the hero's enemy, leading into the action proper, is still less of a standard form, but it is present in Saint-Amant, who takes from the Bible an introductory account of Pharaoh's persecution of the Jews. Its inclusion may have been dictated in the first place by a desire to imitate the Bible, but Pharaoh performs the same structural function as Juno in the *Aeneid*. In both we approach the hero through the machinations of his enemy. Similarly, Marie de Pech follows the setting of *Judith* with a description of Holofernes.

In the consideration of the structure of the poem as a whole, the external division into books, cantos, or parts furnishes at least a starting-point, and a further means of assessing the primacy of religious or literary intention. The strictest fundamentalists do not divide their poems at all (like Sainte-Garde Bernouin); or they may follow the chapters of the Bible (like Saint-Peres and Le Cordier), which tends to destroy any literary unity. Those who aim at reproducing the classical epic ought logically to have adopted a multiple of twelve books on the Homeric or Virgilian model, but among the Biblical poets only Saint-Amant seems to have done so, and he, as we have seen, was obliged to recast his original and more organic plan in the process.[3] (It may not be without significance that Saint-Amant's friend Chapelain constructed *La Pucelle* in twenty-four books, which is again exceptional in the profane epic.) Other Biblical poets have a smaller number of books, usually not less than four.

---

[1] *Susane*, p. 341. [2] *Œuvres*, ii. 152–3. [3] Cf. p. 82 above.

The principle of division and its appropriateness also show some differences which may further illustrate tendencies already observed. Montchrestien's four books are arranged in an exaggerated symmetry, which yet does not correspond exactly to the natural structure of the theme and concentrates most of the narrative interest in the first half of the poem.[1] A similar awkwardness may perhaps be discovered in his plays. In the better of the fundamentalist poets the books are carefully planned. Thus the *David* of Lesfargues is divided into eight books and great care is taken at least over the joints between them. Morillon's *Joseph*, with its six books suitably divided and evenly balanced, is excellent from the point of view of structure. Later, in Perrault's *Adam*, each book has a unity of its own and a well-ordered place in the whole.

On the other hand, a baroque writer like Marie de Pech presents an extreme example of unbalanced structure. All the most significant events—Judith's arrival in the Assyrian camp, her relations with Holofernes, the slaying, and the triumphant return—are crowded into the final part. In some cases asymmetrical planning was the result of adherence to the Bible. Here it is the free choice of the writer, for the other eight parts are taken up mainly with unconnected episodes, even the early history of Judith and the march of Holofernes being comparatively neglected. The object may have been to unite the most potent elements of the story in a final climax. More probably it was the consequence of the temptation of minor narrative and the lack of a single purpose. A similar lack of balance in the *Esther* of Desmarets is largely due to the break between the two editions and the discordant *tempi* of the first and second halves. Apart from this, Desmarets displays real ingenuity in narrative development: he is unique among contemporary Biblical poets in making the story absorbing in itself. He manipulates the division of books so that the reader shall be left in doubt as to the outcome (and this perhaps distinguishes him from writers like Lesfargues and Morillon, who are more concerned to make each book self-contained). In particular the end of Book I, the climax of the temple scene with the defeat of the infernal powers and the destruction of the idol, is unexpected and attains a certain grandeur. Coras, too, arranges his divisions so that each part of the action is at once complete

[1] Cf. p. 58 above.

and suspended, overflowing into the next book. Thus Book V of *Jonas* ends:

> Tandis la mer tranquille, et le vent fauorable,
> Par vn soufle commode, et par vn doux effort,
> Conduisent le Nauire et le poussent au port.[1]

Stillness and movement are united to suggest both an end and a beginning. But in the internal structure Coras, like Marie de Pech, reveals an inability to dominate his material. The great theme of *Samson*, the story of Samson and Delilah, is begun only in the last book, so that the most moving events are compressed in a few pages. *Josué*, in spite of the homogeneity of the subject, has no true poetic unity. Joshua himself is of little importance. The love of Salmon and Rahab is made into the central theme, but it dies away early in the poem to be succeeded by a series of unconnected episodes.

Apart from these superficial (but not insignificant) divisions, internal structure is governed to a large extent by chronological sequence. The unity of time, which had been fixed tentatively by the critics as the duration of one year,[2] does not seem to have preoccupied the poets themselves, except those who were especially aware of literary problems, and they have striven for the greatest restriction possible. So Saint-Amant confines his action within twelve hours (a feat of which he shows himself inordinately proud in the Preface) and expands it by means of recitals and the prophetic dream; Desmarets's *Esther* takes place within a single day; and Perrault's *Adam* in two days, expanded by the angelic vision to include the whole of history from the Fall to the Day of Judgement. All these cases illustrate the tendency of some seventeenth-century writers to exaggerate classical principles and carry them to absurd lengths. It may well be a baroque characteristic. On the other hand, simpler poets are untroubled by the rule: Lesfargues and Morillon follow the lives of their heroes from beginning to end, with no essential changes.

More generally, a similar distinction can be observed between those who follow the Biblical chronology exactly and those who distort or dislocate it, and again the latter class is the more interesting. Thus in Gamon's *Semaine* the development of the narrative is entirely subordinate to the dialectical or polemical

---

[1] *Jonas*, p. 105.   [2] Cf. p. 21 above.

objects. The Creation is followed immediately by the Last Judgement, so that the elements of chaos in each may be emphasized by juxtaposition.[1] This is no doubt a survival of the sixteenth century: its purpose is argumentative rather than structural, and it seems unconnected with the literary rules of epic. How the later baroque poets dealt with chronology may be seen in Marie de Pech. After the conventional introduction the narrative goes on at once to Judith herself, omitting (for the moment) the advance of Holofernes and the terror of the Jews. All this is inserted in Part II in a recital. Later the poem is thrown back to a still more distant past, the early life and marriage of Judith, told by her servant Abra. The central narrative thus proceeds in three separate courses with an interrupted rhythm. This chronological disturbance, though much less profound than that of Tortoletti,[2] illustrates a tendency which had become rare in France since the beginning of the century. In Desmarets, Vashti's dismissal and Esther's marriage have already taken place when the poem begins. Dictyne's recital allows the poet to return to them later. The point of division in the story is well chosen, and the principle of *in medias res* faithfully observed by the sacrifice of the Biblical sequence of events.

Saint-Amant (like Perrault) is remarkable for the emphasis on the future rather than the past in the chronological construction of his poem. The reversal of the natural order by recitals means that the reader is left in suspense and uncertainty, since he does not know the origin of what is happening: the references to what is going to happen mean that he has no uncertainty about the future. This is best seen in Jocabel's dream, but there is another instance. After the proposition, which declares that Moses will be saved, a more detailed forecast is given by the angel who appears before Jocabel: the hero will save Israel and receive God's Law. Here we have an example of the influence of Christian material on narrative methods, though an old method is only given a new form (apart from the proposition there are in the classical epic religious means of indicating the future such as oracles and soothsayers, like Calchas or Cassandra). There is yet another such indication at the beginning of the poem: after a parallel has been drawn between Pharaoh and Herod, it is stated that the Nile will save Moses from the murderers.[3] It is in this threefold reference,

---

[1] *Semaine*, p. 12.   [2] Cf. p. 54 above.   [3] *Œuvres*, ii. 156.

where the classical epic normally contents itself with one, that Saint-Amant shows his originality and at the same time conforms to the general tendency already observed, to multiply single structural elements.

Recitals, whether used to break up the chronological sequence of the main narrative, as in some examples already discussed, or to introduce extraneous episodes, play such an important part in epic structure that more detailed consideration seems required. Desmarets employs them with peculiar frequency. They hardly conform, however, to the austere standards of Le Bossu. Thus Iasbel's story[1] is introduced abruptly and without any real justification. Pharsandate's narrative[2] is involved and very difficult to follow: it has no appreciable connexion with the fortunes of Esther, though it does fulfil a structural function in persuading Vashti of Pharsandate's devotion. The recitals generally seem irregular, and not only because of their romantic subjects. Pharsandate's story again supplies a key. It will be noticed that it appears to be fictitious, not only in relation to absolute truth but in relation to the truth of the poem. Artemis, who tells it, is really Pharsandate and lies in order to impress Vashti. So far the pattern is complex but not very surprising: parallels can be found in classical epic. Closer examination reveals, however, that all is not fictitious, that Aman's Macedonian origin is derived from the Bible,[3] that the revolt of Cyrus is an historical fact; in brief that much of the recital was intended to recount the early history of Aman as it was in (poetic) reality. It is thus impossible for the reader to decide where truth ends and fiction begins. The grafting of the story of Artemis on the main recital means that the narrator's personality is doubled and another element of confusion is added. This duplicity perhaps throws some light on the poet's moral character, but more is involved than the critical problems of truth and fiction or the relations between recital and central narrative. The whole formal structure is changed: instead of a clearly defined path which winds backwards and forwards to a fixed object, we are suddenly confronted with a prospect receding into infinity. It may be suggested that there is an intimate relationship between this phenomenon and the tricks of perspective and *trompe-l'œil* employed in baroque architecture.

Saint-Amant and Coras furnish examples (there are many others)

---

[1] *Esther*, 1673, p. 61.   [2] Cf. p. 124 above.   [3] Esther xvi. 10 (Vulgate).

of the use of recitals as a means of drawing on Biblical sources outside the main story. So in the *Moyse sauvé* the fisherman Merary relates the adventures of Jacob (divided, as we have seen, into two parts)[1]. The mode of introduction is of interest here: Marie appeals to Merary in the same way as Dido invites Aeneas to tell the tale of Troy and a classical form is once more imposed on the Biblical material. In Coras the education of David is a peg for the story of the Hebrew rulers.[2] The whole of the Book of Judges forms a recital in *Samson*.[3] In general, however, there is no organic connexion between episode and main action. The recital from Judges with its monotonous succession of minor battles has no unity in itself and no relation to the life of Samson. In this respect Coras compares unfavourably with Saint-Amant.

Apart from the recital, there are several other methods of introducing episodes, which may be regarded as the vertebrae of epic structure. They may very well be introduced directly by the poet, as in Saint-Amant's Calm or (to take a clumsy example from a fundamentalist) the history of the Gabaonites in Sainte-Garde Bernouin's *Saül puni*, which begins:

> Pour mieux deuelopper la parole diuine,
> Reprenons ce sujet depuis son origine.[4]

They may, as we have seen, be projected into the future: apart from Jocabel's prophetic dream in the *Moyse sauvé*, which gives the whole story of Moses from his rescue by the princess to Mount Sinai and beyond, and the angelic vision of Perrault, we find this done in Coras, where the end of David's life is related in a prophecy.[5] This last case involves no disturbance of time, as there is no break with the main story, which is simply continued. It seems that Coras had become weary and used the prophecy simply as a means of compression. But in all these instances the dream or prophecy is a prolongation of the main story and may be said to belong to it in the same way as the recitals in the *Aeneid* and the *Odyssey*. For the recital is substituted the Biblical prophecy, which introduces what happens after the close of the main narrative instead of what precedes its opening.

Of other devices the most popular is the description of a tapestry, depicting scenes which the poet wishes to introduce.

---

[1] Cf. p. 89 above.   [2] *David*, p. 19.

[3] *Samson*, p. 16.   [4] *Saül puni*, p. 40.   [5] *David*, p. 132.

It is used by Montchrestien (Susanna embroiders a canvas with the subject of Abraham's sacrifice of Isaac); by Saint-Amant (the Deluge); twice by Marie de Pech (Abraham's Sacrifice and the story of Ninus and Semiramis). The tapestry is a convention of Renaissance epic and may go back to the paintings on the walls of Tristano's lodge in Ariosto.[1] In the seventeenth century, however, the convention seems to take on new life under the influence of the conception of *peinture parlante* and *ut pictura poesis*.[2] It involves an attempt to reduce movement to a static verbal picture, as in Montchrestien:

> Le bon vieillard surpris tourne le col en haut,
> De crainte et d'aise ensemble incontinent tressaut.[3]

On the model of the tapestry various less conventional methods are employed, especially by Coras. So the tombs of Jesse's ancestors furnish a pretext for the history of Ruth[4] and, most surprising, the deluge is presented in the form of a sermon preached by Jonah to the people of Nineveh.[5]

The interaction of these different elements, and its structural consequences, may be illustrated from the *Judith* of Marie de Pech, who, with Saint-Amant and Desmarets, furnishes an extreme case of complexity. The tapestry used to introduce the story of Abraham and Isaac is itself enclosed within Abra's recital of Judith's life. By Le Bossu's standards it bears no relation to the main theme, but serves to point a moral. As soon as Abra's story is finished, a new recital begins. The listeners ask for more information about the tapestry, so Abra recounts the history of Abraham and Isaac more extensively.[6] The methods of linking recital and main theme tend to become more ingenious and less convincing. The life of David forms another episode, clumsily inserted to fill in the time while Judith and Abra are waiting for dawn.[7] Like the story of Jacob in the *Moyse sauvé* it is split into two parts. The first goes as far as Goliath's death, the second to David's accession as king. The pattern thus becomes more and more involved. Finally the story of Ninus and Semiramis is introduced by means of a tapestry in the tent of Holofernes.[8] It is more suitable than the others because of the parallel Ninus–Holo-

---

[1] Cf. p. 51 above.
[2] Cf. Sayce, 'Saint-Amant and Poussin', *French Studies*, i (1947).
[3] *Susane*, p. 347.   [4] *David*, p. 11.   [5] *Jonas*, p. 120.
[6] *Judith*, p. 72.   [7] pp. 94 ff.   [8] p. 124.

fernes and Semiramis–Judith, which links it to the action of the poem. But on the whole recitals within recitals and conversations within conversations produce an intricate tangle.

Analogous dislocations of a smooth forward-moving rhythm may be produced, usually on a less extensive scale, by changes of scene or viewpoint, which create effects in space similar to those of the recital in time. Again a distinction may be observed between dislocation and an even progression, exemplified by Saint-Amant and Morillon. In the main story of the *Moyse* there are two scenes of action and two centres of interest (Jocabel and the cradle). After the close of Jocabel's dream we find, instead of a long development of one and then the other, a rapid alternation which recalls Italian methods, though it is less complex. It might be thought that this would damage the unity of the poem. In fact, however, Moses provides a link between them, being the continual theme wherever the action is placed. In Morillon, on the other hand, there is continuity of viewpoint. In the Bible (followed by Saint-Amant) the centre of interest passes from Jacob in flight to Laban in pursuit.[1] In Morillon the action never leaves Jacob, and Laban's arrival is seen through his eyes.[2] Again we may detect signs of a difference between a static and a moving conception of structure.

A particular case of change of viewpoint is presented by the direct intervention of the poet in the narrative, a problem which was to be of great importance in the novel. In the sixteenth century poets had taken sides violently, upbraiding or commending the characters and expressing their opinion freely on events. This is still found in the early seventeenth century (and even later in backward writers like Saint-Peres). So Montchrestien realizes that his reproaches are wasted on the elders:

> Mais ie parle à des sourds, ie perds temps vainement.
> Vous voulez qu'elle meure encor qu'innocemment.[3]

Gamon is more furiously indignant:

> O fureur obstinée! ô destinée amere!
> O desastrez enfans! ô mizerable mere!
> O Thracienne rage! ô crimes desloyaux![4]

This kind of writing seems primitive, but it does reflect genuine

---

[1] Gen. xxxi. 21–25; Saint-Amant, *Œuvres*, ii. 275.   [2] *Joseph*, p. 18.
[3] *Susane*, p. 382.   [4] *Iardinet de poesie*, p. 102.

enthusiasm, a deep interest in the theme of the poem. Later writers maintain to some extent this tradition of personal intervention, but in a different, more distant tone, looking down from a height to bestow approval or reprobation. The difference may be gauged from a comparison between the passage quoted from Montchrestien and the same sentiment expressed by Morillon:

> Mais je vous donne icy des avis superflus,
> Le conseil en est pris, vous ne m'écoutez plus.[1]

Progress has been made, in this as in other respects, towards a classical ideal of restraint. Finally, in an urbane and correct poet like Perrault direct personal intervention is wholly lacking.

Peripeteia, considered necessary in epic by Aristotle and Chapelain, is amply furnished by such stories as those of Joseph, David, Saul, Esther, and Judith, and poets had only to follow their source in order to attain what may be regarded as another means of upsetting a straightforward rhythm. Saint-Amant has probably made the best use of it in the rescue of Joseph from prison in the *Moyse* and, of still greater force, Joseph's revelation of his identity to his brothers in *Joseph*. These incidents, which could not have been omitted, do not concern Saint-Amant's inventiveness, but they do concern the epic nature of the subject and contribute to the epic form of his work.

Another feature of the classical epic is the breaking up of the action by means of the speeches of the characters. The insults of Achilles and Agamemnon, Dido's curse of Aeneas are typical examples. In Saint-Amant the place they occupy is far greater, and their importance for the action on the whole slighter. Thus the lament of Rebecca for Jacob's departure is not necessary to the development of the narrative; and it adds nothing to the indications already given of the characters of Rebecca and the twins, Jacob and Esau. The exaggeration of this element may be attributed partly again to the tendency to multiply classical features, as well as perhaps to the psychological interest and, as also in Montchrestien, the dramatic quality of these long speeches. Most interesting from this point of view is the discussion between Amram and Jocabel, where the sustained dialogue belongs to tragedy rather than epic. It is in sharp contrast with similar instances (much less developed) in classical epic, for example the

---

[1] *Joseph*, p. 25.

quarrel between Agamemnon and Achilles. There the interest lies primarily in the clash between two men, here between two minds, two emotional attitudes. Similarly in Marie de Pech speeches and conversations are multiplied: the brief reference in the Apocrypha to the words of Holofernes is turned into a full classical exhortation.[1] All this gives the poem, like Montchrestien's, a dramatic character. Every new situation or crisis is expressed in dialogue or monologue, and Abra may be regarded as the equivalent of the confidante of tragedy.

As we have seen, the critics had taken some interest in metre as one of the criteria of true epic.[2] The Alexandrine is as firmly established in the poems as it is in works of theory, and no other metre is employed except in the occasional introduction of lyric stanzas, for example by Morillon, who in the oracle and the divine message to Joseph mingles lines of six and eight syllables with his Alexandrines,[3] or by Lesfargues, who uses them to round off some of his books, especially when they end abruptly. This use may be compared with Corneille's in tragedy. It is one more departure from strict classical form. A more interesting one, though there is but a single instance, is the echo, used by Pierre de Saint-Louis. At the beginning of Elijah's ministry his conversation with an angel is represented as an echo, with the prophet's questions and the angel's answers:

> C'est aussi l'oraison, qui doit nourrir mon âme;
> Mais qui nuit plus à l'homme, et qui plus le diffame?
> — Femme.
>
> Sans Eve, cet Adam, le premier des mortels,
> Nous eût-il, comme on dit, rendu tous immortels?
> — Tels.[4]

A similar case has been encountered in the sixteenth century in Didier Oriet,[5] but here the echo is much longer (seventy-five lines) and is worked into the fabric of the poem.

A study of structure, then, confirms observations made from quite different directions. The raw material derived from the Old Testament is manipulated by the more self-conscious poets in order that it may be adapted to classical models. But at the same time the classical models themselves are often distorted in accordance with new aesthetic principles.

[1] *Judith*, p. 34. Cf. Judith vii. 1.   [2] Cf. p. 25 above.
[3] *Joseph*, pp. 105, 108.   [4] *Éliade*, p. 11.   [5] Cf. p. 46 above.

CHAPTER XVI

The Heroic Style

WITH the questions of metre just discussed we are on the threshold of style. Our investigations here must inevitably be directed towards the definition of the epic style of the period, and it will in consequence hardly be possible to do more than touch upon the individual qualities of particular works and especially the poetic originality of Saint-Amant. A full study would transcend the bounds of this inquiry[1].

At the beginning of the century the influence of the Pléiade and Du Bartas is, as might be expected, still dominant, though the effects of Malherbe's reforms are already visible. Gamon's style is directly derived from mon Du Bartas with its compound adjectives *aime-tenebres*, *porte-brandons*, *irrite-Dieu*, its puns:

> As-tu, gentil Gentil . . . [2]

and cacophonies, which in ruggedness surpass the master:

> Si peus-tu les domter en empirant ton ire,
> Car ton ire empirant peut croistre ton Empire.[3]

At the same time it is impossible to deny his vigour:

> Comme quand l'Hyuer porte, en claquetant des dents,
> La bouche creuassée, et les cheueux tous blancs,
> Que les fleuues enflez sur la plaine serrée,
> Poussent, à bleus monceaux, vne glace vitrée.[4]

The combination of realism and abstraction is characteristic. However, even in comparison with Montchrestien, Gamon's style seems a lingering echo of an earlier generation.

The survival of the Pléiade tradition is clearly seen in Anne

---

[1] Though this is a task that remains to be done, some interesting observations may be found in Wencelius, 'Contribution à l'étude du baroque: Saint-Amant', *XVIIe siècle*, 1950; and Le Hir, 'Notes sur la langue et le style du *Moïse sauvé* de Saint-Amant (1653)', *Le Français moderne*, 1951.

[2] *Iardinet de poesie*, p. 104.

[3] Ib., p. 94.

[4] *Semaine*, p. 10.

d'Urfé. A long dissection of Susanna's beauties contains passages like

> Mais quand ils contemploient cette bouche pourprine
> Enflee mollement de couleur coralline . . .
> Et puis son beau menton au milieu fosselu
> Tel comme l'eut Cypris douïllet et pommelu.[1]

Petrarchan, or post-Petrarchan, antitheses and metaphors are used with little sense of fitness:

> Miracle merueilleux qu'vne si chaude flame
> Print naissance de l'eau des pleurs de cette Dame.[2]

The case of Montchrestien is more complex. The evidence of the corrections and their relation to Malherbe has already been examined.[3] Apart from them, we find the appearance of features which attain full development in the middle of the century—heavy periphrasis, as in the description of thunder:

> . . . La bruyante voix,
> Qui meut le pied des monts et la cime des bois[4]

or of the sun as *le grand Astre du Ciel*;[5] frozen metaphors such as *la poison langoureuse*[6] of love; conventional epithets like *les poissons escaillez*; antitheses like

> Ore glacez de haine, ore embrasez d'amour.[7]

None of these devices were invented by Montchrestien, but they show the orientation of the new century.

However, in general and even after the revision, style and imagery are still close to the methods of the Pléiade. Diminutives and obsolete expressions abound:

> Tantost elle contemple vne mignarde Auette
> Cueillir le miel rosin de fleurette en fleurette.[8]

The imagery derived from the dairy, characteristic of Ronsard, is found too in *Susane*:

> Sa gorge vient apres plus blanche que le lait,
> Amassé fraischement en fourmage mollet.[9]

The flowers of the garden have popular country names:

> On voit dans les replis de ce plaisant Dedale
> Le romarin espais, la sauge verte-pale,

[1] *Hymnes*, p. 195. [2] Ib., p. 213. [3] Cf. p. 57 above.
[4] *Susane*, p. 378. [5] p. 355. [6] p. 342.
[7] p. 368. [8] p. 360. [9] p. 376.

La lauande, le thim, et le iaune souci,
La mariolaine franche et la sauuage aussi,
La paruanche, le coq, l'aspic, la sarriette,
L'odorant basilic, la double violette,
Le nard, la marguerite . . .[1]

By their profusion and search for the technical and the obscure
these lists belong to the tradition of the Pléiade. It is clear that
Malherbe's influence on Montchrestien did not penetrate much
below the surface.

Montchrestien is also of his time in the vigorous popular vein
which alternates with the learned terminology of the Pléiade. Low
expressions occur frequently: thus the elders are described as *ces
deux garnemens*,[2] Susanna walking in the garden:

Sur la fin de ces mots ià suante elle arriue.[3]

The tone of such passages falls much below what was soon to be
considered the standard of epic.

Occasionally Montchrestien expresses himself in naïve images
which are generally eliminated in the course of revision. The
astonishing, almost surrealist representation, perhaps derived from
an emblem, of Joachim's first infatuation:

Le cœur à ce propos sortant de la poitrine,
Sous l'escorte de l'œil, vers Susane chemine[4]

is modified considerably in the second edition.

It was only to be expected that the influence of the sixteenth-
century poets should still be strongly marked in Montchrestien
and his contemporaries. It is much more remarkable to find similar
features fifty or more years later: as in other respects, so in style,
the Biblical epic is often an antiquated provincial survival. Thus
Saint-Peres writes:

Se plaindre à Putiphar de l'amoureuse force,
Qu'elle dit auoir fait cet Hebreu jouuenceau,
A leur commun honneur . . . .[5]

The word *jouuenceau* used seriously, the position of the adjective

---

[1] p. 351.   [2] p. 382.
[3] p. 360. This line does not appear in the first edition, which indicates that
refinement of taste was not always a motive in the corrections.
[4] *Susane*, 1601, p. 293.
[5] *Joseph*, p. 12.

Hebreu, the ungainly construction are all surprising in 1648. The comparison of camels to bees:

> „Estoient comme vn Essain qui d'Auettes fourmille[1]

is also in the Pléiade tradition.[2]

Later still, leaving Saint-Amant aside for the moment, there are other poets who remain largely untouched by current fashions, though the sixteenth-century survivals are naturally not so prominent. As his preface suggests,[3] Le Cordier has little use for literary artifice. Though he keeps the syntactic lucidity of his time (and in this way differs from Saint-Peres), there are almost no signs of the conventional poetic vocabulary. Instead we find a succession of images, sometimes complex and unexpected, occasionally catching the directness of the Bible:

> Regardez y l'estat de maint ambitieux
> Qui veut mont dessus mont escalader les Cieux,
> Qui bastit ses chasteaux des mains de l'iniustice
> Et des ruines du pauvre éleve ses caprices,
> Qui porte la semence au champ de sa douleur,
> Afin d'en recüeillir le fruit de son malheur.[4]

In seed, field, and fruit a recurrent theme of Biblical imagery will be noticed. Or the language may be as bare of ornament as the original:

> O mere, ce dit-il, ie sors nud de ton ventre.[5]

The most original of all is Pierre de Saint-Louis, whose sustained extravagance, perhaps the extreme example of baroque influence in French literature, offers a complete contrast to Le Cordier's simplicity. Sometimes, again, his constructions are a survival from the previous century, like the symmetrical arrangement of different verbs and objects (*vers rapportés*):

> Profane, tue, bat, pille, renverse, brise
> Temples, hommes, autels, tombeaux, palais, églises.[6]

The same is perhaps true of the Greek words which fill his verses, producing an effect at once grotesque and marvellous:

> C'est à présent qu'on voit sans feinte et sans fadaise,
> Et la métempsycose, et la palingénèse[7]

---

[1] Ib., p. 6.

[2] *Avette* was already obsolescent by the beginning of the century. The last instance quoted by the *Dictionnaire historique* (Académie) is from Théophile. According to Wartburg (*Französisches Etymologisches Wörterbuch*) it is also found in Scarron.

[3] Cf. p. 109 above.　　　　　　[4] *Job*, p. 24.　　　　　　[5] Ib., p. 9.

[6] *Éliade*, p. 65. On this device cf. Curtius, *Europäische Literatur*, p. 288.

[7] p. 39.

> ... chaque plante
> Est un héliotrope, ou bien une hélianthe[1]
> Qu'en cette grande lice et céleste hippodrome,
> Je puisse pour vous suivre être un héliodrome.[2]

But like the frequent puns:

> De sorte qu'en un sens on pourrait avouer
> Que toutes ces maisons sont maisons à louer[3]

they are also the fruit of an unlimited and highly personal ingenuity. (It will be remembered that Pierre de Saint-Louis could make anagrams by the hundred.)[4] Improbable and inappropriate images flow from his pen. In a few lines he compares the angels to birds of paradise, nightingales, swans dying of love, courtiers, pages, and more still. To give a more complete idea of his method, the whole passage may be quoted:

> Oiseaux de Paradis, rossignols bienheureux,
> Cignes mourans d'amour, aimables amoureux,
> Favorisez mon art avec votre nature,
> Me donnant ma leçon sur votre tablature.
> Premiers pages d'honneur, courtisans de plaisir,
> Toujours en jouissance, et toujours en désir,
> Volez avec vos luths, vos harpes, vos violes,
> Pour animer le ton de mes froides paroles;
> Adoucissez mon chant avec votre bémol,
> Et faites que je puisse aller jusqu'à mon *sol*;
> Réjouissez mon cœur, et recréez mon âme
> Par les divins fredons de votre haute gamme;
> Déployez vos motets, et faites vos concerts
> Pour celui que je chante, et celui que je sers.[5]

The common feature of these ornaments of style is that they all contribute to the agitation which is the abiding characteristic of the poem and derives from the exaltation of the poet:

> Désirant de pouvoir le chanter dans mes vers
> Par tous les carrefours de ce vaste univers.[6]

These, however, are exceptions. Other writers attempt, however feebly in some cases, to achieve the accepted grand style, which can be studied as a whole, with allowances made for indivi-

---

[1] p. 23.   [2] p. 43.   [3] p. 23.
[4] See Follard's life (*Éliade*, p. x); quoted by Gautier in *Les Grotesques*.
[5] p. 2.   [6] p. 2.

dual variations. It depends largely on a system of conventional figures of speech, which tend to recur in almost identical form from one work to another.

Beginning with the single word, we find that an outstanding characteristic of the heroic style is the conventional or frozen epithet, of which an example has already been noted in Mont-chrestien. M. Magendie speaks of the colourless frigidity of style in the *Moyse sauvé*, due to the poet's conviction that he must use only 'l'épithète abstraite, morale, sans couleur et sans vie; elle lui paraît plus distinguée, plus convenable aux nobles personnages auxquels il dédie son poème'.[1] This is perhaps less than half the truth.[2] In Saint-Amant the grand style attains something approaching maturity, but it is by no means fully sustained. It is often relieved by touches of the vigorous realism of the Louis XIII period, more often modified by the particular characteristics of the poet's genius. However, Magendie is right as far as the conventional epithet is concerned and he quotes telling examples like *sentier digne*, *démarche auguste*, *pompe modeste*, *fer pudique*. It may be added that the epithet is often inappropriate as well as conventional:

> Quand le bon Merary, que la fortune indigne
> Reduisoit, quoy qu'illustre, à manier la ligne;[3]
>
> Le bruit confirmatif d'un tonnerre agreable.[4]

The ultimate debasement of such conventions can be observed in Lesfargues, whose epithets are characterized by a falsity and impropriety accentuated by their unnecessary multiplication:

> Doit noyer dans le sang d'vne heureuse blessure
> D'Israël satisfait l'indigne flestrissure.[5]
>
> L'officieux Dauid prend sa fameuse Lyre.[6]

They are associated with an absence of visual imagination, as in the description of Goliath, which might have furnished interesting opportunities for an epic poet:

> Il transporte par tout d'vn port imperieux
> De son enorme corps les membres spacieux.[7]

No picture is evoked.

---

[1] *La Politesse mondaine*, p. 886 n.
[2] For a more balanced view see Le Hir, 'Notes sur la langue et le style du *Moïse sauvé*'.   [3] *Œuvres*, ii. 167.   [4] ii. 179.
[5] *David*, p. 26.   [6] p. 15.   [7] p. 16.

From the conventional epithet we may pass to the conventional image, metaphor or simile. Again Montchrestien has offered an early example and perhaps a link with the generation of the Pléiade;[1] and even the archaistic Saint-Peres uses one of the most familiar of seventeenth-century metaphors:

> Sans se laisser brusler d'vne flamme insensée.[2]

(It is, of course, the complete petrification, and not the metaphor itself, which is typical of the later seventeenth century.)[3] In Saint-Amant and those who follow him such metaphors—*flamme* for love, *appas* for feminine beauty, *flambeau* for sun, *émail* for flowers, *soleil* for eye—recur frequently. Even apparently new images, derived from features of contemporary civilization, soon themselves become fossilized, like the gun, perhaps derived from Ariosto[4] and found, for example, in Saint-Amant and Morillon as well as several times in Coras.

However, against this fixed background individual invention is not excluded. Saint-Amant is not always content with simple substitution of an accepted counter for an accepted object:

> Que d'un fidele tronc un rameau sortiroit
> Dont l'ombrage fatal l'Egipte estoufferoit.[5]

The way in which the primary (and conventional) conception of the tree is used to create fresh metaphors furnishes yet another example of his determination to pursue all the logical consequences of an idea. In Morillon, side by side with the comparisons derived from literary convention (travellers, wolves, eagles, oak-trees, the magnet, the cannon) we find the use of the preacher's homely illustrations—a miser searching for his treasure,[6] a victim of delirium struggling with a physician,[7] lead melted in a furnace.[8] In this respect he comes close to Pierre de Saint-Louis, otherwise almost his opposite.

A deeper originality, though still in harmony with certain tendencies of the period and of the Biblical epic, appears in the author of *Hélie*:

> Que les Astres des Cieux n'égalent pas ses crimes,
> Ny les Eaux de la Mer, ny les feux des abismes.[9]

---

[1] Cf. p. 211 above.   [2] *Joseph*, p. 11.
[3] Cf. d'Urfé, p. 211 above, where the metaphor is still alive, though bearing all the marks of an overworked convention.
[4] Cf. p. 93 above.   [5] *Œuvres*, ii. 154.   [6] *Joseph*, p. 57.
[7] p. 34.   [8] p. 83.   [9] *Hélie*, p. 13.

Retranchés des rameaux, mais pour conseruer l'arbre,
Frapés pour amolir, et pour polir ce marbre,
Frapés ces Cœurs de fer, pour les faire ployer,
Mettés-les dans le feu, mais pour les nettoyer.[1]

The first passage, with its reference to the grandeur of nature, and
the second, with its stern moral application of the terms of hus-
bandry, are clearly Biblical in tone, though there is no question
of servile imitation. They, and others like them, seem to have been
written by a man who had absorbed the spirit of the Bible. At
such points the author draws near to Le Cordier. On the other
hand, we also find cases of a form of *préciosité*, perhaps better
described as baroque, which is marked by the human and psychological transformation of animals or of inanimate objects. An
extreme example is the famine[2] (a conventional descriptive set-
piece), which is recorded entirely in images drawn from human
life: the sun declares war on all flowers, the fields are compared to
tapestries, all greenery is enclosed in a coffin, the waters are dried
up and the fish escape to deep caverns:

Desia tous les poissons se prennent à la main,
Dans leurs antres obscurs ils se cachent en vain.[3]

This last absurdity recalls Saint-Amant's *poissons ébahis* and the
strange juxtapositions of precious style, but the whole passage is
full of life.

Returning to the conventional framework, and approaching
figures involving more than one word, we may find in Saint-
Amant examples, better contrived but not fundamentally different
from others, of precious word-play:

Avoient trompé le temps en trompant le poisson[4]

or

Pensa faire du nord un funeste occident.[5]

Closely allied to these is the artificial repetition (forming a pendant
to an artificial antithesis) of:

La fille, suspendue, observe, non de loin,
Et l'objet de sa flame, et l'objet de son soin.[6]

(The former *objet* is the shepherd Elisaph, the latter the infant
Moses.) The fossilized metaphor *flame* is wholly in keeping with
these surroundings.

[1] p. 29.   [2] From I Kings xvii.   [3] *Hélie*, p. 31.
[4] *Œuvres*, ii. 250.   [5] ii. 243.   [6] ii. 184.

Oxymoron is much more frequent and more significant; it has already been examined in a wider context.[1] From a narrowly stylistic point of view we may observe that in Saint-Amant's *Joseph* the use of oxymoron seems particularly daring:

> Consoloit ce bon pere, et d'un heureux malheur
> Servoit en le blessant à guerir sa douleur.[2]

This suggests a certain evolution in the interval between *Joseph* and *Moyse sauvé*.

Oxymoron may be regarded as a condensed form of antithesis, which is one of the commonest devices and perhaps occupies a place in style equivalent to that of peripeteia in narrative. Habitual ways of thought are reversed and attention is awakened by the shock, though by this time its persistent use had considerably weakened its power to surprise, as we see in Saint-Peres:

> Les jours estoient pour luy de tres-obscures nuits.[3]

This is especially so (and we have here further evidence of the debasement of the conventions) when, as often in Coras, the content does not correspond to the form of the antithesis, for example:

> Du glorieux palmier l'ambitieuse branche,
> Pour leur fournir de mets et s'abaisse et se panche.[4]

The double conjunction suggests a contrast which in fact does not exist. Saint-Amant, on the other hand, occasionally escapes from the overburdened convention to express harmonies which are enhanced by the appearance of violent contradiction, as when he speaks of *les mots flateurs et vrays*[5] or (with oxymoron) of *de la nuit l'effroy tranquille*.[6] The juxtaposition of disparate elements (almost syllepsis) of

> Le blaspheme à la bouche et le glaive à la main[7]

is perhaps an extension of the same principle. It renders action and movement successfully, a point of importance for the heroic atmosphere. In general Saint-Amant tends to accumulate antitheses at emotional crises in order to represent the conflict of psychological forces.[8]

---

[1] Cf. p. 159 above. [2] *Œuvres*, ii. 116. [3] *Joseph*, p. 10.
[4] *Josué*, p. 41. [5] *Œuvres*, ii. 171. [6] ii. 170.
[7] ii. 165. [8] For example in Jocabel's lament (ii. 160–1).

With antithesis and oxymoron, periphrasis may be regarded as the central feature of the heroic style. By its aid a veil of grandeur is spread over objects and actions which are in themselves hardly consonant with the dignity of epic, and this is particularly important when intractable material drawn from the Bible (with its different standards of grandeur) cannot be circumvented.[1] Moreover, in periphrasis a prominent object is not presented to the reader as it appears superficially. Instead its properties are analysed and an attempt is made to uncover the hidden relationships between them. Thus the crocodile in Saint-Amant is not named:

> Quand un monstre cruel, qui nage et qui se treuve
> Tantost dessus la rive et tantost dans le fleuve,
> Un amphibie enorme, un traistre qui se pleint,
> Qui pour l'homme attraper les pleurs de l'homme feint.[2]

These attributes add nothing to the sensory evocation of the beast, but they present a series of intellectual problems (in this case rudimentary). This is not always so—sometimes the periphrasis strengthens the impression made by the object, as in the seven years of Jacob:

> Mais à condition qu'il verroit par sept ans
> Les neiges de l'hyver et les fleurs du printemps,
> Et les biens qu'en l'automne et qu'en l'esté l'on serre,
> Couvrir tour après tour la face de la terre.[3]

It may be thought that the terms used are too abstract (and it will be seen that a second periphrasis—les biens, &c.—is enclosed within the first), but the idea of duration gains in emphasis. The procedure is in harmony with the analytical bent of Saint-Amant, everywhere apparent. Too often, however, it degenerates into automatic dilution, clogged with useless particulars, like the dissection of the crocodile's motives:

> Et, soit que, sous l'instinct d'un desir affamé,
> Il eust senty l'enfant qui reposoit sur l'onde,
> Soit qu'il fist sans dessein sa route vagabonde . . .[4]

Again, later writers carry the debasement of the convention still further, and Coras is distinguished once more by the extreme

---

[1] Cf. pp. 153 ff. above.
[2] Œuvres, ii. 181.
[3] ii. 261.
[4] ii. 181.

impropriety of his periphrases, as when Adine describes *herself* in a well-known formula:

> Souffrons donc, dit Adine, et l'injure, et l'affront,
> Qui fait rougir les lys dont se pare mon front.[1]

Another common ingredient of the heroic style is enumeration, one of the most effective as well as one of the oldest epic devices. It may be seen in Saint-Amant:

> Je ne vous diray point les fleuves qu'ils passerent,
> Les serpens, les lyons, que leurs mains repousserent;
> Les montagnes, les bois, les plaines, les hameaux,
> Que franchirent sous eux les pas de leurs chameaux.[2]

Here it is combined with paralipsis: the poet announces that he will not say what in fact he does say, and so prepares for the compression of what follows. This enhances rather than diminishes the normal effect of enumeration, which is to lend breadth and movement to a description. In this case the discreet use of Oriental detail (*lyons*, *chameaux*) adds to the epic force of the passage. Saint-Amant's imitators are less successful, like Lesfargues:

> Il foule de Sidon les fertiles guerets:
> Il trauerse de Dan les sauuages forests;
> Il approche de Tyr les superbes murailles. . . .[3]

In spite of the particularized proper names, the details chosen seem arbitrary (*guerets* suggests a French scene). We have here another example of Biblical material closely imitated but overdecorated in conformity with the requirements of the heroic style.[4] It is not easy to distinguish enumeration from the catalogue, into which it merges and which is constructed on a larger scale, so as to be perhaps a narrative rather than a stylistic device. Striking examples of the full catalogue are to be found in Anne d'Urfé (the review of the tribes and nations of the Assyrian army in the second book of *Judic*) and Coras (the procession of the twelve tribes of Israel in *Josué*[5]).

If all these features can be summed up in a general observation, it is probably in their common tendency towards abstraction. Saint-Amant, like his predecessors, has not wholly succumbed

---

[1] *Jonas*, p. 150.   [2] *Œuvres*, ii. 177.   [3] *David*, p. 285.
[4] Cf. II Sam. xxiv. 6–7.   [5] *Josué*, p. 38.

to this tendency, and a vigorous, concrete, and sensuous imagination is everywhere apparent in the *Moyse*. The realistic side of the
poem is seen partly in the use of trade and technical terms, which
seem to represent a survival from the theory and practice of the
Pléiade. The use of such terms can also be paralleled in classical
epic, but might none the less be condemned as base by the
standards of decorum current in Saint-Amant's time or shortly
afterwards. An example is Merary's fishing-tackle:

> Qui s'aidoit de la nasse, et qui le plus souvent
> Venoit en cet endroit secher ses rets au vent[1]

or the prosaic details of a comparison drawn from carpentry:

> Ainsi, quand d'une poutre on oste quelque estaye
> Qui se vit autresfois l'honneur d'une futaye.[2]

This sort of realism must not be confused with the conventional
baroque horror of the scenes of carnage:

> Le sang à gros bouillons luy sort de maint endroit[3]

which can be seen more fully developed in Lesfargues:

> ce Roy furieux
> Qui tout à coup roulant ses effroyables yeux,
> Vomit auec effort sans poux et sans courage,
> D'vne bouche escumante et la bile et la rage.[4]

This may seem at first sight to convey realistic vigour, but closer
examination shows the predominance of abstraction (*effroyables,
courage, rage*) and conventional horror (*escumante, bile*). Saint-Amant,
on the other hand, succeeds in introducing sharp visual detail even
into such passages:

> Mais ses ongles enfin s'esclatent et se fendent,
> Et des doigts deschirez les longues peaux luy pendent.[5]

However, abstraction is by no means absent from Saint-Amant's
poetry, and his personal qualities are perhaps best revealed in his
combination of abstract and concrete words, which proves that
abstraction and frigidity are by no means synonymous. The
description of God offers a most splendid example in the union

---

[1] *Œuvres*, ii. 167.   [2] ii. 164.   [3] ii. 197.
[4] *David*, p. 15.   [5] *Œuvres*, ii. 217.

of concrete diadem and abstract eternity (we may be reminded of
Vaughan and especially of *The World*):

> ... je suis le roy suprême
> Qui l'eternité seule a pour son diadême.[1]

But a lower key is almost as effective:

> Elle s'en vient noyer sa chaleur et sa peine
> Dans l'humide plaisir d'une claire fontaine,
> Et veut qu'en mesme temps toutes les vierges sœurs
> Plongent leur lassitude en ses fresches douceurs.[2]

Here five abstract nouns absorb the two concrete (the spring and
the bathing girls): all is made more remote and more unsubstantial.

Saint-Amant perhaps represents a point of balance between the
old concreteness and the growing movement towards abstraction,
which develops rapidly after him and reaches its culmination in
Perrault. Even when he is describing his animals, Perrault asks
questions which never occurred to La Fontaine:

> Mais nous ne sçavons point le fond de leur essence,
> Ce qui fait le Lyon, ce qui dans ses yeux roux,
> Ainsi que dans son cœur allume son courroux.[3]

A particular phenomenon suggests at once an inquiry into its
general significance. More often the particular object is described
in purely abstract terms:

> Toute l'immensité de l'Empire des eaux,
> Ne connoissoit encor ni poissons, ni vaisseaux,
> Et les vents en couroux, de leur soufle inutile
> Ne pouvoient agiter qu'un élement sterile.[4]

Only the fish and the vessels give a concrete impression and they
are merely names of general categories. The method is sometimes
invested with true poetic quality, as in the disincarnate chill of

> Loin des riches Palais, loin du monde et du bruit,
> Dans la rigueur du froid, dans l'horreur de la nuit.[5]

Similarly, the antitheses seem sharper in their contrasts as one
abstract is set against another. These tendencies have been apparent
throughout the century, but nowhere has the lack of contact with
material things reached such an extreme point.

---

[1] *Œuvres*, ii. 179.   [2] ii. 315.   [3] *Adam*, p. 18.
[4] Ib., p. 6.   [5] Ib., p. 74.

Occasionally both earlier realism and later abstraction may attain a certain grave simplicity, which is suited to the majestic themes and provides most of the rare moments of poetry in these works. We find it, for example, in Montchrestien:

> Suffise qu'en ce lieu vient Susane la belle.[1]

And it appears even in Saint-Peres, in the form of Biblical injunction:

> Accueille l'indigent, mange auec luy ton pain,
> Fais asseoir pres de toy celuy-là qui a faim,
> Couure ceux qui sont nuds, et de ta garderobe
> Donne leur des manteaux, couure les de ta robe.[2]

Such moments are naturally much more frequent in Saint-Amant and some have already been discussed, especially where they too are clearly modelled on the Bible.[3] One example may be quoted which owes little to the Bible or to literary sources:

> Si tost que sa lueur reblanchit l'horizon, . . .
> Et que le roy des feux, d'un rayon vif et pur,
> Eut refait le matin d'or, de pourpre et d'azur,
> La faucille à la main, de leur cabanne ils sortent.[4]

The phrase *d'or, de pourpre et d'azur* is not indeed original,[5] but the lines leave an impression of delicate purity.

On the whole, however, for the purposes of this chapter it has been necessary to isolate merely a highest common factor in the poems, which has meant the neglect of much that lies outside it (especially in the case of Saint-Amant). The examination of this common style leads none the less to a conclusion of some interest, the growing technical facility of mediocre or even worthless poets after the middle of the century. Whereas a Saint-Peres, in spite of occasional successful passages, writes badly with confused syntax and is generally feeble, low, and diffuse, his successors, though perhaps less endowed by nature, rarely fall below a moderate level of clarity and elegance. This may be illustrated from the cases of Sainte-Garde and Lesfargues. Both are without poetic talent, but they are capable of writing lines like

> Dauid qui vous sert peu, vous pourra beaucoup nuire[6]

---

[1] *Susane*, p. 352.
[2] *Tobie*, p. 12.
[3] e.g. p. 100 above.
[4] *Œuvres*, ii. 160.
[5] Cf. p. 96 above.
[6] *Saül puni*, p. 15.

with its concise antithesis, or

> Quoy, veux-tu qu'esloigné de la Cour et du monde
> Que traisnant vne vie obscure et vagabonde,
> Tousiours dans les dangers, tousiours dans les douleurs
> Ie n'acheue iamais ma fuite et mes malheurs?[1]

which is not without a sort of pathetic resonance. Both passages
are strongly reminiscent of contemporary tragedy (the first perhaps of *Britannicus*, the second of *Mithridate*). Clearly they are far
below Racine in poetic power, but there is a family resemblance
which is due to the use of a certain vocabulary and to a similar
ease in handling concise or involved syntax.

This may throw some light on the style of Coras, which has been
appraised very differently by the few writers who have considered
it. Chateaubriand praises his simplicity and descriptive power and
prefers him to Saint-Amant.[2] Duchesne goes further:

> Le style a une noblesse continue, une clarté, une correction toutes
> nouvelles, surtout dans l'expression des vérités morales et philoso-
> phiques.[3]

Toinet is equally vehement in the opposite sense:

> Quant au style de Coras, il n'en est point de plus bas et de plus
> prétentieux tout ensemble, de plus aride et de plus impropre.[4]

Duchesne was regarding the question historically: the qualities
which he finds are seen in relation to their absence in Chapelain or
Saint-Amant. His judgement is confirmed by the syntactic facility
which we have observed in Sainte-Garde and Lesfargues, but in
the deeper characteristics which go to make up style Toinet's view
is amply borne out. The explanation of this facility lies no doubt
in the superficial mastery of technique which in periods of highly
developed civilization extends even to artists devoid of talent.

---

[1] *David*, p. 85.   [2] *Génie du Christianisme*, pt. ii, bk. i, ch. 4.
[3] *Histoire des poëmes épiques*, p. 237.   [4] i. 208.

PLATE II

b. Coras, *Jonas*, 1663
Frontispiece

a. Marie de Pech, *Judith*
Second frontispiece

PLATE III

a

b

c

d

Lesfargues, *David*, 1660

PLATE IV

a. Desmarets, *Esther*, 1670

b. From *Bible de Royaumont*, 1670

PLATE V

a

b

c

d

Perrault, *Adam*
a, d Drawings; *b, d* Engravings

PLATE VI

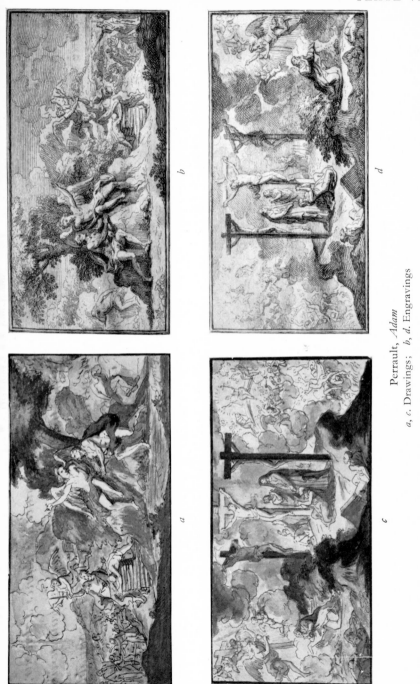

Perrault, *Adam*

a, c. Drawings; *b, d.* Engravings

PLATE VII

b. From *Biblia sacra*, Mainz, 1609

a. From Frizon's *Bible*, 1621

d. From *Bible de Royaumont*, 1670

c. From Frizon's *Bible*, 1621

PLATE VIII

Elsheimer, 'Susanna and the Elders'

CHAPTER XVII

The Epic and the Visual Arts

IT will be apparent that one of the main sources of interest in this study lies in the relation of the poems to contemporary works of art, and through them to the imagination and sensibility of the period. A discussion of this relation may proceed from specific influences to more general affinities. The former are most clearly visible in the illustrations of the poems by contemporary engravers.

Six of the poems are illustrated (excluding mere decorated title-pages and occasional ornament): the *Moyse sauvé*, the *Judith* of Marie de Pech, the *David* of Lesfargues, the *Jonas* of Coras, the *Esther* of Desmarets, and the *Adam* of Perrault. As the Biblical epic was less popular it was not to be expected that this illustration should be on the costly scale of such profane poems as *Alaric* and *La Pucelle*: in most cases the illustration consists of no more than an engraved frontispiece.

The most remarkable example is certainly the frontispiece of the first edition of the *Moyse* (1653), drawn by Claude Vignon and engraved by Abraham Bosse,[1] who were together responsible for some of the best illustrated books of the middle of the century, such as Desmarets's *Ariane* and Chapelain's *La Pucelle*. It is remarkable for its fidelity to both the text and the spirit of the poem.

The scene represented is one chosen by Poussin for at least three, and possibly five, pictures, the discovery of Moses by the princess, 'Moïse sauvé des eaux'.[2] At the left of the engraving the princess appears in a throne-like chariot,[3] drawn, as in the poem, by three yoked unicorns.[4] Dressed in a long robe, with a richly plumed head-dress, bare breasts, and imperiously pointing finger, she towers above the whole scene, a characteristic representative of the feminism of the period which produced the *Grande Mademoiselle* or Saint-Amant's patroness and model, Marie-Louise de

---

[1] See Plate I. The engraving is signed 'A Bosse Seculp. C Vignon jn.' Cf. Blum, *L'Œuvre gravé d'Abraham Bosse*, Paris, 1924, no. 643.

[2] Cf. Magne, *Nicolas Poussin*, Paris, 1914, p. 206.

[3] 'Le beau trosne roulant', *Œuvres*, ii. 318.   [4] ii. 312.

Gonzague. Below her, and only slightly less majestic, is the driver of the unicorns, an Amazon,[1] with the conventional cuirass and plumed helmet. The artists have omitted the accompanying train of Barbary horse (beloved of an elf), dromedary, giraffe, and elephant,[2] but the unicorns supply fantasy enough. Below the chariot four slaves, almost naked (it will be noticed that, although this does not seem to be required by perspective, those still on land are smaller than the princess), spring to seize the cradle, and the leader, a negro,[3] has already reached it. The infant Moses, lying in the cradle, is shown with a halo (a detail not in the poem). This completes the central axis of the picture, which describes an elliptical curve.

On the left, below the chariot, are the eagle and the vulture at the end of the fight, in which the eagle is victorious,[4] one of the many allegorical episodes in the *Moyse* representing by means of animals the conflict between good and evil which is centred on the cradle. In the lower right-hand corner sit Elisaph, Marie, and Merary with their sheep.[5] Elisaph is somewhat oddly dressed, with a plumed cap and an approximation to contemporary peasant costume. In his hand is his shepherd's *houlette* in its characteristic French form, while Merary holds a fishing-rod. The landscape which spreads in the background is obviously imaginary with its vague mountains. The wood on the right might be French, except for the incongruous palm-tree, which alone in the engraving suggests an Egyptian scene (there may be palms on the left, but they are too indistinct to allow precise identification). On the right the sun is setting, and above it two angels and a cherub (no doubt among those who have watched and defended the cradle throughout the poem) hold up a banner with the title.

The frontispiece conveys, it may be said, an accurate impression of the poem, a mixture of exuberant fantasy, allegory, Christian supernatural, and contemporary French realism (though Saint-Amant is occasionally more successful in depicting Egyptian landscape). A comparison with Poussin shows that, in spite of certain general affinities,[6] Saint-Amant and Vignon (Bosse is the executant merely) are here moving in a different imaginative

---

[1] *Œuvres*, ii. 312.   [2] ii. 313.   [3] ii. 322.
[4] ii. 318–20.   [5] ii. 321.
[6] Cf. Sayce, 'Saint-Amant and Poussin', which includes reproductions of the two 'Discoveries' discussed here. For a third, see Blunt, *Art and Architecture*, plate 134.

atmosphere. In Poussin's first 'Discovery of Moses' of 1638 (Louvre) all the trappings of angels, chariot, unicorns, allegorical birds, and plumes are naturally absent. The princess owes her regal dignity to no elaboration of dress or physical elevation: she stands, simply attired, among her handmaidens (though there is the same gesture of the pointing finger). Moses is no more than an ordinary child. There is at least some attempt to secure historical accuracy in the background with the pyramid. The supernatural is represented only by the pagan Nile god. All this applies, though the scene is there wider, the grouping more complex, and palm-tree and sphinx are found as well as pyramids, to the later 'Discovery' of 1645–7 (Louvre). We have here, it may be suggested, a noteworthy example of the contrast between baroque and classical tendencies in French literature and art.

The second frontispiece of the *Judith* of Marie de Pech,[1] showing Judith armed with a sword and holding the head of Holofernes, is unsigned, but of high quality. It may well be the work of an artist of the Toulouse school, probably I. Seguenot, who signed the first frontispiece (a portrait of Queen Marie-Thérèse) and was working in Toulouse in 1659.[2] It is firmly and simply drawn; there are no fantastic elements (it differs greatly from the poem in this respect), and its interest lies principally in the expression of militant feminism.

The illustrations to *David, Jonas,* and *Esther* are the work of François Chauveau, perhaps the most prolific of seventeenth-century illustrators (among the best-known examples of his work are the *Alaric* of Scudéry and the 1676 Racine). There are nine illustrations for the *David* of Lesfargues, all signed by Chauveau.[3] They are lacking in the British Museum and Bibliothèque Nationale copies, but they are preserved separately in the Cabinet des Estampes of the Bibliothèque Nationale[4] and the Arsenal possesses a complete copy.[5] The frontispiece with the title shows David, crowned and playing his harp, supported by cherubs, his foot on Goliath's head.[6] The other subjects are the anointing of David; David receiving the shewbread from Ahimelech (the Roman soldier on the left and the classical architecture will be noticed,

---

[1] Plate II*a*.   [2] Cf. Duportal, *Étude sur les livres à figures*, p. 352.
[3] See Plate III.   [4] Fonds français, Ed. 44 res., I, fo. 6.
[5] Cf. Weigert, *Inventaire*, ii. 474. The Arsenal also possesses a copy of the second issue, with the illustrations.   [6] Plate III*a*.

though there is some attempt at historical accuracy in the costume of the priest and the Hebrew inscription);[1] the death of Saul (a characteristic battle-scene);[2] David playing before the ark; David and Bathsheba (with a fine palm-tree);[3] the death of Absalom; David pouring away the water from the well of Bethlehem; the death of David. All these are close to the Bible and, though much superior, correspond to the spirit of the poem in simplicity of feeling and fidelity. Even so (again as in the poem) there is everywhere a classical colouring which gives a seventeenth-century view of the sacred text. We have here perhaps the best, if not the most interesting, illustrations inspired by the Biblical epic.

Both editions of Coras's *Jonas* (1663 and 1665) have for their frontispiece an engraving signed 'F. Chauveau jn. fec.', representing the prophet Jonah, with outstretched hands, surrounded by a group of repentant Ninevites.[4] Here there is no exact correspondence to the details of the poem, though the scene in general is that of Book X. In the poem Jonah is not actually present when the town performs its act of contrition, so that the frontispiece may be held to render the theme as a whole rather than a particular episode. Apart from Jonah the only identifiable character is the king of Nineveh, who stands with bowed head on the left. In the Bible (Jonah iii. 6), followed by Coras, he has stripped himself of his royal robe and sits in sackcloth and ashes. In the frontispiece, though he is simply dressed for a king, he retains some of the conventional signs of magnificence, the sceptre in his hand, the cuirass, and the decorated buskins. On the step at his feet lies his plumed turban, a conventional adornment of the oriental ruler and indeed his only oriental feature (the rest of his dress is clearly of Roman inspiration). The other figures wear what may pass for sackcloth, but there is no sign of ashes. In brief, we find here a phenomenon common to most of the poems: though no great violence is done to the Biblical account, everything is made more magnificent, and disagreeable details, like the ashes, are tactfully omitted. The architectural background recalls Poussin. Like the king's dress it is of classical and probably Roman derivation and again there is a single concession to the oriental setting, the central obelisk, covered with illegible characters which are probably intended to suggest a Hebrew inscription. Coras (Book X) gives

[1] Plate III*b*.   [2] Plate III*c*.
[3] Plate III*d*.   [4] Plate II*b*.

a detailed description of the temple of Belus, but the engraver has made no attempt to follow him in the building on the left. The frontispiece cannot be regarded as more than a mediocre specimen of Chauveau's work. Indeed, we may suppose that, as was often his practice, he had in this case employed assistants.[1] Figures and buildings are absurdly crowded, and the design has no more shape than the poem itself. This is partly due to the format and therefore to economic considerations. The duodecimo of *Jonas* clearly did not afford the same opportunities as the folios of *Alaric* and *La Pucelle* or the quartos of the *Moyse* and *Judith*. A much superior version of the same theme by Chauveau may be found in Godeau's *Tableaux de la Pénitence*.[2]

Jonas also contains a better engraving signed by Chauveau, which accompanies the dedication. It represents a female warrior (possibly Minerva) with a spear and the conventional helmet, supporting a shield with the arms of Turenne. It bears no relation to the content of the poem, but may perhaps be added to the instances of feminist influence.

The first edition of Desmarets's *Esther* (1670) has an engraving of Esther before Ahasuerus, signed 'F. Chauueau jn. et fecit'.[3] The same plate is repeated above the text at the beginning of each of the four *chants*. Apart from the king's sceptre and crown and the turbans of the figures on the right beyond the balustrade, the dresses and architecture are wholly classical. In particular, the statue of the conventional warrior in the niche should be noticed. An unsigned engraving of the same subject appears in the *Bible de Royaumont*, published by the same printer (Pierre le Petit) in the same year (1670).[4] The identity of the two works is obvious, in spite of some differences (the steps, the balustrade, the absence of statues in the Royaumont version). It seems probable that we have here two different engravings from the same original drawing. The Royaumont engraving is technically superior, though the Desmarets version, with its fuller treatment and greater space, may well correspond more closely to the original design. In any case, it appears that this Royaumont illustration should be added to the works of Chauveau given in M. Weigert's *Inventaire*.[5] The

---

[1] Cf. Duportal, *Étude*, p. 185.   [2] 1654 ed., p. 134.
[3] Plate IV*a*. It had already been used in Arnauld d'Andilly's *Josephus* of 1667 (p. 385) and was not, therefore, made for Desmarets.   [4] Plate IV*b*.
[5] It is not, of course, to be found in the earlier *Icones Biblicae* (cf. p. 232 below).

general conception and treatment bear a fairly close resemblance to Poussin's 'Esther before Ahasuerus' (Hermitage, Leningrad).[1]

Perrault's *Adam* (1697) has four engravings, one at the beginning of each book, signed 'Coypel jn. C. Simonneau Sculp.' They occupy part of the page only, above the text, and represent scenes from the poem, each containing two or more scenes without formal separation (a frequent practice earlier, especially in Bible illustrations, for example Frizon's Bible of 1621). What are in all likelihood the original water-colour drawings from which the engraver worked are to be found in the Bibliothèque Nationale MS.[2] Two of the four are signed 'Coypel f.' Simonneau is obviously the engraver Charles Simonneau (1645–1728). Coypel might be either Noël Coypel (1628–1707) or his more famous son Antoine (1661–1722).[3] Antoine is more probable, since the signatures of the drawings correspond to his normal signature[4] and he collaborated regularly with Simonneau, including a 'Triumph of Galatea' in 1695, the date of the manuscript.[5] This seems to be confirmed by the style, though I am not competent to decide such a point.

A comparison between the engravings and the original drawings[6] affords us the not very common privilege of observing the relation between painter and engraver in a book illustration.[7] It will be seen at once that in this case Simonneau has interpreted his original with great fidelity. There is no appreciable difference in any detail of content or treatment. All that can be said is that the freedom and liveliness of the drawings (anticipating the style of the eighteenth century) are to some extent, and inevitably, lost in translation into a more rigid medium.

In the first drawing[8], followed closely by the engraving, though naturally in reverse, the creation of Adam is shown on the right and the creation of Eve on the left. In the foreground, between the scenes, are two animals, the lion and the fox. The prominence given in the poem to descriptions of these animals,[9] which are not

---

[1] Cf. Grautoff, *Nicolas Poussin*, ii. 173.   [2] Cf. p. 142 above.

[3] Bonnefon (*R.H.L.F.*, 1906, p. 608) attributes the illustrations to Louis Simonneau and Noël Coypel. The former is an obvious error and for neither are reasons given.

[4] As given by Bénézit, *Dictionnaire des peintres, sculpteurs, dessinateurs et graveurs*.

[5] Lieure, *L'École française de gravure, XVIIe siècle*, pp. 82, 133, 152.

[6] See Plates V–VI.   [7] Cf. Duportal, *Étude*, p. 142.

[8] Plate V*a*.   [9] *Adam*, pp. 9, 18. Cf. pp. 144, 222 above.

mentioned in Gen. i and ii, suggests that in this point Coypel was inspired directly by Perrault rather than by the Bible. Other animals (camel and horse) are in the background on the right. God is in the Poussin tradition, massive and scarcely raised above the earth, the divine majesty being conveyed by physical power, the sweeping garment, and the close halo of cloud, rather than by baroque tricks of perspective.[1] The human figures, on the other hand, are more graceful and slender than Poussin's. Eden is merely indicated by the two central trees, and the rest of the landscape appears to be pastoral European rather than Biblical. Most of these features are in harmony with the abstraction of the poem.

The second drawing[2] is rather more complex. On the right Eve offers the apple to Adam; in the centre the angel with flaming sword drives them out of Paradise; on the left, in the foreground, Adam is lying asleep (another detail taken from the poem[3] and not in the Bible), in the middle ground Cain slays Abel, and in the background we see the Deluge and the Ark (two incidents in Adam's dream).

The third drawing[4] is dominated by the scene on the right, where the angel unfolds the vision of the future to Adam, while Eve, remorseful, hides her face.[5] Again this is wholly derived from the poem, with no Biblical justification. On the left we see two episodes from the vision, Abraham's sacrifice and the crossing of the Red Sea.

The last drawing,[6] unlike the others, is to be read from left to right. The left shows Gethsemane, with the kneeling Christ, the sleeping disciples in the foreground, and a cross supported by cherubim with an angel holding the bitter cup (the cross and the cup are not in the poem). The presence of the angel (though authorized by St. Luke), like the angel in the preceding drawing (it is, in fact, the same angel[7]), illustrates the need for continued supernatural intervention, as striking in the art of the period as it is in these poems. In the centre is Calvary, remarkable for the elongated bodies and the arrangement of the crosses, Christ bathed in light, the two thieves in darkness, one turned to the side and the other seen from the back. The asymmetrical organization and the effect of chiaroscuro (obtained even in this simple

---

[1] Cf. Poussin's 'Burning Bush' (Copenhagen) or the frontispiece (by Poussin and Mellan) of the 1642 *Biblia Sacra*.   [2] Plate V*c*.   [3] *Adam*, p. 37.
[4] Plate VI*a*.   [5] Cf. *Adam*, p. 70.   [6] Plate VI*c*.   [7] *Adam*, p. 83.

medium) may be said to spring from baroque feeling. They are due
to the imagination of the artist and have no authority in the poem.
On the right is the Last Judgement, conventionally represented,
but in its radiance and depth a noteworthy attempt to produce
a great baroque ceiling-painting in miniature (not unlike Coypel's
own work in the chapel at Versailles).

So far the relation between poets and artists has been tangible
and unmistakable. When we leave the clearly defined question
of illustration of the texts, the subject expands to large proportions. To give anything like a parallel history of the Old Testament in seventeenth-century art, even in France alone (which
would be inadequate, since the influence or coincidence of Italian,
Netherlandish, or German sources could not be excluded), would
lie outside the bounds of this inquiry. All that can be attempted
is to indicate certain points of contact, which may throw further
light on features already discussed.

However, it may be said in outline that the second half of the
sixteenth century and the first half of the seventeenth are marked
by an efflorescence of Biblical inspiration. Its manifestations in
engraving have already been summarized.[1] It is noteworthy that
Marolles's collection of prints contained, among other Biblical
subjects, 23 representations of the Creation, 121 of Adam and
Eve, 49 of Moses, 96 of David, 83 of Judith, and 43 of Susanna.[2]
In painting Poussin drew extensively on the Old Testament and
was in particular almost obsessed by the life of Moses and the
great themes it presented.[3] Le Sueur and Vouet treat the same
subjects (the former, for example, in the 'Crossing of the Red
Sea' at Limoges, the latter in the Old Testament tapestries).
Claude's Biblical pictures are less numerous than Poussin's and
tend, like the 'Queen of Sheba' (National Gallery), to be mere
variants of his secular works, but there are more independent
examples, such as the 'Burning Bush' (Ellesmere Collection).
After 1650 Biblical inspiration is much less evident. The old
engravings are reprinted:[4] even the *Bible de Royaumont* reproduces
the Strasbourg *Icones Biblicae* of 1625.[5] In painting Le Brun and
Antoine Coypel occasionally paint such subjects (for example, the

[1] Cf. p. 33 above.   [2] *Catalogue de livres d'estampes*, p. 16.
[3] For a fuller treatment see Sayce, 'Saint-Amant and Poussin'.
[4] Cf. p. 34 above.   [5] Duportal, *Étude*, p. 128.

latter's 'Esther before Ahasuerus' in the Louvre), but the emphasis
is now far more on secular magnificence.[1] If this outline corresponds to historical reality, then there seems to be a general analogy between the development of epic and the development of
the graphic arts. Biblical subjects become less fashionable in both
about the time when the force of the great religious movements
of the early part of the century has expended itself and attention
is concentrated on the worldly glories of the court.

Affinities may be discovered between the poems and two kinds
of engraver: those, like Tempesta,[2] who create an epic mode, with
battle-scenes, heroes, and especially heroines, not classically nude
but conventionally accoutred so as to inspire terror or *maraviglia*;
and the illustrators of the Bible, who help to establish an icono-
graphic tradition, including details which are assumed from, or
added to, the sacred text. The combination of the two corresponds to the combinations we have observed in the poems of
Biblical elements and extraneous ornament. When this combination is retranslated into visual terms we have something like the
frontispiece of the *Moyse sauvé*.

As an example of the first category we might consider the
description of the Assyrian soldier in Anne d'Urfé's *Judic*:

> Le guerrier fut arme des pieds jusq'a la teste
> D'ascier resplandissant et portoit sur la creste
> De l'effroyable armet la queue d'un cheual.[3]

It is easy to recognize here the warrior of Tempesta, in particular
in the horse-tail helmet. The conventional epithet *effroyable* may
be considered as an attempt to express verbally the conventional
ferocity of facial expression in the engravings. It is of course impossible to prove an influence here: we can only speak of a close
affinity. Admittedly also this affinity might equally apply to certain
paintings, and it is not easy to distinguish between the contributions of painting and engraving, themselves so nearly connected.
However, the engravings furnish a more satisfactory basis of
comparison from this point of view because in them the icono-
graphic tradition is more stable and individual variations are less
marked.

[1] And Le Brun's Biblical paintings are mostly youthful works of about 1650
(Marcel, *Charles Le Brun*, Paris, n.d., pp. 14–15).
[2] Cf. p. 33 above.   [3] *Judic*, fo. 158.

In the second category may be placed Saint-Amant's description of the death of Pharaoh, for which there is no authority in the Bible, Josephus, or Philo. He remains above the water when all the other Egyptians have been drowned, impotently threatening the Israelites with uplifted sword, till he is swept away by a wave and swallowed by a fish.[1] Now we have already seen that Pharaoh's menacing attitude was derived from Du Bartas.[2] However, the fate of the tyrant was a natural deduction and he often appears, crowned, in Biblical engravings of the scene. The most striking resemblance can be found in the unsigned copper engraving of Frizon's Bible depicting the journey of the Israelites from Egypt to Sinai.[3] Other engravings in Frizon are signed by such artists as Léonard Gaultier, Michel Lasne, Melchior Tavernier, the Pole Jan Ziarnko, and Claude Mellan, so that, although this particular illustration is not identified, we can perceive the milieu which produced it.[4] Here Pharaoh is shown still standing on his chariot, waving his royal sceptre (instead of a sword), while his army is sinking. The poetic tradition and the tradition of the engravers again coincide.

A similar case appears in Perrault's two altars of Cain and Abel,[5] again not mentioned in Genesis, though it was easy, if anachronistic, to infer their presence. The two altars may be seen in Le Clerc's *Figures*, in Johann Theodor de Bry's engraving in the Mainz *Biblia Sacra* of 1609, and in the *Bible de Royaumont* of 1670.[6] It is possible that Perrault had seen these or similar works and had conceived his scene accordingly. It is perhaps more likely that he had arrived at the feature independently or from a literary source.[7] In either case we can appreciate the parallel development of graphic and poetic iconography.

If engraving may have influenced the poets, they in their turn influenced the engravers. Godeau's *Tableaux de la Pénitence* appeared in 1654, the year after the *Moyse sauvé*, with illustrations by Chauveau. The Crossing of the Red Sea,[8] signed 'F. Chauueau. In. Gab le Brun fe', shows a wall of water submerging the Egyptians, the Israelites having crossed safely. In the foreground shells are

---

[1] *Œuvres*, ii. 217–18.   [2] Cf. p. 96 above.
[3] i. 71. See Plate VIIa.
[4] Cf. Duportal, *Catalogue*, p. 124.   [5] Cf. p. 145 above.
[6] For other examples see Ehrenstein, *Das Alte Testament im Bilde*, pp. 88–89; *Das Alte Testament in der Graphik*, pp. 41–48.
[7] Cf. Milton, p. 145 above.   [8] p. 53.

lying on the sand, with a child about to pick them up. Godeau's description runs:

Voila des Meres qui tiennent leurs enfans par la main, et qui les empéchent de s'arrester pour *amasser des coquilles* dont la beauté les charme et leur donne dans la veuë.[1]

This is very close to Saint-Amant's

> *Ramasse une cocquille*, et, d'aise transporté,
> La presente à sa mere avec naïveté.[2]

A common source is not absolutely to be excluded, but it seems probable that Godeau had already read Saint-Amant and had been attracted by this detail, which thus passes from the poet to the prose-writer and from him to the draughtsman and the engraver. Children had usually been included in engravings of the Crossing (as they had been in Du Bartas[3]), but the shells seem to be an innovation.

The most important aspect of the relation between the epic and contemporary painting is certainly the coincidence (and the differences) between the treatment of the Moses story by Saint-Amant and Poussin, and this has been discussed in some detail by the present writer.[4] Here the salient facts only need be repeated: Saint-Amant's declared admiration for Poussin[5] and the use by both of details drawn from Josephus.[6] Apart from this fruitful parallel, seventeenth-century painting shows a general similarity of development rather than exact points of contact. An examination of some of the Biblical works of Vouet, Le Sueur, Claude, and Le Brun has not revealed the specific resemblances which we have discovered in the engravers. This is understandable, since the art of engraving was so intimately connected with literature. Here a few general examples of the expression of visual imagination in the poets will be given.

I have suggested that the angel of Marie de Pech might have come from a baroque painting,[7] and the union of magnificence and luminosity in his person (perhaps rather crudely done in this case) might be an echo of almost any religious work of the seventeenth century.[8] This is a single figure of an angel. The mass effect

---

[1] p. 55. [2] *Œuvres*, ii. 214. Cf. p. 102 above.
[3] Cf. p. 95 above. [4] Sayce, 'Saint-Amant and Poussin'.
[5] *Œuvres*, ii. 241. [6] Cf. p. 28 above. [7] Cf. p. 172 above.
[8] Cf. Mâle, *L'Art religieux*, pp. 301 ff.; and especially Vignon's 'Death of a Hermit' (Louvre) (Blunt, *Art and Architecture*, p. 129).

of a host of seraphim has been seen in Pierre de Saint-Louis, where it prompted a comparison with Rubens,[1] though in fact almost any *gloire* of an ecclesiastical ceiling-painting of the period might furnish a parallel. In particular, an almost contemporary work, though in a very different order of values, Mignard's Val-de-Grâce dome with its angelic musicians, was completed about 1664, four years before Pierre de Saint-Louis began the *Éliade*.

Saint-Amant's predominantly visual imagination has often been touched upon in these pages. In the opinion of Chapelain (shared by some subsequent critics) the value of the *Moyse* lies chiefly in the descriptions:

> Saint-Amand s'est sanctifié par l'entreprise de son *Moïse* dont il fait un idille héroïque tout rempli de descriptions, et belles en vérité, mais il tombe lorsqu'il faut faire parler, si bien qu'il entretient l'imagination et ne remue point les entrailles.[2]

He gives still greater praise to this side of Saint-Amant's work in the preface to *La Pucelle*:

> En effet, qu'est-ce que la *Pucelle* peut opposer dans la peinture parlante, au *Moïse* de M. de Saint-Amant?[3]

Saint-Amant's talent is indeed primarily that of a painter in words. By eliminating dialogue or by introducing such expressions as *je vois* he deliberately emphasizes the pictorial character of his descriptions, which are often isolated from the body of the poem like pictures in their frame. So Marolles, in his discussion of the *Moyse*, is able to enumerate the Crossing of the Red Sea, Moses striking the Rock, the Swimmers, as separate visual units.[4] Like a painter (and especially like Poussin) Saint-Amant analyses his subjects into groups and individual figures, which explains his most successful passages, as well as the absurdities castigated by Boileau.

As an example outside the Biblical cycle we may take the almost wholly pagan description of the return of the cradle to its resting-place:

> Les esprits bien-heureux qui luy servoyent d'escorte
> Pour ayder à son cours s'estoyent placez en sorte

---

[1] Cf. p. 199 above.
[2] Chapelain to Balzac, 3 Jan. 1639 (*Lettres*, i. 353–4).
[3] *Opuscules*, ed. Hunter, p. 278.
[4] *Traité du poëme epique*, p. 121. Cf. Sayce, *French Studies*, 1947, p. 241.

Que l'haleine du calme, en leurs plumes donnant,
Faisoit d'un jonc vogueur un spectacle estonnant.
Leurs beaux cheveux, emus en diverses manieres,
Du triomphe naval composoyent les banieres, . . .
L'auguste gardien . . .
D'un dard traisnant en pouppe en Typhis agissoit,
Et comme d'un timon la proue en regissoit.[1]

The *esprits* and the *auguste gardien* are attendant angels, but their
Christian character is all but lost in the pervasive classical atmosphere. The whole passage inevitably suggests a painting—a birth
of Venus or a triumph of Neptune or Thetis, in which the shell
or chariot is escorted by Nereids and Tritons.[2] Baroque elements
may perhaps be detected in the combination of Christian and
classical, in the incongruous magnificence of the cradle and its
accompaniment, and especially in the attempt to force the reader's
admiration with *un spectacle estonnant*.

Some of the leading painters of the seventeenth century, especially those who were royal directors of artistic production, Vouet
and Le Brun, were makers of tapestries as well as of paintings.
We have seen that the tapestry was a favourite device of the poets
for the introduction of episodes.[3] The finest example, showing
a clear reflection of contemporary tapestry, is again in Saint-
Amant, the Deluge embroidered by Jocabel. After the description
of the different figures, desperately striving to escape by climbing
trees and swimming or lifting children above the water (very much
as in Poussin's 'Deluge' or the Deluge in Godeau's *Tableaux*),
comes the border:

Et, sans le beau rempart d'une riche bordure
De fruits, de papillons, de fleurs et de verdure,
Qui sembloit s'opposer au deluge depeint,
Un plus ample ravage on en eust presque craint.
Les plus proches objets, selon la perspective,
Estoyent d'une maniere et plus forte et plus vive;
Mais de loin en plus loin la forme s'effaçoit,
Et dans le bleu perdu tout s'evanouissoit.[4]

The border of fruit and flowers is a constant feature of the
seventeenth-century French tapestry, and Saint-Amant clearly

---

[1] *Œuvres*, ii. 240–1.

[2] e.g. Le Brun's 'Triumph of Neptune and Amphitrite' (Louvre) or Poussin's
picture of the same title (Hermitage, Leningrad).

[3] Cf. p. 206 above. [4] *Œuvres*, ii. 190–1.

appreciates its aesthetic function as well as the working of perspective. Throughout the description the reader is reminded that he must imagine a piece of tapestry and only indirectly the flood. Combined with the gradation of perspective in the scene itself, this produces a vision in depth.

Sculpture naturally presents fewer instructive parallels. With Anne d'Urfé's Rumour[1] we might compare Jean Goujon's statue on Lescot's Louvre front or Biard's 'Renommée de Cadillac' of about 1597 (also in the Louvre), which has the trumpet, though not the eyes, since they would obviously be displeasing in sculpture. However, we are dealing here with a literary commonplace and it is only possible to say that it has found parallel expression in poets and sculptors.

A more interesting case is the fountain of Susanna's bathing-pool in Montchrestien:

> Qui toute se r'amasse au ventre d'vn vaisseau
> De Iaspe bigarré fait en figure ouale.
> D'vne tour esleuee en ce vaisseau deuale
> L'onde coulante en bas, par la bouche et les yeux
> De deux marmots d'airain qui regardent les Cieux.
> Cette tour est de marbre, et par des interuales
> Se bossent hors de l'œuure vn nombre de medalles.[2]

The two bronze boys with water flowing from their mouths, and the embossed medallions are typical of a Renaissance fountain. Only jasper perhaps lends a faintly Biblical tinge to the passage. The engravers (and occasionally the painters[3]) usually include a similar fountain in the scene. So de Bry in the 1609 Bible has a fountain with a boy riding a winged dolphin;[4] in Frizon there is a lion's head spouting water into a bowl;[5] and in the *Bible de Royaumont* there is a figure, half boy, half fish, playing a trumpet from which water emerges.[6] A still closer resemblance may be found in Elsheimer's 'Susanna and the Elders' (Dulwich), where the fountain has three boys with water flowing from their mouths.[7] Elsheimer is an almost exact contemporary of Montchrestien,[8]

---

[1] *Judic*, fo. 163v⁰. Cf. p. 179 above.   [2] *Susane*, p. 361.

[3] There are fountains in the versions of the subject by Rubens and Van Dyck (Munich).

[4] ii. 148. See Plate VII*b*.   [5] ii. 366. Plate VII*c*.

[6] Plate VII*d*.   [7] Plate VIII.

[8] The painting apparently dates from about 1598–1605 (cf. Weizsäcker, *Adam Elsheimer*, Berlin, 1936, i. 133–5).

though the engravings are later. All serve to illustrate the complex interaction of literary (Biblical) and artistic (pictorial and sculptural) influences.

The fountain is part of Susanna's garden, the literary sources of which we have already discussed.[1] But it also reflects the contemporary state of garden architecture. The stream running into the fountain is perhaps too classical:

> Elle demeure au chef de ce ruisseau sacré,
> D'où n'aproche iamais la cohorte alteree
> Des moutons ramenez sur la tarde seree:
> Les Chéures et les Boucs, les Vaches, les Toreaux
> De leur baue à longs fils n'infectent point ses eaux.[2]

It is easy to recognize here the spring of Bandusia seen through the eyes of the Pléiade. But the arrangement of trees and shrubs is more to our purpose:

> Et peuplent d'arbrisseaux et d'arbres differens,
> Disposez au cordeau par cent sortes de rangs,
> Si bien que du Soleil les fléches rayonnantes
> Ne peuuent trauerser leurs branches verdoyantes.[3]

We have here the Renaissance (or perhaps mannerist) garden, with its strict formality and absence of open vistas, something like what has been called the *jardin-bibelot*.[4] It may be seen in schematic form in the Frizon engraving[5] or, perhaps more as it was, in Tintoretto's 'Susanna'.[6] Although the painting is earlier, its combination of heavy shade and formality (the trellises in the background) suggests that the painter and the poet were inspired by the same kind of garden.

The princess's retreat in the *Moyse sauvé* reveals the progress in the art of gardening in the half-century which separates Montchrestien from Saint-Amant. It is at once natural and artificial:

> On y voyoit des pins se hausser jusqu'aux nues;
> Cent files d'orangers formoyent ses avenues,
> Où les yeux admiroyent, sous un ciel pur et beau,
> Le printemps et l'autonne en un mesme rameau.[7]

---

[1] Cf. p. 63 above.
[2] *Susane*, p. 361. [3] Ib., p. 349.
[4] Cf. Crump, *Nature in the Age of Louis XIV*, pp. 2–4 and ch. i *passim*.
[5] Plate VII*c*.
[6] Vienna, Kunsthistorisches Museum. [7] *Œuvres*, ii. 292.

The avenues of orange-trees probably come from a seventeenth-century garden: it was at this time that they began to be extensively used as garden ornaments in the north of France.[1] The disturbance of the natural order of things (spring and autumn on the same bough) has already been encountered in Montchrestien and may be presumed to derive from the same literary tradition.[2]

The seventeenth-century form is still clearer in the description which follows of a garden which is presumably inside the retreat itself:

> Tantost, dans un jardin enrichy de statues,
> De grottes, de canaux et de masses pointues,
> Où l'on voyoit l'orgueil d'un porphire eclatant
> Dedaigner son pié mesme et se perdre en montant . . .
> Tantost, sous des lauriers repliez en arcades,
> Elle prenoit plaisir à voir mille cascades,
> Que, par art et de front, les claires eaux faisoyent . . .
> Tandis que d'autres eaux, par le plomb divisées,
> Sortoyent de cent bassins en forme de fusées,
> Et que d'autres encore alloyent en cent façons
> Grossir un bel estang plein de rares poissons,
> Un estang precieux dont seulement les cygnes
> Entre tous les oyseaux s'osoyent reputer dignes,
> Pour la belle raison de la conformité
> Qu'avoit leur innocence avec sa pureté.[3]

The column of porphyry may be an attempt to suggest an Egyptian atmosphere. On the other hand, grottoes, cascades, swans were generally used in seventeenth-century gardening, even though they do not belong specifically to it. And the rest—statues, arcades of laurels, the fish-pond—can be said to be typical of the Renaissance and seventeenth-century garden. The canals deserve special mention: they too are typical. *Masses pointues* may refer to shaped box or yew. Most of all, the water machinery with its lead pipes and basins belongs to the seventeenth century. It is typical of Saint-Amant that he should describe not only the final result but the technical means by which it is achieved. These conclusions are confirmed by the description of the part of the

---

[1] André Le Nôtre and his father Jean were in charge of the orange-trees in the Tuileries garden about 1638 (when the *Moyse* was beginning to take shape). Cf. Corpechot, *Parcs et jardins de France*, Paris, 1937, p. 58.

[2] Cf. p. 63 above.   [3] *Œuvres*, ii. 293.

Nile which has been made into a swimming-pool for the princess. Here Saint-Amant declares directly that the surroundings are enriched with

> Tout ce qu'ont *nos* jardins d'exquis et de superbe.[1]

The *long et droit canal* which follows inevitably suggests Versailles (though the gardens did not exist when Saint-Amant wrote).

Five poets have been considered here as expressing a baroque tendency in French literature. (This classification is not of course hard and fast. Similar elements are to be found, to a lesser degree, in many of the others.) Here the word is used to denote the fantasy and taste for luxuriant decoration which distinguish the period of Louis XIII and the Regency from French classicism proper, though unlike the individual extravagance of the Romantics, it follows fairly rigid conventional patterns. Other characteristics may emerge from a closer examination.

In the course of this chapter many parallels have been noted between the poems and contemporary work in the visual arts. Some may appear far-fetched, but some are so close as to be inescapable. Such are, for example, Anne d'Urfé's Rumour with trumpet and swelling cheeks, the angel of Marie de Pech, Saint-Amant's *peinture parlante*. Their source was not necessarily the baroque painters and sculptors, but they were trying to do in words what had been done in paint and stone. It may be assumed then that there is a general relationship between these poems and the visual arts.

Their formal qualities confirm this relationship. The chronological manipulations of some poets, the straightforward narrative of others, correspond to the tortured masses of baroque architecture or the plain severity of classical buildings. We have noticed the strange tricks of perspective, which Desmarets derives from these disturbances, and their architectural counterparts.[2] We have here perhaps the essential formal characteristic of baroque art. It is not (as is sometimes supposed) diametrically opposed to classicism. On the contrary, it accepts the basic forms of classicism and distorts them. The most familiar example is the treatment of the pediment in baroque architecture, where the simple classical form, triangle or segment of a circle, is broken, inverted (two

---

[1] ii. 313. [2] Cf. p. 204 above.

halves of a triangle back to back), or convoluted. In the poems this
may be seen, for instance, in the new handling of the conventional
classical proposition, a distortion which may take the form of
bombast or parody.[1]

Distortion may consist in no more than the multiplication of
single elements. Thus the poems reveal a tendency to multiply
features which were originally simple. The invocation is doubled,
tripled, and then repeated throughout the work.[2] In Saint-Amant
three Messianic prophecies are inserted where one would have
sufficed; the familiar angelic flight appears, but with two divine
messengers instead of one.[3] Similarly in architecture columns and
pilasters, originally single, are grouped in clusters of two and three,
or pediments appear all over a building. The action of a fully
developed epic, like the *Moyse sauvé* or the *Esther* of Desmarets,
moves on three planes, the human, the allegorical, and the supernatural, all advancing simultaneously. Here again we see effects of
repetition and perspective which are more complex than those
of classical epic, where there are only two planes, clearly distinguished. With multiplication may be associated movement, the
agitation which we have observed at its most violent in Pierre de
Saint-Louis.

Or distortion may assume the form of exaggeration, as when
Saint-Amant, Desmarets, and Perrault interpret the unity of time
rule with excessive rigour and compress vast historical themes
within the framework of a day or two.[4] The overlaying of a
classical foundation with non-functional ornament perhaps belongs
to the same category. It is best seen in the elaborate descriptions
which aroused the classical displeasure of Boileau and are here
most prominent in Saint-Amant.

Exaggeration is not confined to classical features. The emphasis
which so often transforms the Biblical atmosphere of the poems
finds a parallel in the accentuated gestures and expressions of a
Bernini. The basis of such exaggeration is the desire to produce
astonishment, that *maraviglia* which we have often encountered.
On a small scale it appears in the constant use of adjectives like
effroyable, *merveilleux*, *étonnant*.[5] Actions are not allowed to speak

---

[1] Cf. pp. 196–8 above.

[2] Though the last point must not be overemphasized in this connexion. For the
history of the repeated invocation, cf. Curtius, *Europäische Literatur*, p. 243.

[3] Cf. p. 180 above.   [4] Cf. p. 202 above.   [5] Cf. p. 237 above.

for themselves, their emotional effect must be intensified. On a larger scale we find it in the taste for magnificence illustrated, to take but a few cases, in the angel of Marie de Pech, in the chariot, attire, and retinue of Saint-Amant's princess (closely followed by Vignon and Bosse), or in the triumphant progress of the cradle.

A pendant to magnificence is horror, the fondness for scenes of carnage and repugnant pictures of wounded and dying, which we have found in the poems and which have their counterpart in baroque art, especially in the martyrdom paintings (though martyrdom itself is not treated as a main theme after Gamon's *Poëme tragique*). The place of such scenes in baroque aesthetics is best expressed in Marino's poem on Tempesta's engraving 'La battaglia de' Lapiti' (again showing the close relations between literature and the visual arts):

> Chi non sà, come in uero
> Possa da lo spauento uscir diletto,
> E l'horrore esser bello,
> Miri quì di pennello
> Bellicoso, e guerriero
> Mirabil magistero,
> De la Guerra sanguigna il crudo aspetto,
> Vedrà nel fiero oggetto
> (Miracolo d'artefice sagace)
> Ira ch'alletta, e crudeltà che piace.[1]

In the Italian poet the principle is carried to its extreme conclusion, which is less clear in the French works. It is indeed often assumed that in architecture and painting there was a French resistance to the formal influences of baroque, culminating in the substitution of Perrault's plans for Bernini's at the Louvre. It must be admitted that a similar resistance exists in Biblical poetry. We have seen that fabulous or romantic additions penetrated far more deeply into the structure of Italian poems than of French, where they remained superimposed. Similarly chronological dislocation was never so violent in France as in such works as the *Judith* of Tortoletti. The technical features of baroque in the French epic are unmistakable, but they are never (except perhaps in Desmarets and Pierre de Saint-Louis) so fully developed as in the Italians.

In drawing conclusions from formal detail, or the aspects of content most closely connected with it, we are on fairly sure

---

[1] *La Galeria del Cavalier Marino*, Venice, 1630, p. 54.

ground. Comparisons based on broader ideas are subject to caution but none the less suggest interesting results. The humanizing of inanimate objects and animals is a perennial poetic device. But its exaggerations here—Saint-Amant's fish at the windows, the fish in *Hélie* taking each other by the hand—are so extraordinary as to demand a special explanation. They are partly the result of a 'metaphysical' or *précieux* search for recondite relationships. But more particularly, they may spring from the mentality which represents the Nile or the Jordan as old men, half human, half aqueous. Once again the poets touch the visual world of the baroque artists.

There is here a tendency to mix opposites, and another outstanding baroque characteristic in the poems is a deep contradiction or conflict. We have seen its manifestations in minor details, the oxymoron which expresses the discord between Biblical and contemporary morality,[1] the elaborate precautions by which the poets attempt to nullify the effect of the pagan deities whose poetic prestige they are none the less eager to exploit.[2] This is in miniature a reflection of the greater problem of the Christian and classical *merveilleux*, with its largely unresolved tensions. The curious relations between classical muse and Christian angel in Saint-Amant's guardian[3] may serve as one extreme example of a struggle which runs all through these poems. Boileau's reaction against the mingling of sacred and profane shows once more the classical point of view opposed to the manifestations of the baroque spirit.[4]

There is a related conflict, for the most part illusory, between the forces of Heaven and Hell, good and evil,[5] and this element of illusion is another feature of baroque art, Wölfflin's *Kunst des Scheins*. It is more convincingly manifested in the intricate mixture of truth and falsehood in Pharsandate's recital;[6] in the enormous importance of Jocabel's dream in the structure of the *Moyse sauvé* (almost the whole of the hero's active life is presented in this unreal form); and in Jocabel's tapestry, where we find the characteristic baroque device of the picture within a picture[7] (it can be

---

[1] Cf. p. 159 above.
[2] Cf. p. 167 above.   [3] Cf. p. 173 above.
[4] The baroque character of the French epic is briefly indicated, with special reference to this aspect, by Schürr (*Barock, Klassizismus und Rokoko*, p. 19, n. 1).
[5] Cf. p. 175 above.   [6] Cf. p. 204 above.
[7] Cf. p. 237 above.

discovered elsewhere, but, as we have seen, Saint-Amant lays great emphasis on this aspect).

The tendency to mix opposites may also be seen in the expression of mystical love or religious sentiments in terms of human erotic feeling, a phenomenon which has often been observed in Bernini and Crashaw, but which is perhaps characteristic of baroque religious art in general.[1] Here it is most obvious in Pierre de Saint-Louis,[2] though there are traces in Saint-Amant and Coras.

This is perhaps one aspect of the desire to 'unite heaven and earth', which we have considered as an explanation of the importance of allegory in all the arts of the period.[3] Professor Hatzfeld has stressed the widespread use in baroque poetry of the Jacob's ladder theme with its 'Hin- und Herwogen zwischen Himmel und Erde'.[4] Saint-Amant furnishes an excellent example, also noteworthy for the magnificence of the description.[5]

With these features we may tentatively link the expression of militant Catholicism. Four of our baroque poets—Marie de Pech, Coras, Desmarets, and Pierre de Saint-Louis—stand out as supporters of a crusade against heretics and infidels. Their exaltation is in sharp contrast to the austere piety of Gallicanism and Jansenism.

It may also be suggested, with rather less assurance, that the feminism of the epic, eloquently summarized in the frontispiece of the *Moyse* but equally present in all the Susanna, Judith, and Esther poems, is a baroque characteristic. At any rate the Renaissance shows in the *Querelle des Femmes* two positions, which are later reflected on the one hand in the works of Du Bosc and Le Moyne as well as in the poems, where no distinction is made between masculine and feminine virtues, on the other in Molière and in Boileau's satire, where the differences are vigorously maintained. We may see here again the baroque tendency to break down barriers and mix opposites, the classical attachment to firm divisions and the rule of common sense.

The questions of historical accuracy and local colour are closely connected with similar problems in the visual arts. We have been

[1] Cf. Weisbach, *Der Barock als Kunst der Gegenreformation*, Berlin, 1921, pp. 32 ff., 142 ff.; also Croce, *Storia della età barocca*, pp. 305 ff.

[2] Cf. p. 193 above. [3] Cf. p. 32 above.

[4] 'Der Barockstil der religiösen klassischen Lyrik', p. 33.

[5] Cf. p. 169 above.

able to distinguish two kinds of atmosphere—an ideal magnificence, made up of disparate classical and modern elements but really unsituated in time or space; and an authentic if limited orientalism, seen in Saint-Amant's crocodile and ichneumons or Morillon's description of Arabia.[1] Both have affinities with baroque art. The first is the strange world, neither heaven nor earth, of engravers like Tempesta, the second is symptomatic of a general fondness for the exotic and the bizarre.

A point that must be stressed, however, is the preoccupation with historical accuracy, proved by numerous references to learned authorities and in particular by Saint-Amant's letter to Bochart, which probably indicates the standpoint of most of the poets. It is assumed that in principle a poem should be historically true and every deviation requires to be justified by serious poetic motives. By our standards this accuracy seems rather mechanical. Certainly it implies no understanding of the differences between historical epochs. The Biblical poets were perhaps unaware of the existence of such differences, except in terms of degrees of refinement. They regarded all men in accordance with a universal pattern of humanity. In this respect, perhaps, the baroque and classical spirit are one.

It would be a simplification to regard the Biblical epic, or seventeenth-century literature in general, as a conflict between extravagance and simplicity, between ultramontane luxury and Gallican austerity. However, the striking coincidence between the literary artifices condemned by Boileau in his predecessors and certain contemporary developments of painting, architecture, and sculpture confirms the need for a term which embraces tendencies not confined to literature nor to France.

[1] *Joseph*, pp. 54–55.

CHAPTER XVIII

Conclusion

The Writers

A CURSORY examination of the poems studied here is sufficient
to show that the Biblical epic was above all the product of a
provincial literature. Only Saint-Amant, Desmarets, and Perrault
truly belong to the main literary stream of the capital. The rest
lived and wrote in distant country places or, when they had come
to Paris, retained, like the unfortunate Lesfargues, unmistakable
traces of their origin. One explanation of this phenomenon is
evident and has already been indicated: the epics of 1650, and
especially the *Moyse sauvé*, began a fashion, which soon died in
Paris but which lingered on where people were naturally less
sensitive to changes in critical opinion and taste. There were,
however, other reasons, as the geographical distribution of the
works suggests.

Of all these authors a considerable majority (two-thirds) came
from Normandy or from the south. At first sight there seems little
to relate the two. The large number of Normans is no doubt
partly due to the importance of Rouen as an independent publishing centre and the general literary activity which shortly before
produced Malherbe and Corneille. However, Normandy, like the
provinces of the Midi, was then a stronghold of Protestantism.
The origins of the Biblical epic in Du Bartas, the religious ante-
cedents of Montchrestien, Saint-Amant (both Normans), and
Coras thus take on an added significance. It may be conjectured
that in these provinces even Catholics were impelled to study the
Bible, perhaps by way of reaction or as a measure of defence.
On the other hand, it would be quite wrong to assume (at this
period) any hostility of the Catholic Church towards Bible-reading
among the laity. The predominance of Catholics among the
Biblical poets, as well as the numerous contemporary translations,
clearly proves the contrary.

Another point of interest arises from this distribution. Throughout the century the Midi (though not of course Normandy) was

marked by an artistic autonomy, expressed for example in the painters of Toulouse and the sculpture of Puget. More easily accessible to Spanish and Italian influence, they reveal baroque and realistic features in strong contrast to the official doctrines of Paris and Versailles. Literature offers no exact parallel, but we find here, in the works of Du Bartas, Gamon, Marie de Pech, and Pierre de Saint-Louis, at least the elements of an independent *méridional* tradition, characterized by multiplicity of invention and lack of restraint.

On the whole, however, the provincial poets imitate their more successful brethren in the capital. This leads, as always, to survivals and archaisms which disturb a too rigid chronological evolution. Thus we have seen Gamon and Anne d'Urfé employing the language and forms of thirty years earlier. As the century proceeds this difference is perceptibly narrowed, and the provincial repercussions of Saint-Amant's success appear seven or eight years later. The age of the writer must be taken into account as well as his distance from the centre, but we may reasonably conclude that increasing centralization and improved communications were accompanied by a quickening of intellectual exchanges.

In the same way the persistent influence of Du Bartas is partly the result of provincial backwardness. Our poets were frequently unaware of the disfavour which had overtaken his work. In his search for models a writer, it is true, may easily turn to a book which has been forgotten by the general public, and the fact that Biblical poets made use of *Judith* or the *Semaine* does not prove that those books were still widely read. But in spite of such reservations the continued life of Du Bartas throughout the century throws some light on the hardy nature of literary reputations, which perhaps are never completely obliterated.

The Subjects

Considering the variety of material offered by the Old Testament, it is remarkable that the choice of subjects was so restricted. The poets return again and again to the same figures—Susanna, Judith, Esther, Joseph, and especially David. To these must be added the Creation poems, which reflected the scientific interests of the late sixteenth and late seventeenth centuries. The exceptions are, it is true, important. Thus Saint-Amant takes Moses, Coras Joshua and Samson. It is all the more surprising that their example was not widely followed, since these three have great epic qualities which were lacking in the more popular heroes—even David's exploits have not the breadth of the vast migrations led by Moses and Joshua or the legendary character of Samson's victories. And in Saint-Amant's Moses the truly heroic elements are subordinate (structurally at least) to the idyllic theme. Moreover, certain subjects are neglected altogether—Gideon, for example, or the violent history of the Kings of Israel and Judah (which furnished the source of *Athalie*), or the rebellion of the Maccabees. On the whole, then, suitability for epic treatment was not the principal criterion.

Nor does it seem to have been religious significance. All the subjects chosen were capable of bearing a general allegorical interpretation and often a specific reference to the events of the Gospels. But the allegories were so elastic that they could have been applied to almost any story.

It is hardly an accident that the Biblical tragedy drew on the same narrow group of subjects. The frequent recurrence of the three heroines is, we have seen, a reflection of feminism, and especially of the success of feminist doctrines under Anne of Austria's regency. Joseph's history—the well, the years of slavery, the reversal of fortune—is closely related to the themes of contemporary fiction. David is perhaps not quite of full epic stature, but his battle with Goliath, his complex relations with Saul, the ebb and flow of the war against the Philistines, the love-stories of Michal and Bathsheba (one romantic, the other darkly tragic), all present numerous themes for the dramatist or the novelist. It appears then that in spite of high literary pretensions and affirmations of religious intention, these subjects were chosen with the object of *pleasing*—of attracting a public which looked for varied adventure and sentiment.

The Evolution of the Biblical Epic

We have already followed the changes in conception and technique which appear from poem to poem. Here it will only be necessary to summarize the principal developments. The central feature remains the gap between 1620 and 1650, which breaks the epic into two clear divisions. However, a line of development has been traced from the Pléiade and Du Bartas to Perrault. The transformations which accompany it are sometimes instructive.

Duchesne sees a difference too between the works of 1650 (*La
Pucelle, Moyse sauvé,* and so on) and the imitations which followed
ten years later, marked by modesty and simplicity.[1] This he
attributes to the discouragement of the writers and the growing
scepticism of the public. This is only partly true. We have seen
that it sprang from a much wider movement of taste.

We have already studied the difference between the first and
second group of epics, those deriving directly from Du Bartas and
those which followed Saint-Amant. The most important is the
treatment of the Bible, the change from sympathetic understanding to moral deformation. With it goes the new magnificence, which
replaces contemporary dress and modern French atmosphere.
We may also notice a relative decline of faith in the classical
gods and a decided evolution in political outlook. The sixteenth-
century poet is not afraid to confront and upbraid the most
powerful princes, to treat the institution of monarchy itself with
disrespect. In the seventeenth century this gives way to flattery and
an almost superstitious reverence, though towards the end of the
period Morillon and especially Perrault reveal a new attitude of
urbane scepticism.

Within the second group itself the evolution is principally a
matter of style. We have seen at the beginning of the century the
gradual elimination of Ronsardian features, which, however, seem
to have had a longer life in the epic than elsewhere. At the same
time a heroic style takes shape, becoming more and more set in
stereotyped forms as the century progresses. After 1660 the most
remarkable change is the technical facility which even the least
talented poets display in the handling of prosody and syntax.
We may see here a reflection of the work of Vaugelas and the
Academy. The phenomenon suggests two conclusions: one, evidently, that there is no necessary connexion between technical
skill and even moderate literary talent; the other that in a great
period the work of the supreme masters rests on the obscure
labours of countless minor artists, who bring their medium to
perfection.

With the heroic style goes the hero himself. We have seen how
a code of heroic conduct is gradually formulated, founded on the
suppression of all those flaws and human frailties which are still
discernible in the early poets. Both style and heroic code form part

[1] *Histoire des poëmes épiques,* ch. ix.

of a general tendency towards rationalizing abstraction and systematic order which culminates in the theories of Le Bossu and the poem of Perrault. It is again a movement away from baroque extravagance to the opposite pole of reason and harmony.

The Enterprise and its Significance

In spite of the advantages which they appeared to enjoy, the writers of Christian epic failed disastrously in their main task (for the beauties of the *Moyse sauvé*, the gay adventures of *Esther* or the *Éliade*, hardly lie within their declared programme). Yet surely no enterprise could have been more in tune with the religious and aesthetic aspirations of the time. It is for this reason that the problem of their failure has attracted the attention of many critics. All throw some light on it, none perhaps touches the core of the matter.

The first and the most penetrating was Saint-Évremond, who blames servile imitation of the ancients:

. . . ils donnent l'air de *Mercure* à nos Anges, et celui des Merveilles fabuleuses des Anciens à nos Miracles. Ce Mêlange de l'Antique et du Moderne leur a fort mal réüssi: et on peut dire qu'ils n'ont sû tirer aucun avantage de leurs Fictions, ni faire un bon usage de nos Verités.[1]

This is indeed the crux of the question, but the reader is left wondering why they did not make better use of fiction and truth. Duchesne considers the problem in greater detail. He attributes the weakness of the poems partly to the deficiencies of the French language in descriptive vocabulary and special poetic terms,[2] partly to the fact that taste had not kept pace with reason.[3] It is true that the vocabulary is restricted, which is perhaps an advantage in tragedy but leads to monotony in epic. It is equally true that critical conception surpassed poetic execution, but again the reason remains obscure. M. Cottaz[4] blames the pernicious influence of Tasso—the poets followed the chimerical fantasies of Italian romance instead of the true wonders of Christianity. But we have seen that Tasso's influence was limited and that the poets who were free from it were on the whole inferior. Mornet[5] considers that rigid attachment to the rules strangled original

---

[1] *Œuvres meslées*, London, 1705, ii. 419. Cf. Cottaz, *L'Influence des théories du Tasse*, p. 202.   [2] *Histoire des poëmes épiques*, p. 19.
[3] Ib., p. 73.   [4] *L'Influence des théories du Tasse*, passim.
[5] *Histoire de la littérature classique*, pp. 88 ff.

talent. It is certain that a man of Saint-Amant's temperament was unhappy in the strait-jacket of regular form, but a system which produced (or at least permitted) admirable results in tragedy should not have exercised such a deleterious effect in epic. André Barbier[1] places the question in its social perspective when he says that a period in which literature was governed by a polite society could hardly be favourable to the production of epic. Virgil, Ariosto, and Tasso, however, wrote during periods which, from this point of view, were very similar. Finally Sir Maurice Bowra[2] makes two incidental suggestions which are full of interest. Literary epic, he says, flourishes just after and not during periods of political greatness. Thus in the age of Louis XIV men looked to the present and the future, not to the past. This is probably true, though the inclusion of the Augustan age of Rome among the declining periods is perhaps a little forced. In conclusion he compares Milton's synthesis of Humanism and Puritanism in England with the unresolved antagonism between Humanism and Jansenism in France. This might be criticized in detail (the Jansenists did much to further the development of Humanism in the narrower sense), but its general implications correspond closely to the tendencies we have observed.

Bearing these opinions in mind, we may now return to the poets themselves. It is doubtful whether, in spite of Boileau, a faultless sonnet is worth a long poem. At any rate epic makes far more exacting demands on the writer than does a 'minor' form. Weaknesses which in a short poem might escape unnoticed are here magnified until they become intolerable. Only a poet of the very highest order can survive such a test. Montchrestien, Saint-Amant, Perrault, excellent though they were in their limited fields, clearly did not possess the requisite qualities.

It seems natural therefore that the almost universal defect of these poems (the one exception is Perrault's *Adam*) should be a lack of structural sense. Everywhere we find servile attachment to the Bible or ill-conceived additions and transformations. The material is rarely mastered or viewed as a whole.

Passing from the writers to their public, we must qualify the estimate of their success. The repeated editions show that the more important poems were widely read, but they tell us little

---

[1] *French Studies*, 1947, p. 32.
[2] *From Virgil to Milton*, pp. 28 and 244.

concerning the quality of the readers. It is noteworthy that the epic was not greatly encouraged by the principal patrons of letters. The duc de Longueville's interest in *La Pucelle* was largely the consequence of family vanity, Marie-Louise de Gonzague was as eccentric as her protégé. Neither could be said to enjoy very high consideration. Similarly the critics who received the poems with favour, Sorel or Marolles for example, had no considerable reputation. On the whole it may be assumed that the readers of epic were to be found mainly among the provincial *bourgeoisie*. This tends to confirm Barbier's view: the dominant class in letters was indifferent or hostile.

It seems then that the failure of epic can be explained very simply by the inadequate qualities of the writers and by certain social conditions. However, we must ask why, in view of the critical prestige of the epic, it did not attract the great writers and the great patrons. It is impossible to give a precise answer to this question, but it shows the need for a more general explanation.

Le Bossu suggests one clue when he says that tragedy depicts passions, epic manners (*mœurs*).[1] The second part of the statement would scarcely occur to us and it is of course coloured by Le Bossu's moral bias. It probably represents, none the less, what many seventeenth-century readers sought in, say, Homer or Virgil. In current literature new forms had developed, which had the portrayal of manners as their object—the loose reflections of La Rochefoucauld or later La Bruyère, and even the youthful novel. These were more suited to the taste of an age which found in the word *plaire* the secret of literary attraction.

However, the true reason lies deeper. We have seen the discordance between the Bible and the modern spirit which interprets it, between two sets of religious beliefs which are never quite reconciled. The poems in consequence are built on unresolved conflicts, which serve to explain the structural disharmonies, the violent distortions of reality, the puerile disproportion between means and ends in the treatment of the supernatural. We are again driven to a comparison with baroque art, also founded on conflict and distortion. But we may equally well see a reflection, or rather a parallel expression, of the social and religious tensions of the century—of Catholicism and Protestantism, of Jesuitism and Jansenism, of Fronde and absolute monarchy.

[1] Cf. p. 9 above.

French classicism mastered these dissensions and resolved the discords. *Athalie* and *Esther* bring to these very problems the harmony which the Biblical poets had sought in vain. By this time, however, the epic enterprise itself had come to be regarded as an aberration of the baroque spirit and was abandoned by serious writers. In his championship of the epic and the moderns Perrault is perhaps a survival of the past as much as a prophet of the future.

Bibliography

THE bibliography omits standard works of reference, such as histories of literature, Brunet's *Manuel du libraire*, or Lanson's *Manuel bibliographique*, which have supplied much useful material. Otherwise its aim is to present as complete a review as possible of literature connected with the subject. Editions of the Bible have also been omitted, except in a few special cases. A library press-mark has been given for the epic poems themselves and for other rare or little-known books (though no attempt has been made to produce a census). The following abbreviations are used: Ars., Bibliothèque de l'Arsenal; Bam., Staatliche Bibliothek, Bamberg; BM., British Museum; BN., Bibliothèque Nationale, Paris; Bod., Bodleian Library; Méj., Bibliothèque Méjanes, Aix-en-Provence; St. G., Bibliothèque Sainte-Geneviève.

A. MANUSCRIPTS

PERRAULT (Charles), *Adam ou La Creation de l'homme, Sa chûte Et sa Reparation. Poëme Chrestien. M. DC. XCV.* BN.: MSS., fonds français 24324 (8 unnumbered leaves, 100 pp., 5 unnumbered leaves).

PIERRE DE SAINT-LOUIS (R.P.), *L'Éliade* in *Recueil de poésies françaises*, 3 vols. Méj.: MSS. 363–5 (200–2—R. 417,807). Vol. iii, pp. 1–105.

D'URFÉ (Anne), *Judic* in *Œuvres moralles et spirituelles.* BN.: MSS., fonds français 12487, fols. 149–68.

B. PRINTED BOOKS

I. BIBLIOGRAPHICAL WORKS

DARLOW (T. H.) and MOULE (H. F.), *Historical Catalogue of the Printed Editions of Holy Scripture in the Library of the British and Foreign Bible Society*, 2 vols. London, 1903–11.

DUPORTAL (J.), *Contribution au catalogue général des livres à figures du XVIIe siècle (1601–1633).* Paris, 1914.

FRÈRE (E.), *Manuel du bibliographe normand*, 2 vols. Rouen, 1858–60.

GOUJET (abbé), *Bibliothèque françoise*, 18 vols. Paris, 1741–56.

JACOB (R.P. Louis), *Bibliographia Gallica Universalis . . . Annis 1643, 1644 et 1645; Anno 1646; Anno MDCLI; Annis M. DC. LII et M. DC. LIII.* Parisiis, 1646, 1647, 1652, 1654.

—— *Bibliographia Parisina . . . Annis 1643 et 1644; Anno 1645; Annis 1647 et 1648; Anno 1649; MDCL.* Parisiis, 1645, 1646, 1649, 1650, 1651.

LACHÈVRE (Frédéric), *Bibliographie des recueils collectifs de poésies, 1597–1700*, 4 vols. Paris, 1901–5.

MAGNE (E.), *Bibliographie générale des œuvres de Nicolas Boileau-Despréaux et de Gilles et Jacques Boileau, suivie des Luttes de Boileau*, 2 vols. Paris, 1929.

MAROLLES (Michel de), *Catalogue de livres d'estampes et de figures en taille douce*. Paris, 1666.

NYON L'AÎNÉ (Jean-Luc), *Catalogue des livres de la bibliothèque de feu M. le duc de la Vallière*, vol. iv. Paris, 1784.

TOINET (R.), *Quelques Recherches autour des poèmes héroïques-épiques français du dix-septième siècle*, 2 vols. Tulle, 1897, 1907.

VAN EYS (W. J.), *Bibliographie des Bibles et des Nouveaux Testaments en langue française des XVᵉ et XVIᵉ siècles*, 2 vols. Geneva, 1900–1.

VIOLLET-LE-DUC (E.-N.), *Catalogue des livres composant la bibliothèque poétique de M. Viollet le Duc*, 2 vols. Paris, 1843–7.

WEIGERT (R.-A.), *Inventaire du fonds français: Graveurs du XVIIᵉ siècle*. Paris, 1939– (*in progress*).

II. THE BIBLICAL EPIC[1]

a. *Sixteenth Century*

DU BELLAY, *La Monomachie de David et de Goliath*. Paris, F. Morel, 1560. 4to. [BN.: Ye. 1030]

BELLEAU, *Les Amours de David et de Bersabee* in *La Seconde Iournée de la Bergerie*. Paris, G. Gilles, 1572. 8vo. [BN.: Ye. 7396–7]

—— *Œuvres poétiques*, ed. Marty-Laveaux, 2 vols. Paris, Lemerre, 1878.

BRACH (Pierre de), *La Monomachie de David et de Goliat* in *Les Poemes*. Bordeaux, S. Millanges, 1576. 4to. [BN.: Rés. Ye. 865]

—— *Œuvres poétiques*, ed. Dezeimeris, vol. ii. Paris, Aubry, 1862.

PETREMAND (Thierry), *Paraphrase de l'admirable Histoire de la Saincte heroyne Iudith*. Lyon, 1578. 8vo. [Ars.: 8° BL. 10364]

DU BARTAS, *La Sepmaine, ou Creation du Monde*. Paris, J. Février, 1578. 4to. [BN.: Rés. Ye. 536]

—— *Les Œuvres poetiques*. Rouen, L. Loudet, 1616. 12mo. [BN.: Ye. 7451]

—— *The Works of Guillaume de Salluste, sieur Du Bartas*, ed. Holmes et al., 3 vols. Chapel Hill, Univ. of North Carolina Press, 1935–40.

—— *La divina Settimana*, trans. Ferrante Guisone. Tours, G. Metaieri, 1592. 12mo. [BM.: 11474 aa. 40]

ORIET (Didier), *La Susanne*. Paris, D. Du Val, 1581. 4to. [BN.: Ye. 1039]

—— *Livre de l'Esther*. Paris, 1584. 12mo. [Ars.: 8° BL. 10367]

COIGNARD (Gabrielle de), *Imitation de la victoire de Iudith* in *Œuvres chrestiennes*. Tournon, pour J. Faure, 1595. 12mo. [BN.: Rés. Ye. 2008]

GAMON (Christofle de), *Le Verger Poétique*. Lyon, 1597.

PERRIN (François), *Histoire tragique de Sennacherib, Roy des Assyriens....* Paris, A. L'Angelier, 1599. 8vo. [BN.: Rés. p. Ye. 371]

GAMON (C. de), *Le Iardinet de Poesie de CDG*. Lyon, C. Morillon, 1600. 12mo. [BN.: Ye. 7583]

---

[1] Arranged chronologically. For a list of epics other than Biblical, see Toinet, op. cit.

b. Seventeenth Century

MONTCHRESTIEN (A. de), *Susane ou la Chasteté* in *Les Tragedies.* Rouen, J. Petit [1601 ?]. 8vo.   [BN.: Yf. 2083–4]

——— Rouen, J. Petit, 1603. 8vo.   [Ars.: 8° BL. 12622]

——— Rouen, J. Osmont, 1604. 12mo.   [BN.: Rés. p. Yf. 90]

——— Nyort, J. Vaultier, 1606. 12mo.   [BN.: Yf. 2085]

——— Rouen, P. de la Motte, 1627. 8vo.   [BN.: Rés. p. Yf. 91]

D'URFÉ (Anne), *Hymne de Saincte Susanne* in *Le premier livre des Hymnes.* Lyon, P. Rigaud, 1608. 4to.   [Ars.: 4° BL. 3108]

GAMON (C. de), *La Semaine, ou Creation du Monde . . . Contre celle du Sieur du Bartas.* Lyon, C. Morillon, 1609. 12mo.   [BM.: 240 c. 43]

——— [Geneva], G. Petit, 1609. 12mo.   [BN.: Ye. 7584]

——— *Excerpta,* ed. J. Roche. Paris, La Connaissance, 1927.

D'ANCHERES (Daniel) [Jean de Schelandre], *Les trois premiers de sept tableaux de penitence tirés de la saincte escripture . . . .*[1] Paris, 1609. 4to. [BM.: C. 44 c. 12]

SAINT-PERES (sieur de), *La Vie du Saint Patriarche Tobie. . . .* Paris, 1648. 12mo.
                                                                  [St. G.: 8° Y. 1242]

——— *La Vie de Ioseph, Viceroy d'Egypte . . . .* Paris, 1648. 12mo. [BN.: Ye. 32824]

SAINT-AMANT, *Moyse sauvé, idyle heroïque.* Paris, A. Courbé, 1653. 4to.
                                                                  [BN.: Rés. Ye. 648]

——— *Fragment d'un Poeme de Ioseph et de ses Freres en Egipte* in *Dernier Recueil de Diverses Poësies.* Paris, A. de Sommaville, 1658. 4to. [BN.: Ye. 1298]

——— *Œuvres complètes de Saint-Amant,* ed. Ch.-L. Livet, 2 vols. Paris, Jannet, 1855.

SAINTE-GARDE BERNOUIN, *La Providence ou les deux exemples.* I. *Saül puni.* II. *Suzanne deliurée.* Paris, R. Soubret, 1660. 8vo.   [BN.: Ye. 7984]

LESFARGUES (Bernard), *David, poeme heroïque.* Paris, P. Lamy, 1660. 12mo.
                                        [BN.: Ye. 7978; Ars.: 8° BL. 10370]

——— Paris, J. Guignard, 1687. 12mo.   [Ars.: 8° BL. 10371]

PECH DE CALAGES (Marie de), *Iudith, ou la Délivrance de Bethulie, poeme saint.* Tolose, A. Colomiez, 1660. 4to.   [BN.: Ye. 1277]

[JACQUELIN ?], *Helie, poëme heroïque.* Paris, C. de Sercy, 1661. 12mo.
                                                                  [BN.: Ye. 7869]

CORAS (Jacques de), *Ionas.* Paris, C. Angot, 1663. 12mo. [BN.: Ye. 7951]

——— *Samson.* Paris, C. Angot, 1665. 12mo.   [BN.: Ye. 8057]

——— *Iosué.* Paris, C. Angot, 1665. 12mo.   [BN.: Ye. 8055]

——— *David.* Paris, C. Angot, 1665. 12mo.   [BN.: Ye. 8056]

——— *Œuvres poëtiques . . . .* Paris, C. Angot, 1665. 12mo.[2] [BN.: Ye. 19059]

LE CORDIER (Hélie), *L'Illustre Souffrant ou Iob.* Paris, J. Cochart, 1667. 12mo.
                                                                  [BN.: Ye. 8059]

SAINT-MARTIN (sieur de), *La Nature naissante ou les merveilleux effets de la puissance divine dans la creation du monde . . . .* Paris, V. Du Moutier, 1667. 8vo.   [BN.: Ye. 8137]

MORILLON (dom Gatien de), *Paraphrase sur le livre de Iob . . . .* Paris, L. Billaine, 1668. 8vo.   [BN.: A. 6739]

---

[1] The title-page of the BM. copy is in MS.
[2] All four poems, including the 2nd edition of *Jonas.*

SAINT-MARTIN, *Le systeme des cieux et des elemens* .... Paris, 1670. 8vo.
[Ars.: 8° BL. 11063]
—— —— Paris, U. Coutelier, 1690. 8vo. [BN.: Ye. 8139]
BOISVAL [Desmarets de Saint-Sorlin], *Esther*. Paris, P. Le Petit, 1670. 4to.
[BN.: Ye. 1352]
DESMARETS, *Esther*. Paris, J. Guignard, 1673. 12mo. [Ars.: 8° BL. 10368]
MORILLON, *Paraphrase sur le livre de Tobie* .... Paris, L. Billaine, 1674. 12mo.
[BN.: A. 10327 bis]
[MORILLON], *Joseph, ou l'esclave fidele*. Turin [Tours], B. Fleury et J. le Brun,
1679. 12mo. [BN.: Ye. 8069]
—— Breda [Tours], chez Pierre, Jean, Jacques, 1705. 12mo. [BN.: Ye. 8833]
[DESMARETS], *Abraham ou la vie parfaite*. [no place], 1680. 12mo.
[BN.: Ye. 35226]
SAINT-MARTIN, *L'Univers tiré du neant* .... Paris, U. Coutelier, 1690. 8vo.
[BN.: Ye. 8138]
PERRAULT (Charles), *La Création du Monde*. Paris, 1692. [Toinet, i. 274]
—— *Poëme de la Creation du Monde* in *Recueil de pieces curieuses et nouvelles* . . .,
vol. i, pt. i, pp. 1–28. La Haye, A. Moetjens, 1694. 12mo. [BM.: 241 c. 42]
—— *Adam* .... Paris, J. B. Coignard, 1697. 12mo. [BN.: Ye. 8119]
PIERRE DE SAINT-LOUIS (R.P.), *L'Éliade, ou triomphes et faits mémorables de
saint Élie, Patriarche des Carmes* .... Aix, A. Pontier, 1827.
[BN.: Ye. 30102]
D'AUBIGNÉ (A.), *La Création* in *Œuvres complètes*, ed. Réaume and Caussade,
vol. iii. Paris, Lemerre, 1874.

III. MODERN LATIN EPIC

SANNAZARO (J.), *De partu Virginis*. Romae, 1526.
—— trans. Colletet, *Les Couches sacrées de la Vierge*. Paris, J. Camusat, 1634.
VIDA, *Christiados libri sex*. Cremonae, 1535.
FRACASTORIUS (Hieronymus), *Joseph* in *Opera omnia*. Venetiis, apud Juntas,
1555.
TORTOLETTI (Bartolomeo), *Iuditha vindex et vindicata*. Romae, Typis Vaticanis,
1628. [BN.: Yc. 1148]
MILLIEU (Antoine), *Moyses Viator seu imago militantis Ecclesiae* . . ., 2 vols.
Lugduni, G. Boissat, 1636–9. [BN.: Yc. 8368–9]

IV. ITALIAN EPIC

ARIOSTO, *Orlando Furioso*. Ferrara, 1516; Ferrara, 1532.
—— ed. Zingarelli. Milan, 1944.
DOLCE (Lodovico), *La vita di Giuseppe*. Vinegia, 1561. [Ars.: 4° BL. 3079]
ALFANO, *La Battaglia Celeste tra Michele e Lucifero*. Palermo, 1568.
TASSO, *Gerusalemme Liberata*. Casalmaggiore, 1581.
—— *Di Gerusalemme conquistata*. Roma, 1593.
—— *I due primi giorni del Mondo Creato*. Venetia, 1600.
—— *Le sette giornate del Mondo Creato*. Viterbo, 1607.
MURTOLA (Gasparo), *Della creatione del mondo*. Venetia, 1608.
[BN.: Rés. Yd. 948]

Passero (Felice), *L'Essamerone, ouero l'opra de' sei giorni.* Napoli, 1608.

Cebà (Ansaldo), *La Reina Esther.* Genova, 1615. [BN.: Yd. 16]

Abbondanti (Antonio), *La Giuditta.* Liegi, 1630. [Ars.: 8° BL. 6041]

Marino (Giambattista), *L'Adone.* Parigi, 1623.

—— *La Strage degli Innocenti.* Venetia, 1632.

Bianchi (Giacinto), *La Giuditta Trionfante.* Verona, 1642.

Tortoletti (Bartolomeo), *Giuditta Vittoriosa.* Roma, 1648.

[Ars.: 4° BL. 2226]

V. THEORETICAL WORKS[1]

Beni (Paolo), *Comparatione di Homero, Virgilio e Torquato et a chi di loro si debba la Palma.* Padova, 1607.

Carel de Sainte-Garde (Jacques), *Reflexions academiques sur les orateurs et sur les poëtes.* Paris, 1676.

Castelvetro (Lodovico), *Poetica d'Aristotele.* Vienna, 1570; Basilea, 1576.

Cebà (Ansaldo), *Il Gonzaga, overo del Poema heroico, dialogo.* Genova, 1621.

Chapelain (Jean), *Lettre ou discours à Monsieur Favereau.* Paris, 1623.

—— *Opuscules critiques,* ed. Hunter. Paris, 1936.

Desmarets de Saint-Sorlin (Jean), *La Comparaison de la Langue et de la Poësie françoise.* Paris, 1670.

—— *L'Excellence et les Plaintes de la poesie heroïque* in *Esther.* Paris, 1670.

—— *Traité pour juger des poetes grecs, latins, et françois.* Paris, 1670.

—— *Epistre au Roy* in *Clovis* (3rd edition). Paris, 1673.

—— *Discours pour prouver que les sujets Chrestiens sont les seuls propres à la poësie Heroïque* in *Clovis* (3rd edition). Paris, 1673.

—— *La Deffense du poeme heroïque.* Paris, 1674.

Du Bellay (Joachim), *La Deffence et illustration de la langue françoyse.* Paris, 1549.

Du Rivage, *Lettre contenant quelques observations sur le poëme epique et sur le poëme de la Pucelle.* Paris, 1656.

Giraldi Cinthio (G. B.), *Discorsi.* Vinegia, 1554.

Godeau (Antoine), *Poësies chrestiennes.* Paris, 1646.

Lamy (Bernard), *Nouvelles réflexions sur l'art poëtique.* Paris, 1668 [1678].

Laudun d'Aigaliers (Pierre de), *L'Art poetique françois.* Paris, 1597.

—— ed. Dedieu. Toulouse, 1909.

Le Bossu (père René), *Traité du poëme épique.* Paris, 1675.

Le Laboureur (Louis), *Sentimens sur la poësie chrestienne et prophane* in *La Magdelaine pénitente.* Paris, 1643.

Le Moyne (père Pierre), *Dissertation du poëme heroïque* in *Saint Louys.* Paris, 1653.

Mambrun (père Pierre), *Dissertatio peripatetica de epico carmine.* Parisiis, 1652.

Marolles (Michel de, abbé de Villeloin), *Traité du poëme epique.* Paris, 1662.

Minturno (Antonio), *L'Arte Poetica.* Venetia, 1563.

Peletier du Mans (Jacques), *L'Art poëtique (1555),* ed. Boulanger. Paris, 1930.

[1] Arranged alphabetically.

PERRAULT (Charles), *Paralelle des Anciens et des Modernes*, 4 vols. Paris, 1688–97.

PICCOLOMINI (Alessandro), *Annotationi di M. Alessandro Piccolomini nel libro della Poetica d'Aristotele*. Vinegia, 1575.

RAPIN (père René), *Réflexions sur la poëtique d'Aristote et sur les ouvrages des poëtes anciens et modernes*. Paris, 1674.

—— *Comparaison des poëmes d'Homère et de Virgile*. Paris, 1664.

ROBORTELLUS (Franciscus), *In librum Aristotelis de arte poetica explicationes*. Florentiae, 1548; Basileae, 1555.

SAINTE-GARDE: *see* CAREL DE SAINTE-GARDE.

SCALIGER (Julius Caesar), *Poetices libri septem*. [Lyons], 1561.

—— —— trans. Padelford. New York, 1905.

TASSO, *Discorsi dell'arte poetica; et . . . del Poema Heroico*. Venetia, 1587.

—— *Le prose diverse*, ed. Guasti, 2 vols. Florence, 1875.

TRISSINO (Gian Giorgio), *La Poetica*. Vicenza, 1529.

VAUQUELIN DE LA FRESNAYE (Jean), *L'Art Poetique françois* in *Les Diverses Poesies*. Caen, 1605.

—— —— ed. Genty. Paris, 1862.

VIDA (Marcus), *De arte poetica libri tres*. Romae, 1527.

VI. MISCELLANEOUS

ALIZET (Benoît), *La Calliope Chrestienne, ou Sommaire de la pure doctrine touchant la Creation du monde, le peché de l'homme, la Redemption et Glorification des enfans de Dieu*. [no place], 1596. [Ars.: 8º BL. 10328]

D'ARGENT (Abel), *La Semaine*. Sedan, 1629. [BN.: Ye. 14332]

D'ARTIGNY (abbé), *Nouveaux Mémoires d'histoire, de critique et de littérature*, 7 vols. Paris, 1749–56.

D'AVITY (Pierre), *Les Empires, Royaumes, Estats . . . et Principautez du Monde*. Saint-Omer, 1614. [BM.: 10004 ccc. 11]

BAILLET (Adrien), *Jugemens des Savans sur les principaux ouvrages des auteurs*, 8 vols. Paris, 1722–30.

Biblia Sacra . . . cxxxx figuris . . . illustrata a de Brÿ . . . . Moguntia, 1609. [Bod.: 4º A. 66. Th.]

BOCHARTUS (Samuel), *Geographia sacra . . . cui accedunt variae dissertationes philologicae, geographicae, theologicae*. Cadorni, 1646.

—— —— Enlarged edition. Lugduni Batavorum, 1692.

CALVIN (Jean), *Sermons . . . sur le v. liure de Moyse nommé Deuteronome*. Genève, 1567.

CAREL DE SAINTE-GARDE: *see* LERAC.

CHAPELAIN (Jean), *Lettres*, 2 vols., ed. Tamizey de Larroque. Paris, 1880–3.

CHAPPUIS (Gabriel), *Figures de la Bible declarees par stances*. Lyon, 1582. [BN.: Rés. A. 7633(1)]

COLLETET (Guillaume), *Vies des poëtes gascons*, ed. Tamizey de Larroque. Paris, 1866.

—— *Discours du poëme bucolique*. Paris, 1657.

CORAS (Jacques de), *Le Satirique berné*. Paris, 1668.

—— *Lettres inédites*, ed. Tamizey de Larroque. Paris, 1874.

COWLEY (Abraham), *Davideis* in *Poems*, ed. Waller. Cambridge, 1905.

DES MASURES (Louis), *Tragedies Sainctes — David combattant, David triomphant, David fugitif.* Genève, 1566.

DOROTHÉE: *see* SAINT-RENÉ.

DU BOSC (père Jacques), *La Femme Heroïque ou les Heroïnes comparées avec les Heros en toute sorte de vertus,* 2 vols. Paris, 1645.

DU PLESSIS (A.), *Le livre de Iob traduit en poesie françoise selon la verité Hebraique.* [Geneva], 1552. [Ars.: 8° BL. 10349]

DU RYER (Pierre), *Saül.* Paris, 1642.

FRIZON (Pierre), *La Saincte Bible françoise,* 3 vols. Paris, 1621.
[Bod.: Douce B. subt. 13–15]

GIRARD (Antoine), *Les Peintures sacrées sur la Bible.* Paris, 1653.
[BN.: A. 1388]

GODEAU (Antoine), *Les Tableaux de la Penitence.* Paris, 1654. [BN.: D. 5638]

GOURNAY (Marie de), *Egalité des Hommes et des Femmes.* [no place], 1622.

GUARINI (Giovan Battista), *Il Pastor Fido.* Venetia, 1590.

D'HERBELOT, *Bibliothèque orientale.* Paris, 1697.

HOG (W.): *see* MILTON.

Icones historicae Veteris et Novi Testamenti — Figures historiques du Vieux et du Nouveau Testament. Geneve, 1680. [BN.: Rés. A. 7629]
—— Genevae, 1681. [Bod.: Douce BB. 230]

JACQUELIN, *Paraphrase sur les neuf leçons du Prophete Ieremie.* Narbonne, 1651.
[Ars.: 8° T. 1141]
—— *Soliman ou l'Esclave genereuse.* Paris, 1653. [Ars.: 4° BL. 3652]

JEANGASTON (J. D.), *Les Œuvres poëtiques et chrétienes ....*[1] Orthez, 1635.
[Ars.: 8° BL. 9096]
—— *Les Œuvres chrestiennes.* Orthez, 1639. [BN.: Ye. 7725]

JOSEPHUS (Flavius), *Histoire . . . mise en françois . . . par D. Gilb. Genebrard.* Paris, 1578; Paris, 1609.
—— *Histoire des Iuifs. . . . Traduite . . . par Monsieur Arnauld d'Andilly.* Paris, 1667.

LA MILLETIÈRE (T. de), *De universi orbis christiani pace et concordia.* Parisiis, 1634.

[LE CLERC (Jean)?], *Figures de la Saincte Bible.* Paris, 1614.
[BN.: Rés. A. 1401]

LE CORDIER (Hélie), *Le Pont-l'Evesque.* Paris, 1662.
—— —— ed. Le Verdier. Rouen, 1906.

LE MOYNE (père Pierre), *La Gallerie des Femmes Fortes.* Paris, 1647.
[BN.: Rés. G. 447]

LERAC [Carel de Sainte-Garde], *La Defense des Beaux Esprits de ce temps contre un Satyrique.* Paris, 1675.

LESFARGUES (Bernard), *Apologia pro se Triboniano a censura sospiti nuncupata.* Parisiis, 1660.

MARINO (Giambattista), *La Sampogna.* Parigi, 1620. [Bod.: Vet. F. 2 f. 11]

MAROLLES (Michel de, abbé de Villeloin), *Mémoires,* 2 vols. Paris, 1656–7.
—— *La Prophétie de Daniel.* Paris, 1677.
—— *Les Prophetes Jonas et Nahum.* Paris, 1678.
—— *Le Cantique des Cantiques.* Paris, 1677.

[1] The title (though not the imprint) is in manuscript.

MÉNAGE (Gilles), *Menagiana*. Paris, 1693.

MERAULT (Olivier), *Poëme et bref discours de l'honneur où l'homme estoit colloqué en l'estat de sa creation* . . . Rennes, 1600. [BN.: Rés. Ye. 2022]

MERIAN (Matthæus), *Icones Biblicae*. Strassburg, [1625].
[Bam.: A. symb. 9. 23]

[MILTON (J.)], *Paraphrasis poetica in tria* . . . *poemata* . . . *Autore Gulielmo Hogaeo*. Londini, 1690.

[MORILLON], *Nouveau Recueil de Poësies*. Turin [Tours], 1696.
[BN.: Ye. 28168]

PERRAULT (Charles), *Mémoires de ma vie*, ed. Bonnefon. Paris, 1909.

PERROT DE LA SALE (Paul), *Tableaus sacrez* . . . . Francfort, 1594.
[BN.: Rés. A. 7635]

PHILO JUDAEUS (Philon Juif), *Les Œuvres* . . . *en François, par Pierre Bellier*. Paris, 1575.

—— *Les Œuvres* . . . *Reueuës* . . . *Par Fed. Morel*. Paris, 1612; Paris, 1619.

PIERRE DE SAINT-LOUIS (R.P.), *La Muse bouquetiere de Notre Dame de Laurete*. Viterbe, 1672. [BM.: 11474 aa. 32]

QUILLIAN (Michel), *La Derniere Semaine, ou Consommation du Monde*. Paris, 1596. [BN.: Rés. Ye. 1967]

RONSARD, *Les quatre premiers livres de la Franciade*. Paris, 1572.

—— *Œuvres complètes*, ed. Laumonier, 8 vols. Paris, 1914–19.

—— *Hymne des Daimons*, ed. Schmidt. Paris, n.d.

ROYAUMONT (sieur de, prieur de Sombreval), *L'Histoire du Vieux et du Nouveau Testament representée avec des figures et des Explications édifiantes* . . . . Paris, 1670. [BN.: Rés. A. 3610]

SAINT-MARTIN, *Ode présentée à Monseigneur le Peletier, controlleur general des finances*. Paris, 1684. [BN.: Ye. 4311]

SAINT-PERES (sieur de), *Le Vray Tresor de l'Histoire Saincte sur le transport miraculeux*... *de Nostre-Dame de Liesse*.... Paris, 1647. [BN.: 4° Lk.[7] 5751]

—— *Histoire miraculeuse de Nostre-Dame de Liesse*. . . . Paris, 1657.
[BN.: 8° Lk.[7] 5752]

SAINT-RENÉ (père Dorothée de), *Commentaire theologique, historique et moral sur les livres des Roys et de l'Apocalipse, ou sont decouvertes les grandeurs des saints prophetes Elie et Elisée*. Paris, 1655. [BN.: A. 1585]

SANNAZARO, *Arcadia*. Napoli, 1504.

SCUDÉRY (Madeleine de), *Artamene, ou le Grand Cyrus*, 10 vols. Paris, 1650–4.

SOREL (Charles), *Bibliothèque françoise*. Paris, 1664.

TALLEMANT DES RÉAUX, *Les Historiettes*, ed. Mongrédien, 8 vols. Paris, [1932–4].

[TASSIN (dom René)], *Histoire littéraire de la congrégation de Saint-Maur*. Brussels and Paris, 1770.

TASSO, *L'Aminta*. Cremona, 1580.

TEMPESTA (Antonio), *Sacra Bella Sanctae Veterum Bibliorum Historiae ordine temporis digesta Antonii Tempestae Apellaea manu delineata*. Antuerpiae apud Petrum de Iode [no date]. [BM.: Maps 18 b. 12]

THOMASSIN, (père L.), *La Methode d'étudier et d'enseigner chrétiennement et solidement les lettres humaines par rapport aux lettres divines et aux Écritures*, 3 vols. Paris, 1681–2.

VII. HISTORICAL AND CRITICAL STUDIES

ADAM (A.), *Théophile de Viau et la libre pensée française en 1620*. Paris, 1935.
—— *Histoire de la littérature française au XVIIᵉ siècle*. Paris, 1948– (in progress).

ALLAIS (G.), *De Franciadis epica fabula*. Paris, 1891.

ASCOLI (G.), *La Grande-Bretagne devant l'opinion française au XVIIᵉ siècle*, 2 vols. Paris, 1930.

ASHTON (H.), *Du Bartas en Angleterre*. Paris, 1908.

AUBIN (R. A.), 'Saint-Amant as Preromantic', *Modern Language Notes*, l (1935), pp. 456–7.

BADOLLE (M.), *Anne d'Urfé, l'homme, le poète*. Paris, n.d.

BALDWIN (E. C.), 'Paradise Lost and the Apocalypse of Moses', *Journal of English and Germanic Philology*, xxiv (1925), pp. 383–6.

BARBIER (A.), 'L'École de 1660', *French Studies*, i (1947), pp. 27–36.

BEALL (C. B.), 'Le père Bouhours et le Tasse', *Modern Language Notes*, l (1935), pp. 434–8.

—— *La Fortune du Tasse en France*. Eugene, Oregon, 1942.

BEAUNIER (A.), 'Un grand poète Louis XIII: Saint-Amant', *Revue des Deux Mondes*, xliii (1918), pp. 210–21.

BELLONI (A.), *Gli Epigoni della Gerusalemme Liberata*. Padua, 1893.

—— *Il poema epico e mitologico*. Milan, n.d.

—— *Il Seicento*, Milan, 1929.

BERGER (S.), *La Bible au seizième siècle*. Paris, 1879.

BLUNT (A.), *Art and Architecture in France, 1500 to 1700*. London, 1953.

BOASE (A. M.), 'Poètes anglais et français de l'époque baroque', *Revue des sciences humaines*, 1949, pp. 155–84.

BOASE (T. S. R.), 'A Seventeenth-Century Carmelite Legend based on Tacitus', *Journal of the Warburg and Courtauld Institutes*, iii (1939–40), pp. 107–18.

BOISARD (F.), *Notices biographiques, littéraires et critiques sur les hommes du Calvados*. Caen, 1848.

BONNEFON (Paul), 'Les dernières années de Charles Perrault', *Revue d'histoire littéraire de la France*, xiii (1906), pp. 606–57.

BORINSKI (K.), *Die Poetik der Renaissance*. Berlin, 1886.

BORZELLI (A.), *Storia della vita e delle opere di Giovan Battista Marino*. Naples, 1927.

BOURGOIN (A.), *Un Bourgeois de Paris lettré au XVIIᵉ siècle — Valentin Conrart, premier secrétaire perpétuel de l'Académie Française et son temps*. Paris, 1883.

BOWRA (C. M.), *From Virgil to Milton*. London, 1945.

BRASPART (M.), *Du Bartas, poète chrétien*. Neuchâtel and Paris, 1947.

BRAY (R.), *La Formation de la doctrine classique en France*. Paris, 1927.

BREMOND (H.), *Histoire littéraire du sentiment religieux en France*, 6 vols. Paris, 1923.

BRIGGS (H. M.), 'Tasso's Theory of Epic Poetry', *Modern Language Review*, xxv (1930), pp. 457–73.

BRUN (Pierre), *Autour du XVIIᵉ siècle*. Grenoble, 1901.

BUFFUM (I.), *Agrippa d'Aubigné's 'Les Tragiques': a Study of the Baroque Style in Poetry*. New Haven, 1951.

BULS (J.), *Das Naturgefühl bei Saint-Amant*. Rostock, 1913.

BUSSON (H.), *La Pensée religieuse française de Charron à Pascal*. Paris, 1933.

—— *La Religion des classiques*. Paris, 1948.

CABEEN (C. W.), *L'Influence de Giambattista Marino sur la littérature française dans la première moitié du XVIIe siècle*. Grenoble, 1904.

CAILLET (M.-A.), *Un Visionnaire du XVIIe siècle: J. Desmarets de Saint-Sorlin*. Paris, 1935.

CAMERON (A.), *The Influence of Ariosto's Epic and Lyric Poetry on Ronsard and His Group*. Baltimore, 1930.

CARRÉ DE BUSSEROLLE (J.), *Dictionnaire géographique, historique et biographique d'Indre-et-Loire et de l'ancienne province de Touraine* (Mémoires de la Société Archéologique de Touraine, xxvii–xxxii). Tours, 1878–84.

CHALMEL (J.-L.), *Histoire de Touraine*. Paris, 1828.

CHAMARD (H.), *Histoire de la Pléiade*, 4 vols. Paris, 1939–40.

CHASLES (P.), *La France, l'Espagne et l'Italie au XVIIe siècle*. Paris, 1877.

CHÉROT (H.), *Étude sur la vie et les œuvres du P. Le Moyne*. Paris, 1887.

CIORANESCU (A.), *L'Arioste en France des origines à la fin du XVIIIe siècle*, 2 vols. Paris, 1938.

COHEN (G.), *Écrivains français en Hollande dans la première moitié du XVIIe siècle*. Paris, 1920.

COLLAS (G.), *Un Poète protecteur des lettres au XVIIe siècle. Jean Chapelain (1595-1674)*. Paris, 1912.

COMPAYRÉ (G.), *Histoire critique des doctrines de l'éducation en France depuis le seizième siècle*, 2 vols. Paris, 1879.

COTTAZ (J.), *L'Influence des théories du Tasse sur l'épopée en France*. Paris, 1942.

—— *Le Tasse et la conception épique*. Paris, 1942.

CROCE (B.), *Storia della età barocca in Italia*, 2nd ed. Bari, 1946.

—— *Saggi sulla letteratura italiana del Seicento*, 3rd ed. Bari, 1948.

—— *Nuovi saggi sulla letteratura italiana del Seicento*, 2nd ed. Bari, 1949.

CRUMP (P. E.), *Nature in the Age of Louis XIV*. London, 1928.

CURTIUS (E. R.), *Europäische Literatur und lateinisches Mittelalter*. Berne, 1948.

DAMIANI (G. F.), *Sopra la poesia del Cavalier Marino*. Turin, 1899.

DEJOB (C.), *De l'influence du Concile de Trente sur la littérature et les beaux-arts chez les peuples catholiques*. Paris, 1884.

DELAPORTE (P.-V.), *Du Merveilleux dans la littérature française sous le règne de Louis XIV*. Paris, 1891.

—— *Les Classiques païens et chrétiens*. Paris, 1894.

DELARUELLE (L.), 'Recherches sur les sources de Du Bartas dans la *Première Semaine*', *Revue d'histoire littéraire de la France*, xl (1933), pp. 320–54.

DELFOUR (L.-Cl.), *La Bible dans Racine*. Paris, 1891.

DESONAY (F.), 'La Réputation littéraire de Ronsard au XVIIe siècle', *Bulletin bibliographique et pédagogique du Musée belge*, xxviii (1924), pp. 133–40.

DIDOT (A.-F.), *Étude sur Jean Cousin suivie de notices sur Jean Leclerc et Pierre Woeiriot*. Paris, 1872.

DU BOYS (E.), 'Marie Puech de Calages, femme poète toulousaine du XVIIe siècle', *Bulletin du bibliophile*, 1891, pp. 18–29.

DUCHESNE (J.), *Histoire des poëmes épiques français du XVIIe siècle*. Paris, 1870.

DUPORTAL (J.), *Étude sur les livres à figures édités en France de 1601 à 1660*. Paris, 1914.

DURAND-LAPIE (P.), *Un Académicien du XVIIe siècle, Saint-Amant, son temps, sa vie, ses poésies (1594–1661)*. Paris, 1898.

—— *A la poursuite d'une date*. Montauban, 1901.

ECKHARDT (A.), *Remy Belleau, sa vie, sa 'Bergerie'*. Budapest, 1917.

EHRENSTEIN (T.), *Das Alte Testament im Bilde*. Vienna, 1923.

—— *Das Alte Testament in der Graphik*. Vienna, 1936.

D'ESPEZEL (P.), *Les Illustrateurs français de la Bible depuis les origines de l'imprimerie, 1499–1950*. Paris, 1950.

FÉLICE (G. de), *Histoire des protestants de France*. Paris, 1850.

FINSLER (G.), *Homer in der Neuzeit*. Leipzig, 1912.

FRIES (L.), Introduction to *Montchrestien's 'Sophonisbe'*. Marburg, 1889.

FUCHS (M.), 'Comment le XVIIe et le XVIIIe siècles ont jugé Ronsard', *Revue de la Renaissance*, viii–ix (1907–8).

FUNCK-BRENTANO (Th.), Introduction to Montchrétien, *Traicté de l'Œconomie Politique*. Paris, 1889.

GAUTIER (Théophile), *Les Grotesques*. Paris, 1844.

GILLOT (H.), *La Querelle des Anciens et des Modernes en France*. Paris, 1914.

GIRARDIN: *see* SAINT-MARC GIRARDIN.

GOURMONT (Remy de), Introduction to *Saint-Amant*. Paris, 1907.

GRAUERT (W. H.), *Christina Königinn von Schweden und ihr Hof*, 2 vols. Bonn, 1837–42.

GRAUTOFF (O.), *Nicolas Poussin, sein Werk und sein Leben*, 2 vols. Munich, 1914.

HAAG (E.), *La France protestante*. Paris, 1846–58.

HALLAYS (A.), *Les Perrault*. Paris, 1926.

HARASZTI (J.), Introduction to Jean de Schelandre, *Tyr et Sidon*. Paris, 1908.

HATZFELD (H.), 'Der Barockstil der religiösen klassischen Lyrik in Frankreich', *Literaturwissenschaftliches Jahrbuch der Görresgesellschaft*, iv (1929), pp. 30–60.

JOLY (A.), *Antoine de Montchrétien, poète et économiste normand*. Caen, 1865.

JUBINAL (A.), 'Coras et Boileau', *Bulletin du bibliophile*, 1847, pp. 3–16.

KAISER (H.), *Über die Schöpfungsgedichte des Chr. de Gamon und Agrippa d'Aubigné und ihre Beziehungen zu du Bartas' 'Premiere Sepmaine'*. Bremen, 1896.

KOHLER (E.), *Entwicklung des biblischen Dramas des 16. Jahrhunderts in Frankreich unter dem Einfluß der literarischen Renaissancebewegung*. Naumburg, 1911.

LACHÈVRE (F.), 'Antoine de Montchrétien, sa religion, son mariage', *Revue d'histoire littéraire de la France*, xxv (1918), pp. 445–54.

—— *Glanes bibliographiques et littéraires*, vol. ii. Paris, 1929.

LAHONDÈS (J. de), *Une Poétesse épique toulousaine*. Toulouse, n.d. (Extract from *Revue des Pyrénées*, xv, 1903.)

LANCASTER (H. C.), *A History of French Dramatic Literature in the Seventeenth Century*, 9 vols. Baltimore, 1929–42.

LANSON (G.), 'La Littérature française sous Henri IV: Antoine de Montchrétien', *Revue des Deux Mondes*, cvii (1891), pp. 369–87.

LANTOINE (H.), *Histoire de l'enseignement secondaire en France au XVIIe siècle.* Paris, 1874.

LEBÈGUE (R.), *La Tragédie religieuse en France.* — *Les Débuts (1514–1573).* Paris, 1929.

—— 'Malherbe correcteur de tragédie', *Revue d'histoire littéraire de la France,* xli (1934), pp. 161–84, 344–61, 481–96.

—— *La Tragédie française de la Renaissance.* Brussels, 1944.

—— *La Poésie française de 1560 à 1630,* 2 vols. Paris, 1951.

LE HIR (Y.), 'Notes sur la langue et le style du *Moïse sauvé* de Saint-Amant (1653)', *Le Français moderne,* xix (1951), pp. 95–108.

LEMERCIER (A.-P.), *Étude . . . sur les poésies de Jean Vauquelin de la Fresnaye.* Nancy, 1887.

LICHTENSTEIN (J.), *Racine poète biblique.* Paris, 1934.

LIEURE (J.), *L'École française de gravure, XVIIe siècle.* Paris [1931].

LOISEAU (J.), *Abraham Cowley, sa vie, son œuvre.* Paris, 1931.

LOUKOVITCH (K.), *L'Évolution de la tragédie religieuse classique en France.* Paris, 1933.

MCBRYDE (J. McL.), 'A Study of Cowley's *Davideis*', *Journal of Germanic Philology,* ii (1898–9), pp. 454–527.

MCCANN (G. L.), *Le Sentiment de la nature en France dans la première moitié du dix-septième siècle.* Nemours, 1926.

MAGENDIE (M.), *La Politesse mondaine et les théories de l'honnêteté en France au XVIIe siècle de 1600 à 1660.* Paris, 1925.

—— *Le Roman français au XVIIe siècle.* Paris, 1932.

MÂLE (E.), *L'Art religieux après le Concile de Trente.* Paris, 1932.

MANGO (F.), *Le Fonti dell'Adone di Giambattista Marino.* Turin, 1891.

MARNI (A.), *Allegory in the French Heroic Poem of the Seventeenth Century.* Princeton, 1936.

MARTINO (P.), *L'Orient dans la littérature française au XVIIe et au XVIIIe siècle.* Paris, 1906.

MAZON (A.), *Notice sur la vie et les œuvres d'Achille de Gamon et de Christofle de Gamon.* Lyons, 1885.

—— 'Les Gamon d'Annonay', *Revue du Vivarais,* ii (1894), pp. 289–302, 337–45.

MEOZZI (A.), *Il secentismo e le sue manifestazioni europee in rapporto all'Italia.* Pisa, 1936.

MOORE (O. H.), 'The Infernal Council', *Modern Philology,* xvi (1918), pp. 169–93.

MORNET (D.), *Histoire de la littérature française classique (1660–1700).* Paris, 1947.

MOURGUES (O. de), *Metaphysical, Baroque and Précieux Poetry.* Oxford, 1953.

PANNIER (J.), *L'Église Réformée de Paris sous Louis XIII de 1621 à 1629,* 2 vols. Paris, 1931–2.

PASCOE (M. E.), *Les Drames religieux du milieu du XVIIe siècle (1636–50).* Paris, 1932.

PATTERSON (W. F.), *Three Centuries of French Poetic Theory: a Critical History of the Chief Arts of Poetry in France (1328–1630),* 2 vols. Ann Arbor, 1935.

PELLISSIER (G.), *La Vie et les œuvres de Du Bartas.* Paris, 1882.

PÉTAVEL (E.), *La Bible en France.* Paris, 1864.

PETIT DE JULLEVILLE (L.), *Notice sur Montchrestien* in *Les Tragédies de Montchrestien.* Paris, 1891.

PEYRE (H.), *Qu'est-ce que le classicisme?* Paris, 1942.

PIERCE (F.), 'La Creación del Mundo and the Spanish Religious Epic of the Golden Age', *Bulletin of Spanish Studies*, xvii (1940), pp. 23–32.

—— 'Hojeda's *La Christiada*: a Poem of the Literary Baroque', *Bulletin of Spanish Studies*, xvii (1940), pp. 203–18.

REIBETANZ (A.), *Jean Desmarets de Saint-Sorlin, sein Leben und seine Werke.* Leipzig, 1910.

RIGAULT (H.), *Histoire de la Querelle des Anciens et des Modernes.* Paris, 1856.

RONDOT (N.), *Bernard Salomon, peintre et tailleur d'histoires à Lyon au XVI⁰ siècle.* Lyons, 1897.

RONZY (P.), 'Une Imitation du Tasse: Le conseil infernal dans la *Judith* d'Anne d'Urfé', *L'Italie classique et moderne*, no. 1, pp. 8–9. Grenoble, 1908.

ROUSSET (J.), *La Littérature de l'âge baroque en France.* Paris, 1953.

SAINTE-BEUVE (C.-A.), *Tableau de la poésie française au XVI⁰ siècle*, 2 vols. Paris, 1876.

SAINT-MARC GIRARDIN, *Tableau de la littérature française au XVI⁰ siècle suivi d'études sur la littérature du Moyen Age et de la Renaissance.* Paris, 1862.

SAINTSBURY (G.), *A History of Criticism and Literary Taste in Europe from the Earliest Texts to the Present Day*, 3 vols. Edinburgh, 1900–4.

SAMARAN (C.), 'A propos de Saint-Amant', *Journal des Débats*, 16 August 1911.

SAYCE (R. A.), 'Saint-Amant's *Moyse sauvé* and French Bible translations', *Modern Language Review*, xxxvii (1942), pp. 147–55.

—— 'Saint-Amant and Poussin', *French Studies*, i (1947), pp. 241–51.

SCHMIDT (A.-M.), *La Poésie scientifique en France au XVI⁰ siècle.* Paris, 1938.

SCHÖNHERR (P. B.), *Saint-Amant, sein Leben und seine Werke.* Oppeln and Leipzig, 1888.

SCHUBART (H.), *Die Bibelillustrationen des Bernard Salomon* (Hamburg thesis). Amorbach, 1932.

SCHÜRR (F.), *Barock, Klassizismus und Rokoko in der französischen Literatur.* Leipzig, 1928.

SEIVER (G. O.), Introduction to: Antoine de Montchrestien, *Aman, a critical edition.* Philadelphia, 1939.

SEZNEC (J.), *La Survivance des dieux antiques.* London, 1940.

SPINGARN (J. E.), *A History of Literary Criticism in the Renaissance*, 2nd ed. New York, 1908.

STERLING (C.), 'Un Précurseur français de Rembrandt: Claude Vignon', *Gazette des Beaux-Arts*, 1934 (ii), pp. 123–36.

STROWSKI (F.), *Pascal et son temps*, 3 vols. Paris, 1907.

TAMIZEY DE LARROQUE (P.), 'Jacques de Coras', *Revue de Gascogne*, 1874, pp. 459–71.

TELLEEN (J. M.), *Milton dans la littérature française.* Paris, 1904.

THIBAUT DE MAISIÈRES (M.), *Les Poèmes inspirés du début de la Genèse à l'époque de la Renaissance.* Louvain, 1931.

TIEGHEM: see VAN TIEGHEM.

TRÉNEL (J.), *L'Élément biblique dans l'œuvre poétique d'Agrippa d'Aubigné.* Paris, 1904.

VAGANAY (H.), 'Un sonnet de Ronsard peu connu', *Revue d'histoire littéraire de la France*, xxiii (1916), pp. 562–3.

VAN TIEGHEM (Paul), *La Littérature latine de la Renaissance*. Paris, 1944.

VAUDICHON (G. de), *Montchrestien (1575–1621)*. Amiens, 1882.

VIANEY (J.), 'La Bible dans la poésie française depuis Marot', *Revue des Cours et Conférences*, 1922.

VISSAC (abbé), *De la poésie latine en France au siècle de Louis XIV*. Paris, 1862.

WENCELIUS (M. S.), 'Contribution à l'étude du Baroque: Saint-Amant', *Bulletin de la Société d'Étude du XVIIe siècle*, 5–6 (1950), pp. 148–63.

WENZEL (G.), *Aesthetische und sprachliche Studien über Antoine de Montchrétien*. Weimar, 1885.

WILL (J. S.), *Protestantism in France*, vol. ii. Toronto, 1921.

WILLIAMS (R. C.), 'Italian Influence on Ronsard's Theory of the Epic', *Modern Language Notes*, xxxv (1920), pp. 161–5.

—— 'Two Studies in Epic Theory: I. Verisimilitude in the Epic. II. Plagiarism by Scudéry of Tasso's Epic Theory', *Modern Philology*, xxii (1924), pp. 133–58.

—— *The Merveilleux in the Epic*. Paris, 1925.

WILLNER (K.), *Montchrestiens Tragödien und die stoische Lebensweisheit*. Berlin, 1932 (*Romanische Studien*, Heft 32).

ZANTA (L.), *La Renaissance du Stoïcisme au XVIe siècle*. Paris, 1914.

Index